Y

A

CAT

YOUNG ADULT CATHOLICS

*Religion in
the Culture of Choice*

DEAN R. HOGE
WILLIAM D. DINGES
MARY JOHNSON, S.N.D. DE N.
JUAN L. GONZALES, JR.

UNIVERSITY OF NOTRE DAME PRESS

Notre Dame, Indiana

Copyright © 2001
University of Notre Dame
Notre Dame, Indiana 46556
All Rights Reserved
http://www.undpress.nd.edu

Reprinted in 2002

Manufactured in the United States of America

Library of Congress Cataloging-in-Publication Data
Young adult Catholics : religion in the culture of choice / Dean R. Hoge
 . . . [et al.].
    p.   cm.
    Includes bibliographical references and index
    ISBN 0-268-04475-9 (cloth : alk. paper)—ISBN 0-268-04476-7
(pbk. : alk. paper)
    1. Catholic Church—United States.   2. Young adults—Religious life.
3. United States—Church history.   I. Hoge, Dean R., 1937–
BX1406.2 .Y68   2001
282'.73'0842—dc21   2001000490

∞ *This book is printed on acid-free paper.*

Contents

Acknowledgments

Throughout the study we have been helped by many friends. During the design of the study we were advised by Dolores Leckey, Nancy Ammerman, Regina Cole, Eugene Hemrick, Peggy Steinfels, Sharon Euart, James Davidson, Patrick McNamara, Ronaldo Cruz, Anthony Stevens-Arroyo, Allan Figueroa Deck, Orlando Espin, Gary Riebe-Estrella, and Veronica Mendez. During data collection we were helped by many others, including Maria Elena Gonzalez, Marcos Sanchez, Jorge Presmanes, Ovidio Pecharroman, and John Brogan. We want to thank the thirty persons who did interviewing for us. Also we had capable research assistance from Annmarie Perez, Xiaoyan Wang, Dan Kuntz, Janice Kraus, Michele Wilsusen, Lisa Renee Dinges, Tom O'Connor, and Andrea Herdelin. We thank Ellen Coughlin, Susan Van Cuyk Grunder, and Michelle Dillon for comments on early versions of the manuscript.

Financial assistance came from the Lilly Endowment. We thank Fred Hofheinz and Jeanne Knoerle, program directors for religion, for their aid and encouragement over many months.

Each member of the research team has family members, friends, and colleagues who sustained and supported us. We dedicate this book to all of these wonderful people.

Introduction

Leaders of the American Catholic community want to reach out to young adults. The Conference of Bishops in their 1997 statement called young adults to be "sons and daughters of the light," that is, a reflection of the light of Christ to the world.[1] They stated that the Church must actively invite young adults into the full life of the Church. And the Church must give special attention to the needs of young adults in parishes, in communities, and on college campuses.

This is urgent, since evidence shows that commitments of Catholics to the Church are weakening. For example, the highly reliable General Social Survey of the University of Chicago found in its 1998 poll of American Catholics that 37 percent described themselves as "strong" Catholics and 29 percent said they attend Mass weekly. Back in the 1970s the results on the same questions were that 46 percent said they were "strong" Catholics and 48 percent claimed they attended weekly.[2] The trends are downward.

Today we also see reports that Latino Catholics are often switching to evangelical and Pentecostal churches, thus departing from the long-term traditions of their families. How many are switching? Why is this?

Thoughtful Catholics need more information. Effective ministry to young adults requires that everybody be acquainted with the needs and attitudes of this generation of Catholics. This is the main reason we undertook a study of young adult Catholics. We hoped to gather reliable information on how young adult Catholics, both European-American and Latino, live their Catholicism. Are they alienated from the Church?

Are they cynical about Church moral teachings? Do they take the pope's statements seriously? Do they attend Mass? Have large numbers left Catholicism for other churches? Do they experiment with non-Catholic spiritual groups and therapies? Do they want Catholic religious education for their children? Too many broadstroke journalistic reports of what young adult Catholics are "really like" have been circulating, and some are misleading. Research that is reliable and illuminating is needed.

We undertook the project for a second reason also. A study such as this provides an opportunity to gather new information on the religion of young adults more generally. We designed the study to produce data useful to social scientists who are asking questions about spiritual seeking, privatization, institutional authority, denominational identity, and so on among the young. Our new data clarify present-day debates about assimilation of immigrants, religious identity formation, and generational differences. In the final chapters of the book we enter the current sociological debates over relativism, pluralism, and identity theory.

With financial help from the Lilly Endowment we began work in 1995. We decided to do a study on two levels, first, a careful sampling of young adults throughout the nation in a short interview survey, and second, a series of in-depth interviews with individuals. We added focus groups to study particular types of persons. We also decided to gather two samples, one of Latino young adults and the other of "everyone else," that is of European, African American, and Asian American Catholics.

We made a separate sample of Latinos because of their growing importance in American Catholicism. Students of American Catholicism today need to look at specific ethnic and nationality groups as much as possible, and the main ethnic group to look at is the Latinos—actually a collection of diverse national groups growing rapidly. The best estimates today are that about 30 percent of American Catholics are Latinos.[3]

We could not look at every nationality group reliably, so as a compromise we decided to create two random samples, one of Latinos and the other of "everybody else," and to include the different ethnic and nationality groups in correct proportions in each sample. Thus, for example, the Latino sample has correct proportions of Mexican Americans, Cuban Americans, and so forth. Both samples are nationwide in the contiguous forty-eight states.

How would it be possible to get interviews with a good random sample of young adults? After reviewing several options we chose to do a survey of young adults who were confirmed some years earlier in Catholic parishes. It would be a study of "where are they now?" We decided to get random samples of names of confirmands in past years from Catholic parishes, so that the persons would be twenty to thirty-nine years old today, and then to find as many as possible and ask them about their lives.

This type of research is revelatory in that it begins with a definite category of people who were all at the same place during adolescence—in confirmation classes—and who might be relatively easy to find and interview today. It has a disadvantage in that not every Catholic adolescent in the 1980s and 1990s was confirmed, and thus our sample would be of a restricted group; we would be describing confirmands but not *all* young Catholics. We felt the advantages outweighed the limitations. We tried out the method in five cities in 1995, then received a grant from the Lilly Endowment in 1996 to proceed.

This book is the result. Throughout the project we have tried above all to gather trustworthy data and to report it clearly. During the research we developed our own viewpoints on various issues facing the Church, and in the final chapter of the book we introduce our own perspectives when we make several recommendations to Church leaders.

The phone survey of confirmands was by far the most difficult part of the study. We worked in forty-four parishes in eleven dioceses throughout the nation. In each parish we randomly selected names from the confirmation books, then hired local people to help us find the people today and also did our own search using nationwide computerized phone directories and thousands of calls. Most of the data were gathered in 1997.

Gathering the Latino interviews required extra effort. In some regions of the United States, finding the Latino confirmands was difficult. Our searches using phone calls to locate the Latinos had mixed success, and the process took a long time. Our eighty personal interviews and six focus groups were much easier, since we chose available persons for them rather than picking subjects by careful sampling. But in all our research we limited our attention to young adult Catholics twenty to thirty-nine years old who had been confirmed during adolescence. Appendix A gives details of the research methods.

Our hope is, first of all, to convey an accurate portrait of young adults. Insofar as our research methods introduced possible biases, we have tried to estimate their size. Our second hope is to have interpreted the findings in a way which is practically useful and conceptually fruitful. Much is at stake here. It is not an exaggeration to say that the future blossoming of American Catholicism depends on how the Church responds to young people.

CHAPTER 1

· ❦ ·

Catholicism in American Culture

·   ·   ·   ·

Charles Morris notes in the subtitle of his influential study of Catholicism in the United States (1997) that the story of American Catholics is one of "saints and sinners" who transformed a beleaguered immigrant faith into one of America's largest and most powerful religious institutions. Poised on the threshold of the Third Christian Millennium, these "saints and sinners" now constitute a church with sixty-two million members. A substantial percentage is thoroughly ensconced in the American middle and upper-middle classes, well-educated and with significant—if uncoordinated—political clout.

The Catholic Church in America also continues its traditional multicultural look. In the wake of the nation's new wave of immigration, the number of Asian and Latino Catholics has increased dramatically. Within the first quarter of the new millennium, Latino Catholics will constitute a near majority of the Church in the United States.

The story of American Catholic "saints and sinners" is a dizzying array of subtexts surrounding the engagement of a faith tradition and its host culture. This story illuminates the complex relationships between ethnic and religious identity, between "sect" and "church" tensions within the tradition, and between Catholicism and the forces of social change.

Central to these subtexts is the issue of Catholic identity: What does it mean to be Catholic today in this particular cultural milieu? What are the defining characteristics of Catholic identity? By what authority is this identity defined? And, perhaps most importantly, how is Catholic identity maintained by the twenty million young adult Catholics who are the future of the Church and for whom, in many cases, the Second Vatican Council is an unknown event? While the question of a coherent identity is a perennial one in all religious traditions, it has a special urgency for Catholics today.

Most observers agree that more than any other time in the past, American Catholics now have a confused sense of belonging and not belonging. The kinds of religious expression that can be subsumed under the name "Catholic" are less clear today than in the decades prior to the Second Vatican Council. The criteria surrounding Catholic identity—what is "core" and obligatory to the faith, what is and what is not legitimate in belief and practice, who does and who does not belong—have become more problematic in the last four decades. Catholic identity, once confined to clearly defined categories, is now as loosely marked as that of other mainline religious traditions. As the lines of Catholic identity become more blurred and diffuse, confusion and disputes as to the limits of that identity arise. Many young adult Catholics today appear uncertain as to whether there is anything *truly distinctive* about their religious identity—while the vast majority continue to identify themselves as "Catholic" and to admire the person, if not always the policies, of Pope John Paul II. Among many young adult Catholics today, the popular pope of papal visits and compact disks may not be the pope forming individual conscience. Nor has it gone unnoticed that in the diffusion of religious identity, Catholicism appears to be recapitulating patterns similar to the Protestant and Jewish encounter with modern American culture.

FIVE PERIODS OF AMERICAN CATHOLIC HISTORY

As a necessary prelude to the study that follows, we describe American Catholic history as having five general periods.

I. The Republican Period

In the late eighteenth and early nineteenth centuries, Catholics were few in numbers, relatively homogenous in their ethnic and national origins, and dutiful in their support of the emerging American Republic. The main issues facing the nascent Church during this first "Republican period" included establishing the faith in a new political and cultural environment, clerical shortages, conflicts over lay vs. clerical authority (trusteeism), and widespread anti-Catholicism. In addition, early Church leaders such as John Carroll, the first Catholic bishop in the United States, faced the formidable task of "constant exhortations to piety" as a way of engendering fervor in a population of Catholics who, with the exception of a number of prominent Maryland Catholic families, were mostly poor and illiterate farmers.

II. The Immigrant Church

The second period lasted roughly from the mid-nineteenth century through the first quarter of the twentieth century. This era of the "immigrant church" saw millions of Catholics pour into the United States from southern and eastern Europe. It was also a time when the number of Mexican Catholics increased due to American expansionism, having been initially converted beginning in 1565 by Spanish priests in the western regions of the United States.

Although sharing a common working-class identity and in spite of Protestant perceptions of a monolithic Catholicism, Catholic immigrants were not a homogeneous group, ethnically or linguistically. By the end of the nineteenth century, there were nearly thirty different Catholic nationality subgroups in the United States.

During this immigrant era, Church leadership faced the practical challenge of meeting the social and educational needs of the waves of Catholic immigrants. Other tasks focused on combating outbursts of anti-Catholic prejudice and discrimination and on building religious unity in the face of Catholicism's ethnic and cultural diversity. In addition, in the context of the "Americanist" controversy over the compatibility of Catholicism with religious liberty, church-state separation, and the call for a more Americanized church, American Church leaders were also swept into the conflict surrounding the Vatican's ideological struggle with a world increasingly shaped by the forces of liberalism, nationalism, materialism, scientism, and other "isms" deemed inimical to the faith.

III. The Triumphal Church

From the early twentieth century through the 1960s, the American
Catholic saga entered a third phase marked by social mobility, accel-
erating assimilation, participation in the broader American society, and
a growing Catholic cultural presence. This "triumphal stage" of the
1920s, 1930s, and 1940s saw the pinnacle of Catholic neighborhood,
parish, and parochial life in the United States (Dolan 1985). As Catholicism's ethnic diversity waned under the pressures of assimilation, and
as the Vatican pressed toward centralization and standardization in
Catholic religious life, the Church in America evolved into a more
homogeneous institution. Catholic identity developed distinct and
generally uniform institutional and symbolic boundaries. This uniformity was achieved theologically through the imposition of neo-
scholasticism and standardized doctrinal teachings; ritually through the
promotion of uniform modes of piety, devotionalism, and liturgical
life; ecclesially through a focus on papal authority; and socially through
a vast structure of Catholic institutions, especially Catholic schools.
These developments, combined with the social solidarity born of feelings of being outsiders in America, contributed to a distinct and vital
Catholic presence, as did Catholicism's conservative views of family
and married life, repressive sexual ethic, and reflexive anticommunism
(Tentler 1993).

During the post–World War II era, Catholic identity was also impacted by new forms of anti-Catholicism that arose in the public concern about "Catholic power" and the emerging Catholic influence on
American public affairs (Walch 1989:81). Catholics were especially considered a threat on church-state questions and issues surrounding
parochial schools. As McGreevey has shown (1997), the concern over
"Catholic power" became one of the defining characteristics of twentieth-century American liberalism. Thus, while upward mobility and
ethnic assimilation moved Catholics closer to the common culture, lin-
gering anti-Catholic animosities in the wider society limited this movement and reinforced a distinct Catholic identity. Other factors also
contributed to these developments.

For example, the ethos of Catholic spiritual and devotional life remained relatively medieval, save for a decline in certain ethnic-based

forms of devotionalism, a few innovations associated with the liturgical movement, and lay initiatives such as the Christian Family Movement. To many Protestants and nonreligious observers, Catholics were different, in large part because they prayed differently. Their spiritual and devotional life, which intensified with the spiritual resurgence of the 1950s (Walch 1989:77), remained preeminently otherworldly, centered around a complex of official and unofficial devotional practices, and dominated by clerical models of spiritual piety and virtuosity. Catholic spirituality also separated the sacred and profane spheres while promoting a highly objectified sacramentalism focused primarily around parish-based devotional life (Forty Hours, First Fridays, novenas) and on the holy sacrifice of the Mass.

Catholic social action also contributed to Catholic religious and cultural distinctiveness. Although Catholics took an active part in efforts to reform the American labor movement, Catholic social concerns were typically acts of charity aimed at spiritual solutions, and concentrated on Catholic working-class populations. Following the establishment of the National Catholic War Council (1917) (transformed into the National Catholic Welfare Council in 1919), any broader social initiatives remained confined to a minority of socially active bishops, to officially sanctioned "Catholic Action" ("the participation of the laity in the apostolate of the hierarchy"), and to a small and marginalized Catholic radicalism embodied in the Catholic Worker Movement.

IV. The Post–World War II Era

Catholic social mobility accelerated dramatically in the wake of the GI Bill. Under its provisions, millions of Catholic veterans attained college educations—the ticket into the American middle class. Catholics moved from urban enclaves into middle-class suburbia. This move dismantled much of the social ecology of the Euro-American ethnic and parochial neighborhoods that had long undergirded Catholic identity. By the mid-1950s Catholicism increasingly appeared as another full-fledged American religion, distinct in some ways from Protestantism and Judaism, but professing many values increasingly similar to them (Herberg 1960). By the 1960s, social mobility had produced a largely suburbanized and assimilated population of middle-class Euro-American Catholics now

fully engaged in American life and culture. John F. Kennedy symbolized this "new breed" Catholicism. Although a privileged political
mandarin himself and not part of the emergent Catholic middle class,
Kennedy typified the come-of-age independent lay Catholicism of the
day. By the 1970s and 1980s, American Catholics were among the most
highly educated, most occupationally privileged, and most prosperous
Americans (Davidson et al. 1997).

Lest the above picture of pre–Vatican II Catholicism seem overly
idealized, we are reminded that American Catholics were never without
their share of internal conflict, whether over trusteeism during the Republican era, the national parish conflict during the immigrant era, or
the debate over Catholic intellectual life in the mid-1950s. Not long after
World War II, Catholic intellectuals began calling for the Church to
break out of its self-imposed ghetto posture. This dissent focused on
Catholicism's clerical paternalism, the deficiencies of its scholastic intellectual capital, the authoritarianism of its ecclesial structures, and the
parochialism of Catholic culture in general (Callahan 1963, O'Dea 1958).
It called for a more culturally congruent Catholicism. The ensuing conflict echoed elements of the turn-of-the-century "Americanist" controversy that divided Catholic elites over issues of assimilation, allegiance
to American institutions and ideals, American nationalism, church-state
separation and religious liberty, and the wisdom of sponsoring parochial schools. By the mid-1960s, however, the conflict of the previous
decade was overshadowed by the storms erupting over the meaning and
implementation of the Second Vatican Council (1962–65).

V. Post-conciliar Catholicism

The fifth era of the American Catholic story runs roughly from the
pontificate of John XXIII to the present. Bob Dylan's counter-
cultural anthem of the early 1960s proclaimed that "The times, they
are a'changing." For Catholics the changes were wide-ranging and
dramatic. Like many of their non-Catholic compatriots, American
Catholics experienced the cultural crisis of the 1960s; the travail of
America's civil religion; the emergence of an anti-establishment,
youth-oriented counterculture; widespread drug usage; urban riots; political assassinations; and other paroxysms that eroded much of the

public symbolism and moral capital that had once defined the meaning of the American experience (Bellah 1975).

The morally-driven political struggles of the times—especially the civil rights movement and to a lesser degree the anti-Vietnam war movement—changed Catholic institutional and religious self-understanding. The civil rights movement and the controversies over desegregation and forced busing focused attention on the resistance of many Euro-American Catholics to the growing number of Latino and Afro-American Catholics. In addition, the civil rights movement cast many clergy, nuns, and parishioners, energized by Vatican II, into new social roles and relationships with far-reaching implications for the Church's own internal life. The focus of Catholic attention on power, authority, equality, and discrimination in the public sphere invariably turned back on the Church itself. In time, many Catholic liberals adopted a rights-based language that raised the question of the rights of Catholics in the Church itself (McGreevey 1996:245).

In addition to these events, the cumulative effects of broad social and cultural changes in American society in the 1960s, 70s, and 80s produced a convergence in Catholic attitudes and practices with the American population as a whole. Analysis of attitude trends over the last quarter century shows both marked decline in distinctive Catholic attitudes and behaviors and striking similarities between Catholics and the population at large. In the former regard, between 1970 and 1991, Protestants had no overall change in self-estimated commitment to their religion, but the proportion of Catholics saying they were strong declined from 45 percent to 37 percent. By the 1990s Catholics were no different from Protestants in their rates of church attendance (25 to 30 percent reporting weekly attendance). And, regarding age strata, in all surveys the youngest group of Catholics was much less likely than the others to say they were "strong" Catholics. Catholics also expressed a more tolerant view of freedom of speech, with important differences in levels of toleration from young (more tolerant) to older (less tolerant) Catholics. Catholics and Protestants were also virtually the same in all nationwide surveys regarding confidence in organized religion, with both showing a strong decline in confidence, especially prior to 1985.

With regard to family size and sex role issues, Catholics, especially the young and college-educated, have followed national trends indicating a desire for smaller numbers of children, support for women in leadership roles, and attitudes toward greater support for women's rights and freedoms. Catholics have also moved in the direction of greater tolerance for various sexual behaviors such as premarital sex, homosexuality, and the use of birth control (Hoge 1998).

Vatican II Aggiornamento

Along with the political and cultural turmoil of the time, Catholics in the 1960s also found themselves in an institution embarking upon its most significant reform since the Reformation. The Second Vatican Council articulated a more positive Catholic assessment of the world, launched a reform of how the Church renewed itself (especially in regard to its liturgical life), and encouraged local churches to achieve more culturally relevant expressions of Catholicism. The dominant themes and images of Vatican II *aggiornamento* ("updating") included Catholics as the "people of God" who were members of a Pilgrim Church that now embraced a more collegial (and less clerical) ecclesiology. All baptized Catholics were called to holiness, to active transformation of the world, and to reading the "signs of the times." Catholics were also called to a new ecumenical outreach and to the priority of individual conscience over coercion in matters of religion (Komonchak 1997).

American Catholics responded in overwhelmingly positive ways to Vatican II *aggiornamento,* even where implementation of the conciliar decrees came slowly and hesitantly. By the late 1960s, however, disputes over the Council's meaning and implementation had hardened into ideological lines and interest group agendas overshadowing much of the initial euphoria. This conflict reflected, in part, the difficulties caused by the sheer speed at which Catholicism's seemingly unchanging and uniform religious culture was replaced by new forms that sometimes seemed contradictory of previous church life. The ensuing battle for the American Church brought to the fore many issues of ecclesiology, assimilation, and authority that had simmered below the surface of the Church's institutional life—including issues of lay autonomy, clerical authority, and control of Catholic institutions (Kelly 1979, Hitchcock 1979).

The growing divisiveness after Vatican II pitted liberal and progressive Catholics, who saw the Council as a long-overdue accommodation of the Church to the world and a starting point for more wide-ranging reforms, against conservative and traditionalist Catholics who were much more resistant to accommodation (Weaver and Appleby 1995). The symbolic context for much of this conflict over Vatican II centered around implementation of the *Novus Ordo Missae*, the New Order of the Mass introduced in 1967 in the wake of the Council's call for a reform of the liturgy (Dinges 1991).

Conflict among American Catholics in the wake of the Council was also fueled by the liberalizing social trends noted earlier, and by other developments on the religious landscape, notably the restructuring of American religion in the 1960s, 1970s, and 1980s along liberal and conservative lines (Wuthnow 1988). In addition, the growing Latino presence in the Church in America began to take on a new significance and aroused new tensions as Latinos and Latinas began, in the latter 1960s, to press for a more enculturated expression of their faith and for alternative ministries and structures that utilized an ecclesiology different from the Euro-American church. Many saw their religion as a major source of social and symbolic capital to enhance their distinctive identity in American society (Diaz-Stevens and Stevens-Arroyo 1998). In time, Latino theologians came increasingly to emphasize popular religion as a key concept for Latino religious experience (Espin 1994).

After the Council, dramatic declines also occurred in many elements of Catholic institutional life. Vocations, Mass attendance, confessions, and the number of converts all diminished significantly. These developments, which reinforced conservative Catholic anxieties over *aggiornamento*, were also attended by a collapse of Catholicism's neo-scholastic intellectual edifice under the influence of social science, existentialism, a new emphasis on orthopraxis, growing pluralism in theology, and a spreading historical consciousness. In addition, much of what had once passed for virtuosity and holiness in Catholic spiritual life seemed unfashionable and unhealthy in light of contemporary psychological criteria, especially new theories emphasizing personal fulfillment and a more holistic understanding of the human person (Downey 1994). Nor can the turmoil over Vatican II be understood independently from the protracted conflict over Pope Paul VI's *Humanae Vitae* (1968), an encyclical that generated a tidal wave of frustrated expectations and dissent that carried over into controversies surrounding implementation of the Council reforms.

THE CATHOLIC IDENTITY ISSUE

At the beginning of the new century we are well into the fifth period of American Catholic history. Much of the polarization and interest group conflict among Catholics of the previous three decades has abated, not because the various sides have softened their positions, but for other reasons. The most radicalized elements have turned to more passive forms of protest, or they have been removed from teaching jobs or other positions of authority as in the case of clerics and theologians. Some have simply left the Church.[1] Since the mid-1980s, much of the public discourse on American Catholics has shifted from the debate over Vatican II to the collateral question of Catholic identity. The identity issue has attracted a broad spectrum of concerns both within and outside the Church, from those simply decrying (or celebrating) the loss of Catholicism's distinctiveness to those advocating a more radical re-imagining of Catholic identity in the Third Christian Millennium. Few discussants, however, disagree that the Church in America has experienced a profoundly destabilizing moment in what American Catholic historians have come to describe as the "collapse of Tridentine Catholicism" (Tentler 1993).

Before turning to a brief description of what some of these voices are saying about Catholic identity, we note two additional factors that contextualize the problem of contemporary Catholic identity.

Postmodern Globalism

The broader cultural context today is one of postmodern globalism. The postmodern world is a world of cultural mixing of symbols and codes, a rising tide of pluralism, suspicion of totalistic ideologies, and the deconstruction of traditions (Beyer 1994, Lakeland 1997). It is also a world dominated by electronic mass media, the information explosion, and by free-market capitalism's ethos of commodification and consumption. These conditions challenge all religious traditions.

Young adult Catholics in the United States have grown up in a time of unprecedented affluence. They have more educational and occupational opportunities than ever. They enjoy more freedom and have found more doors open to them. They have traveled more than any Catholics in history. They have a more global outlook. They have also grown up amid radical changes in sexual morality, in the roles of women, of marriage, community, and family, and in other forms of institutional life—including religious institutions.

Many aspects of popular culture today involve a loosening of social ties. From the mid-1960s to the early 1990s, social conditions deteriorated as measured by rising crime, illegitimate births, declining fertility, and declining trust and confidence in institutions. Large numbers of young adults have experienced parental divorce and other family breakdowns. Many feel insecure about long-term relationships and long-term commitments. These trends are compounded by the cultural assault on the authority of tradition by exaggerated individualism—including religious individualism.

Religious Individualism

It is widely recognized today that although religion and spirituality have traditionally been the province of institutional religion, they are increasingly viewed as individual and private matters with few connections with communities or institutions. The values of free choice and experimentation in religion have been part of the American cultural tradition, as has the legacy of the Protestant notion that there should be no mediator between the individual and God. The social revolution of the sixties, however, had a pronounced impact on elevating the values of free choice and experimentation in the religious context (Hammond 1993). Large numbers of people now experience the sacred outside the sanction of religious institutions. Spirituality has become increasingly uncoupled from religion (Roof 1999).

This is the cultural setting in which young adult Catholics now live. In this context, many do not perceive their Catholic identity as an inherited tradition per se, but, like other forms of social identity, as a self-constructed process of choosing among religous-spiritual options. This individualist religious identity construction is undertaken in conjunction with perceived spiritual needs. It utilizes the symbols and doctrines of the tradition, but only insofar as young adults know and appropriate them and find them pragmatically useful. This process also involves drawing on other forms of spiritual merchandizing in the American cultural emporium. This highly subjective and individualist understanding of changing identity and obligation is at the heart of the "seeker" syndrome and "new volunteerism" in religion (Roof and McKinney 1987). It also expresses the contractual and individualistic assumptions of contemporary American culture.

What Are Today's Voices Saying about Catholic Identity?

In chapter 2, we describe contemporary research perspectives on young adult Catholics. Here we summarize a few overall findings and assertions.

Recent studies of identity diffusion among American Catholics suggest that the gap continues to grow between what official documents and ecclesiologists say about the nature of the Church and Catholic identity, and the practical ecclesiology of voluntary associations espoused by many Catholics today (Searle 1986:332, McNamara 1992, D'Antonio et al. 1996, Davidson et al. 1997). Young adults have a more selective sense of a "consumer Catholicism" than a practicing or institutionally validated Catholicism. Their knowledge of the faith and of its traditional symbols and root metaphors is limited, fragmentary, or nonexistent (Imbelli 1982:524, Coleman 1982:158). Many appear to have lost much of the core narrative of the tradition and to have little connectedness with Catholic institutional life (Rohr and Martos 1989). As a consequence, young adult Catholics have a difficult time articulating a coherent sense of Catholic identity and expressing Catholicism's distinctiveness. Nor, with the exception of Latinos, are many young adult Catholics able to fall back on ethnic or tribal identity as a reinforcement of religious identity. As the boundaries of Catholicism become weaker and more diffuse, preserving and transmitting the tradition's norms become more difficult. We discuss these problems in chapters 9 and 10.

Liberal Catholic reform groups, such as Call to Action, have warned of the growing number of young adults and children of Catholic families who are reluctant to affiliate with a Church they view as authoritarian and hypocritical (1990). Other progressive observers such as Robert Ludwig, director of ministry and professor of religious studies at De Paul University, decry the number of young Catholics who have never experienced any compelling connection to their religious heritage, who have little or no meaningful socialization into the Church, and who have "almost no definition delimiting Catholicism nor any exclusive allegiance to it" (1995:40). As Ludwig notes, this disconnection from the Church—which is often perceived by young adults as a conflicted institution—is particularly detrimental. It occurs in the cultural context of radical alterations in family life, rising divorce and suicide rates, widespread drug abuse, changing gender roles, and, as we have noted, in a culture in which individualism has expanded dramatically at the expense of community and institutional life once nurtured by religious traditions.

Others have argued that the problem of Catholic identity has taken on more urgency because the new sense of choice seems to de-emphasize faithful observance of prescribed beliefs, behaviors, and practices (Phan 1998:160). The selective nature of Catholic identity today has also been highlighted, suggesting that there is little difference between core Catholics and those who are unchurched or non-practicing ones in making up their own minds which Church positions to accept and which to reject (Greeley 1977, 1990).

One of the most problematic trends among young adults is the decline in the perceived importance of being Catholic. Studies consistently show that the salience of Catholic identity has steadily waned (McNamara 1992, D'Antonio 1995, Davidson 1997). *Fewer young adult Catholics believe that it is important to be Catholic.* Many have developed a loose commitment to a vague "cultural Catholicism" or have espoused a more generic Christian lifestyle. Some have simply reduced their religious identity to being a good person. Others approach institutional Catholicism tentatively and intermittently. This decline in the salience of Catholic identity has important behavioral consequences, not only in the realm of moral choices, but in choices about marriage partners, childrearing, the education of children, and church attendance.

In a recent analysis of American Catholics, James Davidson and his colleagues point to the "cohort effect" (relating changing beliefs and behaviors to age differences) as a factor relevant to the declining salience of Catholic identity and to generational differences among Catholics today. Davidson notes in a foreboding summary that young adult Catholics

> are less religious in childhood than their parents and grandparents; they report fewer experiences of God's presence in their lives; and they are less committed to the Church. Unless steps are taken these trends portend a future of dwindling faithfulness among young Catholics, diminishing awareness of God's presence in the lives of Catholic adults, further erosion of Catholic identity, and a declining sense that the Church is worth supporting. These trends, in turn, signal a continuation of recent tendencies to disagree with traditional faith and morals and to embrace religious ideas that are incompatible with Church teachings. (204)

Alternative Views

Not everyone agrees with this bleak scenario. Andrew Greeley has insisted that there is nothing in his data to suggest that the generation of Catholics who have grown up since the Second Vatican Council are "any less loyal, any less committed, any less devout than their predecessors" (1990). John Coleman, another sociological observer, while recognizing that young adults are less practicing and less committed to the Church, attributes much of this detachment to the life cycle syndrome (1990). That is, with marriage and families, they will become more connected later. A similar positive evaluation of young adult commitment to the Church can be found in the *Sons and Daughters of the Light*, the United States Catholic Conference document we noted in the introduction.

Observers differ over the reality of young adult Catholics today in terms of their sense of identity, boundaries, and institutional affiliation. These are some of the complex questions which we will try to answer in the chapters that follow.

CHAPTER 2

Past Research
on Young Catholics

· · · ·

To help explain the new research results we need to look at earlier studies. A constant finding of earlier research has been that Catholic older adults and Catholic young adults are different in many ways. Investigators have found this repeatedly, so we can accept it as proven: young Catholics are different, and they represent something American Catholicism hasn't seen until now (D'Antonio et al. 1996, Davidson et al. 1997). Young Catholics tend to be independent thinkers on religious and moral topics. We will expand on this below.

The uniqueness of young adults would be enough reason to look at them in depth. But there are other reasons also. One is that the early adult years have a strong influence on the remainder of life. Social scientists have identified late adolescence and young adulthold as an especially "impressionable period" during which social, political, and religious attitudes are formed. The leading sociologist studying young adults was Karl Mannheim, who identified the years after seventeen as the most impressionable period of the European youths he studied.[1] For American youth this is also true. Political scientist Karl Deutsch identified the special years for political development as twenty plus or minus five, that is, fifteen to twenty-five. For whatever reason, these years are more formative for values and attitudes than any time before or after. Some recent observers have guessed that the impressionable years have moved downward in recent years, that is, to younger and younger ages; our impression is that this is true.

Research has found, furthermore, that the values and attitudes developed during the fifteen to twenty period tend to remain throughout life. That is, after about twenty-five years of age there is a solidification of values making them resistant to change, and researchers studying the life cycle find that people in their forties, fifties, or sixties tend to have the same values they had back in their twenties (Glenn 1980, Braungart and Braungart 1986). This is not to say that everyone maintains the same attitudes and values during the adult years, since for some persons it is not true. But the overall pattern is of stability more than change, and the persons who do change tend to be those who experience extreme changes in their lives, as for example, marriage to a person much different than themselves, radical change of place of residence, change of career, or the like. Such people are the minority; for the majority there is a momentum in the life cycle so that the values inculcated during their twenties remain for many decades.

Thus, widely heard sayings such as "old people turn conservative" or "yesterday's radicals all go straight later" are for the most part untrue. It *is* true that older people in the American population are more conservative than the young on many topics (a good example: the rules of sexual behavior), but this is not because the older people have changed with age. It is because they acquired more conservative values when *they* were in their twenties and have kept them. In short: the differences between old and young are mostly the result of the different life experiences of these groups when they were young. They are not because older people change in one direction or another.

Sociologists studying social change have found that attitude change in the population is a product of two processes, first, the entrance into the adult population of new young people who have different attitudes from their elders, and second, a general shift in attitudes in *all* age groups. Of the two, the first is relatively more powerful in such attitudinal areas as race relations, sex-role issues, and political preference, but the second is more important on civil liberties issues (Kiecolt 1988, Firebaugh and Davis 1988). On religious beliefs we do not have enough good research to permit us to make a summary statement. All we can say is that the "age effect," that is, the effect of getting older if all else is constant, is weak.

The important lesson here is that today's young adults predict tomorrow's middle and old adults. Today's old adults *do not* predict tomorrow's old adults. If you want to take an advance peek at tomorrow's adults in the leadership ages (let us say, age forty-five to sixty-five), look at today's adults in their twenties and thirties.

YOUTH AS INNOVATORS

Past research has another lesson: youth are more open to change than older people. This has been shown repeatedly in studies of college students (Lipset and Altbach 1969), and it is true in part because college students tend to be living away from home in special settings which are designed to inculcate new ideas. Colleges were built to influence young adults. Colleges continually try to have an impact, and sometimes, at least, they succeed. College students are the portion of the population most open to change from new ideas. Researchers have found that college student values have a high level of volatility from half-decade to half-decade, a volatility which is not found in the general population. That is, college students change in values and attitudes so much each half-decade that nobody has been able to predict what they will be like in the future. It is worth remembering that no social researchers predicted the student uprisings of the late 1960s, and nobody predicted the return to conservative values in the late 1970s.

In societies undergoing modernization, young adults have played a special role. History demonstrates over and over that young adults, and especially educated young adults, are the shock troops of change. They are the ones who speak out against arbitrary rule, who demonstrate in the streets demanding reforms, who volunteer to lead social movements, and who sometimes clash with established authorities in the streets (Eisenstadt 1956, Gillis 1981). This was true throughout modern European history; it was true in Cuba in the Castro movement; it was true in China in the Tiananmen Square movement; it was true in Indonesia in the overthrow of Sukarno. In each case college students were at the forefront of the movement, asking for more democracy, more justice, and more freedom. The Broadway musical "Les Miserables" showed the typical scene: the idealistic young college students banded together to battle in the streets against the old regime's military guard. The same is true in cultural movements, such as the sexual revolution and the women's movement in the United States since the 1960s: young adults were at the forefront. We should consider it normal that at any time young adults are different from their elders in demanding more freedoms, more democracy, and more innovations. We should expect the same in twenty-first century Catholicism.

We can state a general sociological conclusion: educated young people are disproportionately open to influence from new ideas and experiences. In modernizing nations they are the ones most influenced by modern nations; in immigrant groups everywhere they are the most influenced by the dominant culture; in American Catholicism they are the ones most affected by the surrounding liberal culture—especially as found in American higher education.

Catholics in America today live side by side with Protestants and Jews in suburbs and small towns. They are fully integrated into the mainstream culture. They attend many of the same high schools and colleges. They date each other's brothers and sisters, which results in a high rate of interfaith marriage. Most of them do not feel that they as Catholics are something different or unique. No, at the end of the twentieth century they are full-fledged Americans like everybody else. Being Catholic has less and less impact on young adults' behavior as the years since immigration lengthen. We should expect, as a matter of course, that young Catholics and especially young educated Catholics should be at the forefront of movements asking for more democracy and more freedoms in Catholic life.

The Stage of Youth Now Extended

The stage of American life labeled "youth" (or "adolescence") is not defined with any precision. It has no agreed-on beginning and end. Yet all social scientists agree that this stage is lasting longer and longer. If the end of "youth" is measured by marriage or entry into a permanent occupation, as many sociologists suggest, then "youth" certainly extends longer today than ever before in America. One useful measure is age at first marriage. It has risen sharply since the 1970s. In 1970 the median age of first marriage was 22.5 years for men and 20.6 for women. In 1990 it was 25.9 for men and 24.0 for women, and it has risen by about a year since then (U.S. Census 1998:112). Young people are also having children later. The median age of motherhood rose from 24.6 years in 1980 to 26.8 years in 1996 (U.S. Census 1998:77).

More young people are attending college in America than ever before. In 1970, 10.7 percent of the adult population had received four or more years of college; in 1980 it was 16.3 percent, and in 1990 it was 21.3 percent. Among Latinos the numbers were lower: 7.6 percent in 1980 and 9.2 percent in 1990 (U.S. Census 1998:167).

These trends will affect America's churches. Church leaders need to expect that young adults today will be slower to complete the "youth" stage of their lives than was the case twenty or forty years ago. The geographic and occupational transiency common to people formerly in their early twenties now applies to people throughout all their twenties and even to the early thirties. The age of singlehood now lasts longer, and in addition the social pressure to be married at all has subsided (Cherlin 1996:265). Social changes in the late twentieth century have produced a generation of young adult Catholics different from anything earlier.

RECENT RESEARCH ON YOUNG ADULT CATHOLICS

Five recent investigators have looked at young adult Catholics—Andrew Greeley, Patrick McNamara, Robert Ludwig, Tom Beaudoin, and James Davidson.[2] In this section we will review their main findings.

Andrew Greeley: Communal Catholics

Greeley made several studies of young adults, and in doing so he introduced an important concept—the "communal Catholic." He reported that in the 1970s growing numbers of Catholics were becoming "communal Catholics." He defined "communal Catholics" as persons who describe themselves as Catholic, who like being Catholic, who are at ease with their Catholicism, but who have only minimal expectations of the institutional church, who do not listen very seriously to what the church leaders say, and do not expect to get guidance from the Church. They have a limited knowledge of Catholic doctrine and teachings. They reserve the right to interpret the Catholic worldview to meet their own needs. These persons are not angry with the institutional church; on the contrary they seem to have an affectionate respect for those priests and nuns they have known in the past. Some of these persons show up at church from time to time, many have interest in learning more about the faith, and most of them come for sacramental ministry when they need it. As one young woman told Greeley, "Of course I'm a Catholic. I'm not sure exactly what that means, but I couldn't be any-thing else" (1976:10).

Communal Catholics are not open to changing their denomination:

> It is inconceivable that they would stop being Catholic. That is, I submit, not merely a matter of ethnic loyalty but also a realization that the Catholic symbol system has so shaped their personalities that there is no way they can escape the influence of that shaping. Rather, they make peace with the Catholic symbol system and try to find some guidance from it for their personal problems. (Greeley 1976:11)

Greeley contrasts communal Catholics with "ecclesiastical Catholics." The latter are committed to the institutional church and try either to maintain it unchanged from the 1950s or to reform it. Ecclesiastical Catholics are engrossed in church issues and church politics, including who wins the election of the National Conference of Catholic Bish-ops or who is president of their priests' senate. Ecclesiastical Catho-lics have strong feelings on institutional issues and they cannot com-prehend how anyone can be committed to Catholicism and still be serenely indifferent to the ecclesiastical organization. By contrast, com-munal Catholics never in their lives had much commitment to the institutional church. Generally they like it from a distance with a feel-ing of vague warmth, or they are bemused by its leaders and their pronouncements. The communal Catholic "remains a religious indi-vidualist despite himself" (p. 181).

Communal Catholics are not organized into any movement or party, and Greeley doubts if they can ever be organized. But they are a grow-ing portion of American Catholicism. Greeley guesses that for decades they existed in small numbers, but since the 1960s and 1970s they are growing in numbers, and they will continue to grow in numbers and influence for years to come. They will probably be the wave of the future. The mushrooming numbers will entail a strong challenge to the ecclesial institution:

> Communal Catholics will no longer accept what the church says on social and moral issues merely because the church has said it. Indeed, until the church manages to reassert its credibility they will barely listen to it when it speaks. (p. 185)

We discuss communal Catholics here because later research agreed with Greeley's prognosis. Our own research, as we demonstrate below, agrees partly but not totally. In our study we found a low level of knowledge of the Catholic tradition and limited command of Catholic cultural symbols. These people might be called "communal semi-Catholics" (as we report below).

Patrick McNamara: Study of a Catholic High School

McNamara made annual surveys of seniors in a Catholic high school in the Southwest between 1977 and 1989, and he also surveyed two classes of alumni when they were about twenty-seven years old. His interpretation of differences between these young Catholics and their parents emphasized the personal *selectivity* which the young adults used in accepting the Catholic tradition. These high school seniors and alumni respectfully studied church doctrines and teachings, then they proceeded to make up their own minds about what to accept or reject. They felt little obligation to accept any teachings they did not understand or assent to. Almost all of them remained Catholic but they did so on their own terms. They felt little sense of obligation to carry out church teachings regarding weekly Mass attendance or other participation in the sacraments. For the vast majority, church authority had weakened and had been replaced by personal authority, so they felt it was correct for them as individuals to evaluate authoritative church teachings and to accept or reject them.

McNamara accepted Greeley's concept of "communal Catholic" as being a good description of these young people. Communal Catholics are persons who value their Catholic identity and see no reason to switch denominations. They commit themselves to the portions of Catholic teachings and institutions which they personally select. Many distrust the Church's teaching authority and are unwilling to take it seriously, yet in spite of this sense of distance they continue attending Sunday Mass, and they forge a version of Catholic faith and life which they find acceptable and nourishing. The word "communal" Catholic refers to their identification with the Catholic community and tradition; it is analogous to the concepts "tribal Catholic" or "ethnic Catholic." That is, their commitment and their identity are tied to the Catholic community and heritage, but selectively.

To exemplify: McNamara asked the seniors to select one statement out of three which was closest to their view of church authority. The three were:

1. "As a Catholic, I should form my conscience according to the Church's teaching on religious beliefs and moral behavior." (This was chosen by 11 percent.)
2. "As a Catholic, I should listen respectfully to the Church's teachings on religious beliefs and moral behavior, but then make up my mind according to my own conscience." (Chosen by 78 percent.)
3. "I don't believe any authority has the right to influence the formation of anyone's conscience. That is strictly up to the individual." (Chosen by 11 percent; 1992, p. 106.)

Response no. 2 spoke for the vast majority; it is a forthright statement of the primacy of personal authority. McNamara reflected:

> The religious faith of these young adults . . . is a far cry from the pre–Vatican II devotional Catholicism. The centrality of ritual regularity, and the sense of sin, authority, and the miraculous, have yielded to the tentative, to exploring and testing, to the passing of judgment upon what seems irrelevant, senseless, or even harmful on the one hand, and to what is liberating, fulfilling, and comforting on the other. Many have obviously decided that the world of Catholic ritual, belief, and moral norms passes these tests solidly and can thus be given personal allegiance. But if they do not, they are set aside. (p. 154)

These young adults have no sense of owing loyalty to any institution as such. No institution, simply by making a claim, deserves their allegiance; all institutions need to *earn* it. To accomplish this allegiance, institutions need to appeal more directly to the values these young persons embrace and to explain Catholic teachings.

Of all the Catholic teachings, the ones ignored most by the students were those regarding sexual morality. The students defined these topics as beyond the legitimate range of external authority, whether religious or governmental; in their view, these matters are properly left for individuals to decide.

McNamara talked with the high school teachers and asked them how they coped with this student mentality. How did they handle the teaching of church doctrine? The teachers said that they were unable to convince the students to accept church authority. They needed to adopt a stance of explaining and persuading. One teacher commented:

> Adolescents these days question *all sources* of authority. This generation of kids, especially in the last few years, really had knowledgeable parents, so the kids are more sophisticated. They get it from their parents. So by all means, yes, the tendency is toward questioning and not swallowing something just because you're told to. You know, it's like they're saying, "Any time an authority figure asks me to do something, I'll ask why. You prove it to me." Our job as theology teachers is not just to present but to persuade, these days. We're selling more than telling. (p. 108)

One-third of the students in the school were Latinos, and McNamara investigated how distinctive they were. In general they resembled the other students (whom he called "Anglos"). The only real difference was that the Latinos showed a greater respect for the Church as teacher (p. 91). Also the Latino youth who spoke Spanish at home were different from other Latinos in that they were more orthodox and conservative. McNamara concluded that as immigrant Latino families begin to speak more and more English, their offspring will come to resemble more and more the family's Anglo neighbors and will lose any remaining traits of traditionalism. He predicted that the history of assimilation of earlier European Catholic immigrants is very likely to be repeated in these Latino families (p. 162).

Robert Ludwig: Experience with College Students

Ludwig (1995) wrote a book reflecting on his six years as a campus minister at DePaul University. He found that the students had ambivalent feelings about the Catholic church. Like McNamara, he adopted Greeley's concept "communal Catholic" as a correct description. This form of selective Catholicism is a virtual imperative for young people today, since the prevailing culture is one of suspicion of institutions claiming authority, whether they be religious, cultural, or governmental (p. 41).

Ludwig takes seriously the present-day social context which is fragmented and which provides no personal meaning:

> These young people are reaping the harvest of an age of deconstruction, during which time previous patterns of coherence and meaning came unraveled. Those of us who lived through the 1960s sensed that the changes taking place within and without us were profound and permanent, yet we had little idea of what legacy this would leave our children. (p. 18)

It's not that college students are uninterested. No, they are *hungry* for personal meaning. This spiritual void shows itself in drug and alcohol abuse, reckless sexual activity, eating disorders, clinical depression, apathy, and alienation. Young people feel the need to question *everything* and have a reluctance to commit themselves to anything.

Ludwig's students commonly distinguish spiritual needs from religion, identifying the latter with the organized church. He polled several of his first-year religion courses:

> When asked what the major contemporary *religious* issues are, students consistently bring up the credibility of the church, pedophilia in the priesthood, reproductive rights, the ordination of women, priestly celibacy, and the church's teachings regarding human sexuality— hardly the basics of our tradition! When I push them and ask what the major *spiritual* concerns facing their generation are, I get a very different set of responses: the need to belong and feel loved; concern for interfaith understanding and the self-righteous exclusivity of the Re-

ligious Right; self-esteem, mutual respect, and civility; human rights; increasing violence and abuse; ecological concerns; the problems of addiction; and the loss of meaning and hope for the future. (p. 25)

He reports on his surveys of freshman:

> Two out of forty-five raised their hands when asked if they had "ever heard of the U.S. bishops' pastoral letters on peace and the economy." Only a small minority of incoming DePaul students report an active commitment to an organized religion that they have studied and know something about. (p. 24)

Students feel alienated from the institutional church just like they feel toward other authoritative institutions. Ludwig attributes this partly to the present-day situation of polarization in Catholicism. "Catholic identity is difficult to figure out in such a conflicted situation, and what is attractive and inviting about this church is not very visible to them" (p. 3). A special problem unique to the Catholic church is that it has a heritage of juridical power shared with secular governments. In past centuries the Church governed family life, education, and much of economic life. A tendency toward a juridical mentality lingers in the Church today, and thus many students associate Catholicism with a set of negative constraints on life. Ludwig proposes a reconstruction of Catholicism, giving attention to spiritual experiences and sidelining the older system of governance and rulemaking.

Tom Beaudoin: Analysis of Generation X

Beaudoin makes a unique analysis of young adults and especially of young adult Catholics. His book *Virtual Faith* (1998) pictures the spiritual lives of the members of Generation X. He calls them "GenXers" and defines them as the persons born between the early 1960s and late 1970s. (Elsewhere in this book we do not speak of "Generation X" but prefer to talk more precisely about "persons twenty to thirty-nine years old.") Beaudoin calls his book a description of this generation, while stating that it is not a sociological study. He was born Catholic in 1969, and he was twenty-seven years old and a student at Harvard Divinity

School when he wrote the book. He tells about his own religious development and about the religious and spiritual lives of the friends he came to know while attending college, playing guitar in Christian rock bands, doing volunteer soldiering in Israel, and attending a synagogue for a while.

Actually Beaudoin's book is about a small slice of GenXers, a group of maybe five percent of the total GenX Catholics—those with the most education, cosmopolitan experiences, and freedom. We can call them the "privileged five percent." For example, Beaudoin tells us that he has been "an internet junkie since 1988," when he was nineteen years old (p. 121). It was an expansive experience for him, but such an experience does not occur for the majority of Catholic youth today, who are not frequenters of the internet. To illustrate, a 1997 Gallup poll of students in grades seven through twelve found that only 55 percent had ever had an opportunity to use the internet (Gallup 1997: 213). Clearly the percentage who were "internet junkies" from age nineteen on was not large.

Beaudoin's book pertains to only a thin slice of GenX Catholics, and we are even uncertain if it can be generalized, since the preface to the book tells us that when Beaudoin presented his views to students at Harvard Divinity School it evoked a passionate debate as to whether or not he got it right. Some were sure he got it wrong. His account barely touches on some of the common concerns of Catholic Xers—family relationships, ethnicity, marriage, and children. Nobody should accept Beaudoin's book as a representative portrait of young Catholics today. For that, sociological methods are needed. Our 1997 sample found less educated, less cosmopolitan Catholics, on average, than Beaudoin writes about.[3]

Bracketing for a moment the question of generalizability, what does Beaudoin say? His main message is that popular culture is the voice of GenX today and the key to understanding GenX's deepest spiritual concerns. Although most intellectuals and pastors ignore or deride popular culture, Beaudoin argues that they are making a mistake. They should cherish it for its diagnostic value. Popular culture has molded GenX. This generation grew up surrounded by television, MTV, movies, and the internet, and this technology has produced a "second-layer cultural environment" added on to the more general American experience. Current movies, videos, MTV, and internet web sites are the best ways to know about the spiritual life of the young.

GenX is as spiritual as any earlier generation, but its spiritual quest is broader, more tentative, and more wary about organized religion. Its spirituality can be described under four headings. First, Xers distinguish religion from spirituality. By "religion" they refer to the organized Church, which they view with suspicion. Thus their spiritual quest moves along paths independent of churches.

[An important] theme that emerges from GenX popular culture is deep suspicion of religious institutions. Three types of popular culture suspicion illustrate this distrust. First, Xers challenge religious institutions in general. Second, GenXers specifically assault the Catholic Church. Third, they frequently pit Jesus against the Church. (p. 41)

He quotes a young woman: "What the hell's going to church for? These days you've got to take religion in your own hands." And another: "I still think people can be spiritual or religious without going to churches or synagogues."

The main objections the Xers feel to organized religion are its claims to authority, its blind approval of middle-class culture, and its excessive bureaucracies laboring constantly to maintain the institutional structures intact. The Catholic Church is the most common object of Xer cynicism, partly because it is the biggest target and partly because it has the most layers of distant bureaucracy. An example is the off-putting effect of Catholic diocesan web sites which are decorated with "triumphalistic and outdated images or icons." "Some sites use the keys of Saint Peter or medieval Catholic shields (or subject visitors to several minutes of 'Ave Maria' played on a cheap synthesizer)" (p. 163). These sorts of web sites, Beaudoin says, beg to be parodied.

Second, Xer spirituality is open and unbounded. Xers search for sustenance in many places. Beaudoin told of the spiritualities of the Xers he has known:

These spiritualities, though varied, often consisted of a hodgepodge of theological symbols and traditions. I myself read theology from a variety of sources: the Catholic Hans Küng, the Jewish Martin Buber, and the Protestant Søren Kierkegaard. (p. 13)

This openness is extended by the unbounded modern pop culture, especially the hundreds of religious options in cyberspace. The availability of many religious options invites young adults to an attitude of relativism—the attitude that everything has some measure of truth in it (p. 123). When no credible religious authority exists, the individual is left to himself or herself to make life decisions in any way possible. Religious relativism is ever-present in GenX culture.

Third is the tendency toward *bricolage*. This French word means an improvized, rough assemblage of whatever tools are at hand to solve a problem. Xers have a tendency to take elements from different spiritual sources in constructing a new *bricolage* for themselves, taking from available images, symbols, doctrines, and texts. Pop culture is full of such combinations and juxtapositions, as for example when Madonna in the video "Like a Prayer" uses images of a crucifix, a prayer card, and statues of Jesus, Mary, and Joseph, and she brings to life a statue of Saint Martin by kissing it and being kissed in return.

Fourth, Xer spirituality makes *experience* central. Experience is the arbiter of all religious claims to truth or morality, and lived experience is the main indicator of what counts as religious. It takes precedence over the authority claimed by any institution. This is because, in part, institutional authorities are not credible, and therefore people need to take religious matters into their own hands and sort out religious talk based on what really *feels* to be true and good.

One may ask: is Beaudoin wholly negative, with nothing positive to recommend? No. He calls Xers to reappropriate their religious traditions. He urges them to study Catholic tradition and history so they can use the best parts as weapons against today's church arrangements, in his words, to "reclaim Jesus against Christian churches." The irreverence of GenX pop culture needs to be brought into conversation with "real" religiousness and with religious institutions. He urges church leaders to level their bureaucracies, listen intently to the Xers, and be more open to ecumenism and personal experiences. Both the Xers and the institutions need to begin reaching out.

James Davidson: 1995 Survey of Catholics

The most reliable recent research on young adult Catholics was done by James Davidson and his collaborators (Williams and Davidson 1996, Davidson et al. 1997). The Davidson team carried out focus groups with parishioners of different ages, they surveyed registered parishioners in Indiana, and they commissioned a nationwide poll of Catholics. Among their findings was a clear demarcation between three different generational groups, which they called "pre-Vatican Catholics," "Vatican Catholics," and "post-Vatican Catholics." The pre-Vatican persons (born in 1940 or earlier) had been taught the importance of the institutional Church, and they put emphasis on ritual duties such as attending Mass, confession, praying the rosary, and respecting the Holy Days of Obligation. These persons talked of "doing" their faith more than understanding it. They saw the institutional church as an important mediator in their relationship with God, and many said that the Catholic Church is the "one true church."

The Vatican Catholics (born 1941–1960) had experienced an upbringing similar to the first group, but they tended to define "church" in ways that were a bit different. Some talked about their "spirituality" or their "personal relationship with God." They viewed their faith more in individualistic terms, less in terms of absolute trust in the Church as mediator.

The post-Vatican Catholics (born 1961–1976) were the most individualistic. Many said that being a "good person" is more important than commitment to the Church or participation in the sacraments. Most members of this age group placed great emphasis on having a personal relationship with God and did not see the Church as an essential component of their faith. They did not want to judge others according to criteria set forth by the Church because, as one said, "what really counts is what's in your heart," and "Your religion is within you . . . it's your relationship between you and God. . . . It doesn't matter if you're Catholic, Jewish, or Protestant" (Williams and Davidson 1996: 285). Davidson:

> The post–Vatican II generation is the least committed to the institutional Church. When asked about the essentials of being a "good

Catholic," their concern with whether an individual is a "good person" dominated their responses. When asked outright whether a "good Catholic" needs to attend Mass regularly and accept various Church teachings, these young Catholics answered no. (Davidson et al., p. 138; for a similar analysis see D'Antonio et al., 1996)

The three generation groups varied in their beliefs and moral attitudes. See Table 2.1. On the statements about obligations to attend Mass and obey church teachings, the three generational groups were clearly different, with the young people most individualistic and least likely to stress obedience. On moral questions related to sexuality, the Vatican and post-Vatican generations came out nearly the same. On agreement with church social teachings regarding racism, poverty, and social justice, the three generations were similar.

How about Latino Catholics? The Davidson team conducted enough interviews to make a few summary statements. In most ways the Latinos resembled the whites, but they were a bit more traditional in beliefs and practices. On attitudes about social justice and sexual morality the Latinos and whites were the same.

Davidson concluded that young adults have religious and spiritual interests as strong as anyone else, but their interests are *different*. Young adults place less emphasis on the institutional church and they do not feel that they need to go to Mass to satisfy an obligation. The young adults are not angry; they seem to like being Catholic and appear ready to work out their own personal decisions about how to relate to the institutional church. Some find joy in parish involvement, while others keep a distance. Davidson and his team found nowhere near the same depth of cynicism which Beaudoin described.

If the young post-Vatican Catholics are different today, will they still be different in the future, or will they change as they get older and end up resembling older persons today? Davidson and his colleagues doubt very much if any large future change will occur in this group. Most likely, the older adults of tomorrow will be similar to the young adults of today.

Davidson urges Catholic Church leaders not to take the loyalty and commitment of young Catholics for granted. In America clear trends are underway from a religion of institutional obedience to a religion having individualistic views of faith and morals, with young Catholics

TABLE 2.1

Responses of the Three Generational Groups (*in percents*)

	Pre-Vatican	Vatican	Post-Vatican
The Catholic Church is the one true church. Strongly agree.	58	34	30
It is important to obey Church teachings even when one doesn't understand them. Strongly agree.	38	24	11
One can be a good Catholic without going to Mass. Strongly agree.	26	32	45
Artificial birth control is "always wrong."	20	6	4
Premarital sex is "always wrong."	55	26	20

Source: Davidson et al. 1997, pp. 126–31.

clearly the most individualistic of all. Church leaders need to listen to the concerns of young men and women, and they need to find ways to include them in parish and diocesan decision-making (p. 154).

AGE DIFFERENCES IN THE TOTAL CATHOLIC POPULATION

Above we said that young Catholics are different from older Catholics. But we need to be more specific. To get an overview of age differences our research team collected surveys of American Catholics done in recent years, and we compared attitudes of all age groups on more than one hundred questions.[4] We can draw several conclusions.

The topics with the largest consistent age differences were (a) questions about the morality of sexual behavior, birth control, and divorce, (b) questions about lay participation in church affairs, (c) questions about proper roles of women in society, and (d) frequency of Mass attendance and devotions. The young people were more individualistic on the sexuality issues, more supportive of lay involvement in church decision-making, more open to wider roles for women in all areas of society, and less regular in Mass attendance and personal devotions. On other topics age differences also occurred, but a bit smaller: whether abortion can be a moral choice, whether priests should be allowed to marry, whether women should be ordained, whether the Catholic bishops should consult laity on issues related to sexuality, and whether a Catholic should always obey the pope even when his or her conscience disagrees.

On numerous issues there were no age differences, that is, the age groups agreed. All agreed that in the Mass the bread and wine are actually transformed into the body and blood of Christ, all agreed in their view of how to interpret the Bible, all agreed in beliefs about life after death, all agreed to the same extent with a statement saying that lay people are just as important as priests, all agreed in their evaluation of parishes, and all had similar attitudes about capital punishment. The topics of agreement are diverse, but it is important that they include the central creedal beliefs of Catholicism.

To illustrate the patterns, we depict age differences on seven survey items in Figure 2.1. Three were taken from a 1992 survey, one was taken from a 1996 survey, and three were taken from a 1997 survey.[5] The first item in the figure has the greatest age differences of any in the surveys—on the morality of premarital sex; the young and old differ vastly. The young people seem to see the morality of premarital sex as depending on situations, not a matter of rules.

The second through sixth items in the figure demonstrate the typical age differences on birth control, women priests, and the voice of the laity in parish decision making. On all, the pattern is roughly the same, with a spread of about 30 or 40 percentage points from young to old. The last graph in Figure 2.1 exemplifies a topic on which age differences are small. It asks about the Real Presence in the Eucharist, and the young-to-old gap is small.

The lesson provided by these graphs is that generational differences do not occur on every topic. The young and the old do not disagree on everything. The scope of their disagreement is limited. On most of the basic Catholic doctrines the age differences are slight; they are great only on questions of sexual morals, individual moral authority, and ordination. The young and old disagree not on the basics of the faith but on specific moral teachings and on how the Church should be organized.

With this background we now turn to our new survey findings.

FIGURE 2.1
Catholic Age Differences in Attitudes

Age Group

20–29 30–39 40–49 50–59 60–69 70+

1992
Premarital sexual releations
between persons who are
committed to each other can
be morally acceptable. Agree.

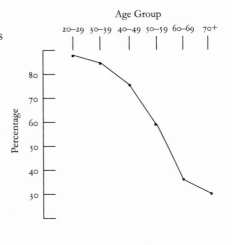

1992
The Church should permit
couples to make their own
decisions about forms of birth
control. Agree.

1992
It would be a good thing if
women were allowed to be
ordained as priests. Agree.

1996
Should Catholic laity have a
voice in selecting the priest
or priests for the parish? Yes.

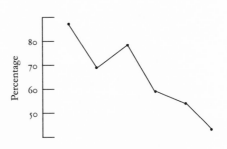

FIGURE 2.1 *(continued)*

Age Group

1997
It is morally wrong to use
artificial methods of birth
control. Disagree.

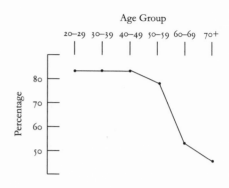

1997
The Catholic Church should allow
women to be priests. Agree.

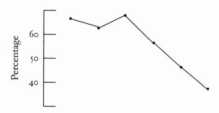

1997 *(this attitude exemplifies
a lack of any age difference)*
The bread and wine used in
Mass are actually transformed
into the body and blood of
Jesus Christ. Agree.

CHAPTER 3

Young Adult Catholics: Survey Results

· · · ·

A major contribution of our research is that we collected a good nationwide sample of interviews with specific types of young adults. A reliable sample provides realism and a sense of proportion in its description of young adult Catholics. It is more credible than any informal or journalistic depiction, however arresting.

In 1997 we collected four samples from forty-four parish confirmation lists, one of Latinos now twenty to twenty-nine years old, one of Latinos thirty to thirty-nine years old, one of non-Latinos twenty to twenty-nine years old, and one of non-Latinos thirty to thirty-nine years old. Our goal was to interview 200 in each sample for a total of 800, but in the end we interviewed 848.

In each parish we randomly chose names from the confirmation record books, then we paid local persons to find as many of the target persons as possible, and afterwards we used professional trackers to find more. Locating the confirmands was the most difficult part of the project. (See Appendix A in the back of this book for details.)

Although our phone interviewers talking to Latinos were bilingual and offered to use either Spanish or English, most of the Latinos preferred to be interviewed in English. Only 4 percent were interviewed entirely in Spanish and another 5 to 10 percent were interviewed in English with some help in Spanish by the interviewer. This low number surprised us. Apparently the second-generation and third-generation Latinos are very fluent in English.[1]

PEOPLE IN THE SAMPLES

Not all Catholic adolescents go through confirmation. We asked veteran pastors and other Catholic experts for estimates of how many were confirmed in the 1980s. They said that in the non-Latino community about 60 to 70 percent of children were confirmed, and in the Latino community it was about 30 to 40 percent. Therefore our samples are not representative of *all* young adult Catholics—only those confirmed as adolescents. Undoubtedly they grew up in homes relatively active in church life.

Our data do not represent all young Catholics for a second reason: we could not interview everyone. Our success in finding Latinos was relatively lower (51 percent vs. 74 percent), thus introducing bias. The Latinos we succeeded in finding were less transient and more church-involved than the average. Thus our Latino data depict a higher level of church involvement than average. The non-Latino sample has a bias in the same direction, but our evidence is that the bias is much smaller.

We sampled nationality groups carefully. The non-Latino sample represents all American Catholics except for the Latinos. Of the persons in our survey, 94 percent were of European white descent, 4 percent African Americans, and 2 percent Asian Americans. In the Latino sample we got 58 percent Mexicans, 13 percent Puerto Ricans, 4 percent Cubans, and 24 percent mixed or others. (See Appendix B, Table B.1.)

Were most of the respondents born in the United States? In the Latino sample 88 percent said yes; this is much higher than the 62 percent of the total Latino population in the United States today. We asked all the Latinos which language they most often speak at home. Sixty-three percent said "English," 13 percent said "Spanish," and the other 24 percent said "both equally." This is more evidence of the influence of U.S. experience on their lives. Our Latino sample is more educated and more assimilated to American culture than average Latinos in the nation.

Early in the data analysis we had a basic finding: the twenty to twenty-nine-year-olds samples were very little different from the thirty to thirty-nine-year-olds. We had not anticipated this, and in fact we had carefully sampled the two age groups to enable us to make exact comparisons. But the answers were similar on most questions, and throughout this chapter we will show age differences only when they occurred. On most topics the differences were small.

Family Backgrounds

We asked about the religious preferences of the subjects' mothers and fathers during their high-school years. Most mothers were Catholic; in the non-Latino sample it was 94 percent and in the Latino sample it was 97 percent. Of the fathers, 84 percent in the non-Latino sample and 92 percent in the Latino sample were Catholic.

The parents were, for the most part, regular Mass attenders. In the non-Latino sample 76 percent said that their mothers attended weekly, and 60 percent said the same for their fathers. In the Latino sample the figures were slightly lower, 66 and 49 percent. These levels of church-going are much higher than found in other research. They are mostly a result of our restricted sample—that is, we interviewed only people who had been confirmed, and they are from churchgoing families.

Catholic Education

Did these young adults attend Catholic elementary school? In the non-Latino sample 50 percent said yes, and in the Latino sample 35 percent said yes. The percent who attended Catholic high school was lower—in the non-Latino sample 28 percent and in the Latino sample 15 percent. The averages for all American Catholics are lower. For 1991 it was estimated by researchers that 20 percent of Catholics of elementary-school age were in Catholic schools, and 14 percent of those of high-school age were in Catholic high schools (Schaub and Baker 1993).

We asked the subjects if they had attended religious education at their parishes, such as C.C.D. classes, when they were in junior high school and high school. In the non-Latino sample 68 percent said yes, and in the Latino sample 74 percent said yes. Thus at least two-thirds of these persons had spent some time in C.C.D. classes or other education classes in their parishes.

How about parish-based Catholic youth programs? Had they been involved in Catholic youth ministry or parish programs when they were in high school? In the non-Latino sample 44 percent said "often" or "occasionally." In the Latino sample 42 percent said the same. These figures are higher than national averages; the 1993 study by Schaub and Baker estimated that 21 percent of high-school age Catholic youth were participating in parish religious education programs.

Finally, how many of the men served as altar boys in the past? In the non-Latino sample 60 percent said they had done it "often" or "occasionally." In the Latino sample it was 45 percent.

Formal Education and Occupation

The levels of formal education were higher than average. Fifty-two percent of the non-Latinos and 20 percent of the Latinos had earned a B.A. or B.S. degree or more. (Details are in Appendix B, Table B.2.) For comparison: among all adult Latinos in the nation in 1991, 9 percent had earned a bachelor's degree (Gonzales 1993b).

How many of the collegegoers had gone to a Catholic college or university? Among the non-Latinos it was only 14 percent, and among the Latinos, 10 percent. We asked the collegegoers if they had ever been active at college in any Catholic campus ministries, Newman Center activities, or any other Catholic group. Of the non-Latinos 14 percent said yes, and of the Latinos, 8 percent.

The present occupation of the sample persons is shown in Appendix B, Table B.3. About half of the non-Latinos and one-third of the Latinos are in white-collar occupations; both proportions are higher than in the total population.

Marital History

In the twenty to twenty-nine-year-old sample, less than half have ever been married, but in the older sample, 82 percent of the non-Latinos and 83 percent of the Latinos have been married. Of the

TABLE 3.1
Marital History (*in percents*)

	Non-Latinos			Latinos		
	All	20–29	30–39	All	20–29	30–39
Percent ever married	65	47	82	61	40	83
Percent currently married	58	40	75	52	35	70
Percent in second or third marriage now	4	0	7	5	0	10
Percent ever divorced	8	2	15	14	5	23
Percent with children, either natural or adopted, living with them now	51	29	69	55	34	78
Percent of persons ever married, whose first spouse was Catholic	50	48	51	76	72	77

persons ever married, half of the non-Latino sample married fellow Catholics, whereas three-fourths of the Latino sample did so. See Table 3.1.[2]

The 50 percent interfaith marriage rate for non-Latinos is a bit higher than found by past researchers. Davidson found a 40 percent rate among young adult Catholics (1997: 192). In an analysis done a decade ago, McCutcheon found a rate of 43 percent for Catholics marrying in the 1970s (1988: 219). McCutcheon found that the intermarriage rate was gradually rising, and we believe it is slowly rising today.[3]

The non-Catholic spouses for the non-Latino sample were mostly Protestants or nonreligious persons; of all the spouses, 14 percent were reported as "no religion or atheist," 7 percent Methodist, 7 percent Baptist, 6 percent Presbyterian, 4 percent "Protestant" unspecified, and others from smaller denominations or nondenominational churches. For the Latino sample the 24 percent of the spouses who were non-Catholic were made up of 5 percent "no religion or atheist,"

5 percent Baptist, 2 percent Episcopalian, 2 percent non-denominational Protestant, and others from different groups. The intermarriage choices of Catholic men and Catholic women were similar.

CHURCH IDENTITY AND INVOLVEMENT NOW

We asked all the subjects, "Are you now Catholic, Protestant, Jewish, another religion, or with no religion?" See Table 3.2.

Most people have remained Catholic. In the non-Latino sample only 11 percent said they are no longer Catholic, and in the Latino sample it was 9 percent. In the older group (thirty-three to thirty-nine years old) the figures are higher: 16 percent of the non-Latinos said they were no longer Catholic, and 13 percent of the Latinos said so, probably because of more interfaith marriages.

The high percentage of persons who called themselves Catholic surprised us, since research on American Protestants has depicted higher rates of switching and lower levels of denominational loyalty than we found here. Catholics are different from Protestants in this respect. Few persons failed to say that they are Catholic, even though (as we shall see) many of them did not attend church regularly and some did not even find the church to be credible. Yet the vast majority have remained Catholic and probably will stay Catholic. Catholics, even if they're unhappy and even if they're disconnected entirely from parish life, tend to continue seeing themselves as Catholics.[4]

Of the persons who told us they are *not* Catholics, the majority said they are now members of other religions. Only a few said they have no religion at all—4 percent of all the non-Latinos and 3 percent of all the Latinos.

The pattern in Table 3.2 surprised us also in a second respect. Since we had read so much about Latinos leaving the Catholic Church, we expected that more Latinos than non-Latinos would have left. But this is not the case. The rates of leaving were nearly the same.

We asked three questions of everyone who said they were not Catholic. First, "Are you now a member of any church?" Forty-five percent of the non-Latinos and 56 percent of the Latinos said they were. Second, if they are now church members, what kind of church? The non-Latinos (twenty-four persons) belonged to diverse denominations: one

TABLE 3.2

Religious Identity Now (*in percents*)

	Non-Latinos			Latinos		
	All	*20–29*	*30–39*	*All*	*20–29*	*30–39*
Catholic	89	93	84	91	94	87
Protestant	6	3	9	6	3	10
Jewish	0	0	1	0	0	0
Another religion	1	1	1	0	0	1
No religion	4	3	6	3	3	2

Episcopalian, two Lutherans, three Methodists, two Presbyterians, four Baptists, six other Protestant groups (including Mormon), and six non-denominational churches. The Latinos (twenty-one persons) belonged more often to evangelical, Mormon, or nondenominational churches, less to mainline Protestant churches. Two said they were Methodists, three were Baptists, nine belonged to other Protestant churches (including Mormon), and seven belonged to nondenominational churches.

Third, do the people who have left the Catholic Church attend church more often than do Catholics? Yes. Of the non-Latinos 40 percent reported that they attend church weekly or more (whether or not they are now church members), and of the Latinos 39 percent reported the same. These figures compare with 31 percent of the people who remained Catholic. The persons who left Catholicism since confirmation have not lost their Christian faith but have for the most part switched to other churches, which they attend quite regularly. (We say more about the non-Catholics in chapter 4.)

Formally Joining Other Denominations

We asked, "Did you ever leave the Catholic Church and formally join another church or religious body?" Only 6 percent of the non-Latinos and 8 percent of the Latinos said yes. (See Appendix B, Table B.4.) For the non-Latinos, about 60 percent of the switchers had gone to evangelical

Protestant denominations, Pentecostal churches, or the Mormons. For the Latinos it was somewhere between 65 and 80 percent. The widespread stereotype that Latinos are switching to evangelical churches while non-Latinos are switching to mainline Protestant churches is partly supported by our data. In our sample the vast majority of Latinos who switched denominations went to evangelical churches, while the non-Latinos who switched had a mixture of destinations—about two-thirds to evangelical churches and one-fourth to mainline Protestant churches.

Why did they switch? They gave two main reasons. The first was interfaith marriage, and second was that the person had been attracted to another church. (We return to this in chapter 4.)

During the interviewing we came across many irregularities in church membership. We talked with numerous persons who were attending non-Catholic churches but who said they were still Catholic, and we found a few cases of persons who were attending non-Catholic churches but were uncertain if they had switched or not. Some of these persons were shopping or experimenting, and we expect that a certain proportion will return to the Catholic church later. We in fact ran into a few individuals who had returned after attending other churches for a time.

Some persons had churchgoing patterns which were truly ambiguous. Among our 848 interviewees we found fourteen persons who said they are Catholics, yet they go regularly to a non-Catholic church. We found ten persons who go to two churches, partly because they are in an interfaith marriage. Thus we estimate that five to ten percent of the people in our samples have inconsistent churchgoing habits, in that they do not attend the denomination of which they are formal members or they attend two different churches.

We expected that a few respondents would have made two denominational switches, so we asked. In the non-Latino sample nobody had made two switches. But in the Latino sample, six persons said they had switched twice, half of whom had returned to the Catholic Church after leaving earlier.

Becoming Inactive

Switching denominations was not the main change in church involvement which these people made. More common was dropping out of church attendance. In our samples a majority of those surveyed had become inactive Catholics in the years after their confirmation. (See Appendix B, Table B.5.) Among non-Latinos, 59 percent had done so, and among Latinos, 62 percent. If we look only at the people thirty or older, the figures were 65 percent for the non-Latinos and 64 percent for the Latinos. The average age for dropping out was twenty.

The pattern of dropping out which we found is similar to what other researchers have found. In all Christian denominations a large number of young people drop out, and some return later. In the 1990 study of Presbyterian youth, Hoge and his colleagues found that 75 percent had dropped out sometime in their teens and twenties, and of these, 49 percent had come back to church involvement by the time they were interviewed at the average age of thirty-seven (Hoge, Johnson, and Luidens 1994:58). In our thirty to thirty-nine-year-old samples the figures for dropping out were a bit lower—65 percent for the non-Latinos and 64 percent for the Latinos.

When we asked *why* the subjects had stopped church attendance, the responses we got were often vague. It became clear to us during the interviewing that cessation of church attendance was seldom due to doctrinal problems or religious doubts; more commonly it was a by-product of changes in these people's lives. Most of the subjects left home during their late teens or early twenties, and many stopped churchgoing at that time. A common pattern was that when they left home for college or work, they also stopped churchgoing. Nineteen percent of the non-Latino sample and 8 percent of the Latino sample told us that the main reason they became inactive was that they left home. But the most frequent reasons given for stopping church attendance were vague and inarticulate, and we grouped them in the category "too busy, lack of interest, or lazy."

Becoming Active Again

About half of the dropouts had become active again by the time we interviewed them—48 percent of the non-Latino sample and 45 percent of the Latinos. (See Appendix B, Table B.6.) The average age was twenty-five or twenty-six years. The most common reasons for resuming churchgoing were spiritual needs (worries or haunting feelings of emptiness, guilt, or a need for renewal) and concerns about family life and children's religious education. All past research has found this same pattern: as adults settle down locally and psychologically, have children, and reevaluate their lives, many return to church involvement.

When the Catholic returnees in our sample came back to church involvement, they did not always return to Catholic parishes. By this time some had been influenced by higher education, marriage, and geographical changes, and we should expect that a few would be making some denominational changes. In both the non-Latino and Latino samples, of the people returning to churchgoing, 86 percent returned to Catholic parishes and the rest went to other churches.

Are Catholics different from Protestants? We can make a rough comparison between Presbyterian young people and Catholic young people in their rates of dropping out and returning. Although the respondents in the earlier Presbyterian study and this Catholic study were not exactly the same ages, we can safely say that fewer Catholics dropped out than Presbyterians (about 65 percent vs. 75), and of the ones who dropped out, a slightly higher percentage returned later (about 54 percent vs. 49). Catholics have a kind of glue holding them holding them closer to their church.

Catholic Activity and Parish Involvement

Persons who told us they are Catholics today were asked three additional questions. First, "Do you consider yourself an active Catholic?" Sixty-three percent of the non-Latinos and 60 percent of the Latinos said yes. Second, "Are you now on the registry list of any parish?" Sixty-nine percent of the non-Latinos and 66 percent of the Latinos said yes. Third, if Catholics are now on the registry list of some parish, *which* parish and why? See Table 3.3.

Young Catholics choose their parishes for two main reasons. The first is where the person grew up. For young Catholics twenty-nine or younger, this is the main factor. The second is where the person *now* lives; it is the main factor for Catholics thirty or older. These two factors determine where about 82 percent of the non-Latinos and 86 percent of the Latinos are registered. For the remainder, the main

TABLE 3.3

Catholics on Parish Lists: Why in That Parish? (*in percents*)

	Non-Latinos			Latinos		
	All	*20–29*	*30–39*	*All*	*20–29*	*30–39*
Why in that particular parish?						
Hometown parish; raised there; parents belong there	43	56	30	51	64	39
The closest, or I live in that parish	39	33	46	35	24	45
Spouse or children attend there	3	1	3	3	4	2
Parish has a good 5-day school	3	1	4	0	0	1
Good parish; good pastor; good fellowship	10	6	12	5	4	7
It is an ethnic parish; it uses my language	2	1	2	2	0	5
Other reason	1	3	1	2	4	2

thing is whether they *like* the parish. About 18 percent of the non-Latinos and about 14 percent of the Latinos belong to parishes they have chosen.

Interviewees in their twenties often told us that they were still registered in the parish where their parents belong, even if the interviewees no longer live in that neighborhood. Some who were now living away from their parental home were uncertain if they were still registered in their home parish or not, but they said that in any event they were not registered in a parish where they now live.

Do these people go to church regularly? We asked all Catholics about their church attendance in the last year. See Table 3.4.

Church attendance rates are nearly the same for the non-Latinos and the Latinos; 31 percent of both said that they attend weekly or more. Older people attended more than younger people.

Are these figures accurate? It is a problem to know how truthful these reports of church attendance are, since several investigators in the last five years have questioned the rates of church attendance which Americans report to pollsters. Self-reported attendance is without doubt higher than the reality, since several careful checks were done by dogged investigators.[5] How much higher? Nobody knows. But we are certain that the self-reported church attendance rate in Table 3.4 is biased upward. A reasonable guess is that the true figure for weekly attendance would be about ten percentage points lower.

How do these young adults decide *where* to attend? For about three-fourths, they attend church where they live. The other one-fourth go to other parishes apparently because of family or friends, or because they like the other parishes better. In a 1996 nationwide survey of Catholics done by the University of Maryland Survey Research Center, 83 percent of Catholics said that they attended Mass at their neighborhood parish, and 17 percent went elsewhere. This indicates that our sample is more likely to shop for attractive parishes than are average American Catholics.

We asked all church-attending Catholics if they had been active in any group or committee in their parish or in another Catholic group in the last six months. Nineteen percent of the non-Latinos and 15 percent of the Latinos said yes. The most common activity was assisting with C.C.D. or the religious education program.

Do these young adults have circles of close friends in their parishes? We asked every Catholic who attends church at all to estimate how many of his or her five closest friends were members of their parishes. Of the non-Latinos, 14 percent said that three or more of their five closest friends were members of their parish, and for the Latinos the figure was 32 percent. These people do not have the majority of their friends in their parishes, but the Latinos have many more than the non-Latinos.

Are they satisfied with their parishes? We asked all the Catholics who have attended church at all in the last year to evaluate their parishes. They gave very favorable evaluations, and even the infrequent attenders did so. This was a surprise. We did not expect such positive attitudes, based on our focus groups and interviews. See Table 3.5.

As the table shows, the evaluations of parishes were positive. Very few of our respondents gave negative ratings to their parishes—in general not over 15 or 20 percent. This outcome is consistent with Greeley's

TABLE 3.4

Catholics: Church Attendance and Parish Involvement (*in percents*)

	Non-Latinos			Latinos		
	All	*20–29*	*30–39*	*All*	*20–29*	*30–39*
Church attendance:						
Once a week or more	31	28	34	31	25	39
Two or three times a month	26	26	26	23	26	21
Once a month	12	15	9	12	11	12
One to six times a year	25	26	24	27	33	22
Never	6	5	7	7	6	7
For persons who attended at all:						
Do you attend Mass at the parish in whose boundaries you reside, or do you attend Mass at another parish?						
Parish where I live	64	61	68	66	62	70
Another parish	21	20	23	22	22	22
Half and half	10	12	8	9	11	7
I go to parents' parish when I am at home	2	3	1	1	1	0
Parish at my college	1	3	0	1	3	0
Don't know	1	1	0	1	1	2
In the last six months, were you active in a parish group or committee?						
Yes	19	18	22	15	12	20

description of "communal Catholics," which says that these Catholics like being Catholic and feel *detachment* from parishes more than they feel any dislike for them. Greeley said that communal Catholics expect little from parish life, but have more positive than negative feelings toward their parishes. Our data agree. Similarly, the 1985 Gallup survey of Hispanic Catholics found that almost nobody criticized the parishes; the 1985 researchers were surprised by this, just as we were.

TABLE 3.5

Catholics Who Attend Church at Least Once a Year:
Evaluation of Their Parishes (*in percents*)

	Non-Latinos	*Latinos*
How well does your parish meet your needs to be closer to God?		
Very well	36	50
Moderately well	47	34
Moderately poorly	7	6
Very poorly	2	2
Don't know	8	8
How well does it make you feel welcome and part of a community?		
Very well	54	61
Moderately well	4	24
Moderately poorly	8	7
Very poorly	1	2
Don't know	3	6
How well does it help you deal with important questions in your life?		
Very well	20	37
Moderately well	44	40
Moderately poorly	16	8
Very poorly	8	3
Don't know	3	12
How well does it meet your need for help in personal and family life?		
Very well	25	43
Moderately well	42	35
Moderately poorly	12	7
Very poorly	8	3
Don't know	14	13

The ratings were positive even by the respondents who seldom attend church. For example, on the first question on how well the parish meets their needs to be closer to God, the overall "very well" and "moderately well" rating, combined, was 83 percent for the non-Latinos and 84 percent for the Latinos. For the people who attend six times a year or less the figures were 64 for the non-Latinos and 67 for the Latinos.

The aspect of parish life given the highest rating was "it makes you feel welcome and part of a community," and this was far ahead of the others. The aspect rated lowest was "it helps you deal with important questions in your life." Possibly the young adults value their parishes more for their feeling of community and their social life than for their spiritual help. The Latinos evaluated their parishes higher than did the non-Latinos, evidently because they have more personal friends there.

Attitudes about the Institutional Church

We read eight statements about the institutional church and asked the people if they agreed or disagreed. Table 3.6 gives the responses of everyone who said they are Catholic now.

The first statement is about the bread and wine in the Eucharist becoming the body and blood of Christ, and nearly everyone agreed. Among the Latinos it was almost unanimous. The high numbers surprised us, since other research found lower numbers. For example, a 1994 New York Times/CBS poll asked Catholic respondents to choose between two statements, one similar to the statement in Table 3.6 and the other saying "The bread and wine are symbolic reminders of Christ." Only 34 percent chose the statement similar to ours, saying that the bread and wine are changed into the body and blood of Christ (Steinfels 1995). By contrast, a 1997 Roper poll asked Catholics if they agreed with the statement, "The bread and wine used in Mass are actually transformed into the body and blood of Jesus Christ," and 82 percent agreed, not much different from our survey.

This is a subtle topic, and the responses to poll questions about it are especially contingent on the way the questions are asked. If the question provides several options, they each receive some assent. We conclude that the high percentage of agreement in Table 3.6 is partly a result of the way we asked the question; a more articulated question

TABLE 3.6
Attitudes of Current Catholics toward the Institutional
Church (*in percents*)

	Non-Latinos	*Latinos*
Percent who Strongly Agree or Moderately Agree:		
In Mass the bread and wine actually become the body and blood of Christ.	87	95
One can be a good Catholic without going to Mass.	64	64
I take seriously the pronouncements of the Pope on social, political, and moral issues.	59	65
Lay people are just as important a part of the Church as priests are.	88	91
The Catholic Church should allow women greater participation in all ministries.	87	87
It is important that the Catholic Church put more women in positions of leadership and authority.	75	75
The Catholic Church should facilitate discussion and debate by the laity on doctrinal issues such as divorce, remarriage, and human sexuality.	80	79
(Different format:) Do you favor or oppose more lay involvement in church affairs at the local parish level, on matters that do not involve questions of faith and morals?		
Favor	71	59
Oppose	10	16
Unsure	19	25

stating several options would have produced a lower level of agreement on the statement we used.

The second statement said that a person can be a good Catholic without going to Mass, and 64 percent in each sample agreed. (In the Davidson study, 73 percent of the same age group agreed.) Here is the first glimpse of a finding we will see repeatedly—that young Catholics tend to have stronger commitment to their own version of the faith than to the rules of the institutional church.

The third statement assesses feelings about the moral authority of the pope, and the results show that the pope's authority is fairly high; it is higher among Latinos than non-Latinos. It is highest of all among the thirty- to thirty-nine-year-old Latinos.

The next four items are about the place of laity and women in the Church. The respondents are almost unanimous in agreeing that "lay people are just as important a part of the Church as priests are" (in the Davidson study it was 86 percent in this age group) and that "the Catholic Church should allow women greater participation in all ministries." For young adult Catholics these topics are beyond serious dispute today.

On the last two items, agreement is also high but not quite unanimous: on putting more women in positions of authority and on including the laity in discussions of doctrinal issues. Seventy-five to 80 percent of the young adults agreed, and differences between the twenty- to twenty-nine-year-olds and the thirty- to thirty-nine-year-olds were small.[6] The last item asks if the respondents favor or oppose more lay involvement in local church affairs, and the majority is strongly in favor. The non-Latinos are more in favor of lay involvement than the Latinos.

Table 3.6 tells us that young adults are ready for greater involvement in church affairs by laity in general and women in particular. These people would endorse a more participatory style church, and they clearly would welcome more ministerial roles for women.

Catholic Social Witness

Next we asked for agreement or disagreement with four statements about Catholic social witness. See Table 3.7.

TABLE 3.7

Attitudes of Current Catholics about Social Witness (*in percents*)

	Non-Latinos	Latinos
Percent who Strongly Agree or Moderately Agree:		
Catholics have a duty to try to end racism.	86	90
Catholics have a duty to try to close the gap between the rich and the poor.	76	83
Catholics have a duty to try to live more simply in order to preserve the environment.	73	80
The Church should stick to religion and not be involved in economic or political issues.	54	52

We see that between 73 and 90 percent of these young adults think that Catholics have a duty to end racism, to close the gap between rich and poor, and to live more simply to preserve the environment. (The Davidson study used one of these statements; the figure for twenty- to twenty-nine-year-olds on closing the gap between the rich and the poor was 60 percent.) Of the three problems, racism is seen as the most urgent. These three statements show that young Catholics today believe they have a duty to apply their faith to improving human society.

The last item in Table 3.7 is different from the first three. It is expressed at a more abstract level than the others, and it states the opposite view—that the Church should *not* engage in social witness or social criticism. This item received agreement from half of the respondents even though the clear majority agreed with the first three items. (In the Davidson study, 60 percent of this age group agreed with the statement.) Here is a puzzle: how could the numbers be so high on the last item? Isn't it stated in opposition to the first three? Our interpretation is that young adult Catholics have mixed views on the abstract question of whether the Church should become involved in economic or political issues, but they are in agreement regarding the three concrete social problems we asked about—racism, inequality, and the environment. We also have evidence, both here and elsewhere, that the respondents in our survey had a tendency to agree rather than disagree

TABLE 3.8

Attitudes of Current Catholics about Other Churches (*in percents*)

	Non-Latinos	Latinos
Percent who Strongly Agree or Moderately Agree:		
I could be just as happy in some other church; it wouldn't have to be Catholic.	23	20
There is something very special about being Catholic which you can't find in other religions.	68	74
I cannot imagine myself being anything other than Catholic.	75	81
The Catholic Church is the one true Church.	48	64

with statements the interviewer read to them, regardless of the content. This is called "yea-saying bias" by researchers, and it is a problem in all surveys. We are certain that some yea-saying occurred in our survey, so all of the numbers in Table 3.7, indicating agreement with the statements, are a bit inflated.

Other Churches

Table 3.8 depicts attitudes toward other Christian churches.

The first three statements have consistent responses: the clear majority think there is something special about being Catholic, and they could not be happy in any other church. For example, 75 percent of the non-Latinos and 81 percent of the Latinos agree that "I cannot imagine myself being anything other than Catholic." The feelings of Latinos and non-Latinos are about the same. We can say, in summary, that about three-fourths of these young adults think that being Catholic is something special, and they cannot envision switching to any other religious group. The last statement in Table 3.8 is different. It asserts that the Catholic Church is the one true church. Forty-eight percent of the non-Latinos and 64 percent of the Latinos agreed. In the 1995 Davidson study the agreement about Catholicism being special was a bit weaker than in our sample, indicating that feelings among *all* young Catholics are not as strong as we found.

We need to add a clarification here: although the fourth statement in the table is an attitude widely held among Catholics, it has not been official Church teaching since the Second Vatican Council. The current teaching states that many churches, not just the Catholic Church, possess *some* divine truth; the Catholic Church is a fuller expression of divine truth than others, but it is not the sole possessor of truth.

Religious Education of Children

Do young adult Catholics want religious education for their children? We asked all the respondents, whether or not they had children, this question: "Would you want a child of yours to receive any religious instruction?" In both the non-Latino sample and the Latino sample, 95 percent said yes. It is *nearly unanimous*. The same result occurred in the 1990 Presbyterian survey, in which 96 percent said they wanted religious education for their children (Hoge et al. 1994:76). Here is a finding of far-reaching importance to the Church: almost all young Catholics want religious instruction for their children. From other responses we know that a good number of these persons are lukewarm about whether they want Catholic worship services for themselves, but *even these* people want religious education for their children. Stated in market terms: there is a vast market for child religious education programs, and it is clearly in the Catholic community's interest to serve this need effectively through Catholic schools and parish programs.

Some of these young adult Catholics have children of school age now. Are the children actually getting religious education? We asked the respondents if they had children living with them, and everyone who had children six to sixteen years old living with them was asked three additional questions: First, "Were your children baptized?" Of the non-Latinos, 91 percent said yes; of the Latinos it was 96 percent. Second, "Do you have any children attending Catholic school now?" Of the non-Latinos, 30 percent said yes, and of the Latinos, 23 percent. These figures are higher than for the total Catholic population in the nation, as we saw earlier. Third, "Do you have any children attending C.C.D., Sunday school, or any other parish-sponsored religious education program now?" Of the non-Latinos, 72 percent said yes, and of the Latinos, 50 percent. These figures are also higher than for the total Catholic population.[7]

Knowledge of Catholic Teachings

We wanted to assess the awareness of Catholic teachings among young adults, so we put four questions to everyone calling themselves Catholic today. See Table 3.9.

About half of the people have heard of the Second Vatican Council; many more non-Latinos than Latinos have. About one-third of the non-Latino respondents have heard about the Council *and* have read about it or discussed it, and this compares with about one-sixth of the Latinos. The greater knowledge among the non-Latinos is no doubt a result of their higher levels of education.

Knowledge of the more recent Church statements is quite low. Less than one-sixth said they had heard about the bishops' 1986 statement on economic justice for all, only one-fourth said they had heard about the pope's 1995 statement criticizing the culture of death. In the process of interviewing we found out that many of the people were unsure if they had heard about the bishops' statement on economic justice and the pope's statement on the culture of death. They often hesitated before answering, and even the ones who said they had heard of the statements were hazy, when we asked, about what the statements said.

Religious Beliefs

We read nine statements of religious beliefs to our respondents and asked if they agreed or disagreed. See Table 3.10. The differences between the younger group (twenty to twenty-nine years old) and the older group (thirty to thirty-nine years old) were important enough to show in the table.

One message of Table 3.10 is the high level of individualism among these young adults. On the first question they clearly said that an individual should arrive at his or her own religious beliefs independent of any churches. The level of individualism in our sample is similar to that in the 1990 study of Presbyterian confirmands, where 63 percent agreed with the same statement.

On the second question the respondents said that the individual's conscience is the final authority about good and bad. This reliance on individual authority is the same found in past research on Catholic

TABLE 3.9

Current Catholics: Knowledge of Church Teachings (*in percents*)

	Non-Latinos	Latinos
Have you ever heard of the Second Vatican Council, which occurred in the early 1960s?		
Yes	56	27
No	42	70
Don't know	2	3
(Of those who said yes:)		
Have you ever read about or discussed any of the ideas from the Second Vatican Council?		
Yes	49	51
No	49	43
Don't know	2	6
Have you heard about or read about the American bishops' 1986 statement on economic justice for all?		
Yes	16	12
No	79	82
Don't know	5	6
Have you heard about or read about Pope John Paul II's 1995 statement criticizing the culture of death?		
Yes	23	28
No	73	67
Don't know	4	5

young people, including studies by Greeley and McNamara. We agree with them: the majority of young adult Catholics believe they as individuals need to rely on their own education and experience in determining what is true and good in their religious tradition. Most do not automatically accept Church teachings as authoritative. The majority viewpoint seems to be that what the Church teaches needs to be heard and studied, but in the end the individual needs to make his or her own important religious and moral judgments.

TABLE 3.10

Current Catholics: Religious Beliefs (*in percents*)

	Non-Latinos			Latinos		
	All	*20–29*	*30–39*	*All*	*20–29*	*30–39*
Percent Strongly Agree or Disagree:						
Individualism						
An individual should arrive at his or her own religious beliefs independent of any churches or synagogues.	61	65	57	69	73	65
In the realm of morality, the final authority about good and bad is the individual's informed conscience.	71	73	68	73	74	71
Relativism and Particularism						
All the major world religions are equally good ways of helping a person find ultimate truth.	70	73	67	76	80	71
All the great religions of the world are equally true and good.	53	54	51	50	54	46
The only absolute Truth for humankind is in the teachings of Jesus Christ.	73	67	79	87	85	89
Only followers of Jesus Christ and members of His church can be saved.	32	29	36	39	32	47
Doctrine						
I believe in a divine judgment after death where some shall be rewarded and others punished.	80	81	79	82	81	84

TABLE 3.10 *(continued)*

	Non-Latinos			Latinos		
	All	*20–29*	*30–39*	*All*	*20–29*	*30–39*
Humans should live with the assumption that there is no life after death.	6	7	4	9	9	10
(Different format)						
Was Jesus Christ God or the Son of God, another religious leader like Mohamed or Buddha, or do you think Jesus Christ never actually lived?						
God or Son of God	91	89	92	96	96	97
Other responses	9	11	8	4	4	3

Items three through six in Table 3.10 assess the levels of relativism vs. particularism felt by these young Catholics. "Relativism" is a belief that various religious teachings carry wisdom and truth, but that no one tradition has priority or leverage over another. It holds, put crudely, that "All religions are really the same." A relativistic person is left with an unsatisfying existential problem: If no one religious tradition can promise authoritative truth, then *no* religious teachings are absolute; all are relative to time and place, and the individual person has the burden of making choices. The obverse of relativism is "particularism"—the belief that one particular religious tradition carries truth and morality which is authoritative for all human beings. Items three and four voice relativism, and items five and six voice particularism. Items three, four, and five attracted agreement from the majority of the respondents, both Latino and non-Latino. Only item six was rejected by the majority.

It is important that official Catholic teachings include a certain level of religious relativism. The documents of the Second Vatican Council affirm that all religions possess some degree of truth. Thus we should not see the high degree of agreement that "All the major world religions are equally good ways of helping a person find ultimate truth" as a radical departure from Catholic doctrine. Catholic teachings do not say that all religious are "equally good," but they also do not condemn other religions. This Catholic teaching may be one explanation for the high level of relativism (which was surprising to us) shown in Table 3.10. Another possible explanation may be that American culture today favors expressions of tolerance and acceptance of pluralism rather than attitudes of religious exclusivism, and this may have influenced the responses of our interviewees. In any event, the persons in our sample accept a high level of religious relativism, and it co-exists alongside specific Catholic commitments.

We can compare the responses on three items with the 1990 Presbyterian sample. On the statement "All the great religions of the world are equally true and good," our sample had about 52 percent agreement, while the Presbyterians had 39 percent. On the statement "Only followers of Jesus Christ and members of His church can be saved," our sample had about 35 percent agreement, while the Presbyterians had 29 percent. There was no great difference between the Catholics and the Presbyterians except that the Catholic respondents were more inclined to agree with *all* of the interview statements regardless of their content (the yea-saying bias).

We expected that persons accepting items three and four would tend to reject items five and six, but this is not how *they* saw it. When we correlated the four items we found that items three and four intercorrelated strongly with each other, as did items five and six. But the items stated in opposite directions did not prove to have strong negative correlations, telling us that many respondents did not perceive them as opposites. For example, item four ("All the great religions of the world are equally true and good") correlated –.14 with item five ("The only absolute Truth for humankind is in the teachings of Jesus Christ"). This is a very weak correlation, much weaker than we expected. We anticipated a strong negative correlation between two statements which we thought were stated in opposite directions, but it didn't happen. Why not? We can only conclude that our respondents did not have clear views on these questions or were not prepared for them. Probably this topic is baffling or ambiguous to many of the interviewees.

The last three items in Table 3.10 affirm central Christian doctrines: a divine judgment after death, life after death (stated inversely), and the divinity of Jesus Christ. Our respondents were overwhelmingly orthodox and traditional. Very few of them questioned or denied central Christian teachings. In sum: few of these Catholic confirmands have turned radically agnostic or non-Christian—at most, 10 percent.

Here again we can contrast the attitudes of our Catholic sample with the 1990 Presbyterian sample. On the statement about a divine judgment after death, our sample had 81 percent agreement, while the Presbyterians had 56 percent. On the statement "Humans should live with the assumption that there is no life after death," our sample had about 7 percent agreeing, while the Presbyterians had 10 percent. On the question about whether Jesus Christ was divine, our sample had about 93 percent agreeing, while the Presbyterians had 78 percent. The Catholics are more traditional in religious beliefs.

The non-Latino and Latino Catholics were similar in these attitudes, and where they were different the Latinos were more conservative. Age differences were weak, but on a few items the older persons were more traditional and the younger persons more relativistic. For example, on item six, saying that "only followers of Jesus Christ and members of His church can be saved," persons over thirty were more conservative than those under thirty.

We compared the Catholics and the persons no longer Catholic. We found that the non-Catholics are more theologically conservative, less individualistic, and less relativistic than the Catholics. This was an unexpected finding, since the study of Presbyterians found that the persons who had left Protestantism were *more* relativistic and *more* hesitant about religious beliefs (Hoge et al. 1994:81–87). But in the present study the people who had left the Catholic Church were not relativists or doubters. The majority have not left the Christian faith; they have merely switched churches.

As we suggested earlier, a question arises as to whether the persons in their twenties are still in a time of transition and will evolve in the next ten years to resemble the respondents currently in their thirties. We have no way of knowing, but the weight of past social research is on the side of saying no. Growing older by itself has no overall effect pushing basic values in one direction or other. We should not expect that today's young people will come to resemble today's older adults "when they mature."

Five Summary Attitude Scales

In data analysis, summary measures are often more useful than individual items, so we created five summary attitude scales from the interviews: (1) *Traditional Doctrine*. This scale measures adherence to Church teachings about the divinity of Christ, life after death, and the Eucharist. (2) *Catholicism Only*. This scale measures the feeling that the Catholic Church is special or superior and that the interviewees could not see themselves as anything but Catholics. (3) *Relativism*. This scale measures the belief that all religions are equally true and good. (4) *Catholic Duty*. This scale measures belief that a Catholic has a duty to try to end racism, reduce the gap between rich and poor, and live simply to help preserve the environment. (5) *Empowerment of Women and Laity*. This scale measures advocacy of greater participation by laity and especially by women in church leadership. (Details of scale construction are given in Appendix B.)

Are these five attitudes associated with each other? Are they so closely related that in reality they are little more than variations on one single viewpoint? No. We correlated the scale scores with each other and found them to be surprisingly independent. (See Appendix B, Table B.8.) Although the correlations were generally weak, they were stronger in the non-Latino sample than in the Latino sample. This is probably a result of the widely-noted tendency of some Latinos to be deferential in interviews (see Appendix A, note 1). As a result, their responses might be less statistically consistent.

In two instances, the scales intercorrelated moderately strongly. The Traditional Doctrine and Catholicism Only scales correlated at .31 in the total sample, and the Catholic Duty and Empowerment of Laity and Women scales correlated at .27. These correlations tell us that people adhering to traditional Catholic doctrines also tend to believe that Catholicism is special, and that people who stress the duty of Catholics to speak out on social issues also desire more participation by laity and women in Church affairs.

The most important lesson we can draw from looking at the intercorrelations of the scales is that advocacy of more Catholic involvement in social issues and of more empowerment of laity and women are independent of traditional beliefs. Both left-of-center and right-of-center Catholics were equally in favor of Catholic involvement in social issues and of lay empowerment; these issues are not the agenda solely of a viewpoint held by one theological faction or the other.

A second important lesson is that relativism is not very strongly associated with the other theological measures. This finding was a surprise. Possibly it occurred because the respondents agree with relativistic statements out of general caution or out of a lack of knowledge about their own faith or other faiths. We also believe that many young persons feel pressure, in American society today, to appear nonjudgmental about other religions. Many respondents have found a way to acknowledge a high degree of religious relativism while remaining committed to the Catholic faith.[8]

Gender Differences

In general, differences between men and women were small, but we found five which are noteworthy. First, the men had dropped out of church attendance more frequently than the women, and they had dropped out earlier. Second, today the women are more active in their parishes; among the women, 67 percent of the non-Latinos and 65 percent of the Latinos consider themselves "active Catholics," while for the men the figures are 58 percent and 53 percent. The women attend Mass more often, and they are more active in groups or committees in their parishes. In the interviews they gave their parishes much higher evaluations than did the men. These gender differences are in line with common observations that Catholic women are more parish-involved than men. Third, on private devotions, women were higher than men. They were higher on making the Stations of the Cross, on saying the Rosary, on reading the Bible at home, and on personal prayer. In addition the Latinas[9] (but not the non-Latino women) were higher in attending Novenas and Benediction services. Fourth, on doctrinal beliefs the non-Latino women were higher than the men (but it was not true among Latinos). Fifth, on Church social action the women were more supportive on one or two items, but not on others. Most decisive on this topic, the women tended *less* than the men to agree with the statement "The Church should stick to religion and not be involved in economic or political issues."

Summary: Five Main Findings in the Survey Results

Our survey has produced five clarifications about the religious beliefs and practices of young adult Catholics.

First, we found that few young adults have left the Catholic community. By an average age of thirty, only 11 percent of the non-Latinos and 9 percent of the Latinos said that they are no longer Catholic. Even among the thirty to thirty-nine-year-old group the proportion who said they are no longer Catholic was only about 15 percent. Of all the no-longer-Catholics, two-thirds now belong to another church and one-third say they are not religious at all. Although we have often heard it said that Latinos are departing Catholicism in especially large numbers, in our sample the rate of leaving was no higher for Latinos than for all others.

Persons who have left Catholicism are not skeptics or secular persons. Though they have left the Catholic Church, they have not left the Christian faith. On most measures they are more religious and devout than others who remained Catholic. These people are basically different than the sample of Presbyterian confirmands done by Hoge, Johnson, and Luidens, in which it was found that the people who had left mainline Protestantism were often relativistic, individualistic, and skeptical in religious beliefs. In the Catholic sample, the majority of the people who left Catholicism remained active Christians but moved to other churches.

Second, the differences between non-Latinos and Latinos were surprisingly small. Keep in mind that our Latino sample was composed mostly of persons born and educated in the United States, and the vast majority preferred to be interviewed in English. These Latinos are fairly acculturated to American life. We return to this topic in chapter 5.

Third, the young adults had some definite opinions about the Church. They favored having more lay participation in parishes, and they were strongly in favor of having more women in all ministries. This puts them in the liberal wing in today's debates about the Church.

Also they strongly felt the importance of religious education for children; nearly all said they want to provide religious education for their
own children.

Fourth, the majority of these young Catholics advocated more
Catholic involvement in social issues. This viewpoint did not depend
on how the people scored on measures of traditional beliefs or beliefs
about the special nature of Catholicism. Respondents with various theological and ecclesiological views all supported social action and lay
empowerment equally.

Fifth, being Catholic is important to these people. Three-fourths
said that being Catholic is special, and they could not envision themselves joining any other religious group. They found it important to be
Catholic, even if many of them could not claim that Catholicism is the
one true Church and even if many don't participate very much in
church life. In some cases their identity as Catholics is apparently tied
to family and ethnicity more than the institutional church. But whatever its source, their Catholic identity is stronger than we expected and
stronger than the denominational identity of Presbyterians.

CHAPTER 4

Five Types of Catholic Involvement

· · · ·

The confirmands are very diverse, and we pondered how best to portray the diversity. A helpful method is to distinguish specific types. The most useful definition of types, we concluded, would be in terms of their relationship to the Church. Hence we distinguished five such types, which we will describe in this chapter. They are: Parish-Involved Catholic, Regular Attending Catholic, Occasional Attender, Non-Attending Catholic, and Not Catholic.[1] We will quote at length interviews with several persons exemplifying the diversity.

I. Parish-Involved Catholic

In constructing the types, we first identified the *most* active Catholics and named them "Parish-Involved Catholics." These are the people who told us they attended church weekly and also have been active in a group or committee in the parish or in another Catholic group in the last six months, such as Confraternity of Christian Doctrine (religious education classes, commonly called C.C.D.), a musical group, a parent-teacher group, a pro-life group, or a social justice group. The largest portion were working in C.C.D. or a religious education program, and another large portion were working in parish committees. Using these criteria we had thirty-three non-Latinos and thirty-nine Latinos who are "Parish-Involved Catholics." They represent the core of the laity in parish life.

II. Regular Attending Catholic

After removing the Parish-Involved Catholics, we had a large group who were irregular in attendance. We broke them into two parts based on frequency of Mass attendance. Persons who attended weekly or two or three times a month but who were not Parish-Involved Catholics, we called "Regular Attendance Catholics." The sample had 179 non-Latinos and 167 Latinos of this type.

III. Occasional Attender

Persons who attended once a month or about six times a year we called "Occasional Attenders." We had ninety-three of these in the non-Latino sample and 102 in the Latino sample.

IV. Non-Attending Catholic

The sample had many people who said they are Catholic but do not attend church. Some told us that they are "spiritual" but not "religious." Others told us that they remain Catholic because of their upbringing, but today they are no longer practicing. Many persons said they attend at least once a year but less than six times a year. We defined these once-a-year attenders as non-attenders, since some people may go to church once a year to a wedding, funeral, or special occasion but at no other time. Thus the "non-attending Catholics" number sixty-four non-Latinos and seventy-one Latinos.

V. Not Catholic

Some respondents identified themselves as not Catholic today. The non-Latino sample had forty-nine such persons (11 percent), and the Latino sample had thirty-nine (9 percent). If we look only at persons thirty- to thirty-nine years old, it was 16 percent of the Euros and 13 percent of the Latinos; this tells us that some of the older interviewees had stopped calling themselves Catholic in the last few years. (Note that we did not ask about religious "preference" or "membership"; we asked only about their current religion.) In sum, 10 percent of our sample are no longer Catholics.

TABLE 4.1
Five Types of Catholics

	Non-Latinos		Latinos	
	Cases	%	Cases	%
I. Parish-Involved Catholic				
Goes to Mass weekly plus is active in the parish	33	8%	39	9%
II. Regular Attending Catholic				
Attends two or three times a month or more, but not a Parish-Involved Catholic	179	42%	167	40%
III. Occasional Attender				
Attends church monthly or about six times a year	93	22%	102	24%
IV. Non-Attending Catholic				
Attends church once a year or less	63	15%	71	17%
V. Not Catholic	49	11%	39	9%

Note: The table does not include seven "irregular" persons who said they are Catholic but now attend only a non-Catholic Church (five non-Latinos and two Latinos). Nor does it include six persons for whom we had inadequate data (five non-Latinos and one Latino).

During data analysis we uncovered some irregularities in the sample. We had about twenty-five interviewees who told us they are still Catholic even though they now attend another church. Some of them attend *two* churches, one Catholic and one non-Catholic. A majority of these persons are in interfaith marriages. In creating our types we considered them Catholics. The types are shown in Table 4.1.

Adding the first two types together, we get 50 percent of the non-Latino sample and 49 percent of the Latinos. We are certain that these numbers are higher than would occur in a random sample, mostly because we surveyed confirmands only. We guess that in a random sample of young adult Catholics the figures would be between 30 and 40 percent in the first two types combined, not 50 percent.

BACKGROUNDS OF THE FIVE TYPES

What life experiences produced these five types of confirmands? Did family life play a role? Did going to Catholic elementary school or high school? Table 4.2 displays the main influences on these persons.

We looked at more factors than are shown in Table 4.2 but deleted those which had only a negligible effect.[2] Probably most interesting (and surprising to us) was that whether a person had attended Catholic elementary school or high school did not at all predict which type of Catholic he or she would be.

We can summarize: of the factors we inspected, the most consequential were (1) whether or not the person had married a Catholic spouse, (2) whether or not the person (if married) now attends the same church as the spouse, and (3) level of church attendance of the person's father and mother. Also having attended a Catholic college (versus another college) and involvement in a Catholic campus group during that time seemed to encourage greater church involvement. For non-Latinos, but not Latinos, it was important if the person had been active in youth ministry during high school, if the person had attended a Catholic college versus a non-Catholic college, if the person had been active in a Catholic campus group, if the person has children living in the home now, and if the person still lives within 100 miles of his or her hometown. The predictors in the table proved to be more influential for church involvement of non-Latinos than of Latinos, and we can speculate that this is due to the stronger social ties and friendships in Latino parishes compared with others, so that *other* factors such as childhood religious education and college experiences have a greater impact on the non-Latinos.

How different are the five types in attitudes and behavior today? Table 4.3 shows the present-day correlates of belonging to each of the types.

TABLE 4.2
Background Influences on the Five Types

| | I | II | III | IV | V |
| | | | | Non- | Not |
	Par. Inv.	Regular	Occasional	Attend	Cath.
Non-Latinos					
Background and Family					
Percent male	24	45	52	56	39*
Percent 30 years or older	55	50	40	52	69*
Percent who lived with both parents during their high school years	91	87	86	79	84
Percent whose mothers attended church weekly	91	83	68	68	65*
Percent whose fathers attended church weekly	81	70	53	44	50*
Percent who were involved in Catholic youth ministry (occasionally or often)	61	50	39	35	31*
Percent who were inactive in churchgoing for a time	24	38	73	94	78*
College and Marriage					
Percent (of those who attended college) who attended a Catholic college	26	17	10	6	8*
Percent (of those who attended college) who were ever active in a Catholic campus group	37	16	7	4	16*
Percent who have children living with them	65	56	43	32	58*
Percent not living more than 100 miles from their childhood home	44	28	17	23	42*
Percent (of those ever married) whose first spouse was Catholic	76	63	40	43	16*
Percent (of those now married) who attend the same church as their spouse	95	79	64	26	47*

TABLE 4.2 (*continued*)

	I Par. Inv.	II Regular	III Occasional	IV Non- Attend	V Not Cath.
Latinos					
Background and Family					
Percent male	28	38	52	52	49*
Percent 30 years or older	62	48	42	41	69*
Percent who lived with both parents during their high school years	97	84	84	78	69*
Percent whose mothers attended church weekly	85	74	59	51	62*
Percent whose fathers attended church weekly	72	55	43	34	47*
Percent who were involved in Catholic youth ministry (occasionally or often)	53	45	40	34	39
Percent who were inactive in churchgoing for a time	23	42	78	99	85*
College and Marriage					
Percent (of those who attended college) who attended a Catholic college	17	9	3	16	11
Percent (of those who attended college) who were ever active in a Catholic campus group	17	8	8	5	7
Percent who have children living with them	62	60	53	47	54
Percent not living more than 100 miles from their childhood home	13	9	13	13	23
Percent (of those ever married) whose first spouse was Catholic	74	82	77	78	44*
Percent (of those now married) who attend the same church as their spouse	78	80	76	44	66*

* Breakdown into types is significant at .05.

The main lesson in Table 4.3 is that people who are involved in parish life are also religious in every other way. These people are higher in belief in traditional doctrine, more loyal to the Catholic Church, more likely to take part in Scripture study groups and prayer groups, more likely to have private devotional practices, and more likely to go for private confession. They tend more often to see themselves as spiritual persons—although the vast majority of our sample saw themselves as spiritual persons, even a majority of every one of the five types.

The strongest single association in Table 4.3 is with going for private confession. This is very strongly associated with level of churchgoing.

Figure 4.1 depicts the average scale scores of the different categories of persons on three of the attitude scales.[3] It shows the strong relationship between parish involvement and attitudes on the Catholicism Only Scale and the moderate relationships between parish involvement and the Traditional Doctrine Scale and Catholic Duty Scale.

Greater parish involvement is associated with a strong belief that Catholics have a duty to try to end racism, reduce the gap between the rich and poor, and aid environmentalism. It is associated with being informed about one's church, exemplified by the percent who have heard of the Second Vatican Council, and *disagreement* that a person "can be a good Catholic without going to Mass."

All five types are roughly in agreement with each other in advocating more empowerment of laity and women in parish leadership. Also all five types have roughly the same level of belief in religious relativism—the belief that all religions are equally true.

After this overview, we introduce five real persons (although we have changed the names). We devote attention to the ends of the spectrum ("Parish-Involved Catholics" and "Not Catholic") rather than the middle, since the people in the two end types are more instructive. Space limitations prevent us from giving one example from each of the five.

I. THE PARISH-INVOLVED CATHOLICS

The typical Parish-Involved Catholic is a female with a strong religious upbringing. If she is a Latina, she is very likely over thirty years old. She has no history of dropping out of churchgoing during her youth. If

TABLE 4.3
Attitudes and Behaviors of the Five Types

	I	II	III	IV	V
				Non-	Not
	Par. Inv.	Regular	Occasional	Attend	Cath.

Non-Latinos

Attitude Scales

Percent high: Traditional
Doctrine Scale

| | 79 | 78 | 65 | 56 | a* |

Percent high: Catholicism
Only Scale

| | 64 | 58 | 45 | 29 | a* |

Percent high: Relativism Scale

| | 36 | 38 | 40 | 46 | 24 |

Percent high: Catholic Duty Scale

| | 70 | 68 | 56 | 46 | a* |

Percent high: Empowerment of
Women and Laity Scale

| | 64 | 62 | 61 | 54 | a |

Behaviors

Percent who attended a Scripture
study group in the last year

| | 36 | 21 | 16 | 5 | 39* |

Percent who attended a prayer
group in the last year

| | 36 | 24 | 17 | 5 | 45* |

Percent who pray daily

| | 62 | 54 | 39 | 28 | 50* |

Percent who have 3 or more of
their 5 closest friends in the
same parish

| | 33 | 13 | 13 | 10 | a* |

Percent who have made a retreat or
a day of recollection in the last
two years

| | 46 | 15 | 17 | 14 | a* |

Percent who have gone for private
confession in the last
two years

| | 64 | 50 | 27 | 6 | a* |

Percent who have read the Bible at
home in the last two years

| | 73 | 60 | 48 | 29 | a* |

Percent who have heard of the
Second Vatican Council

| | 82 | 62 | 47 | 37 | 43* |

Attitudes

Percent who consider themselves a
spiritual person

| | 90 | 89 | 71 | 63 | 81* |

TABLE 4.3 (*continued*)

	I	II	III	IV	V
				Non-	*Not*
	Par. Inv.	*Regular*	*Occasional*	*Attend*	*Cath.*
Percent who agree: "I take seriously the pronouncements of the Pope on social, political, and moral issues."	70	68	53	38	a*
Percent who agree: "One can be a good Catholic without going to Mass."	33	55	79	87	a*

Latinos

Attitude Scales

Percent high: Traditional Doctrine Scale	69	88	70	73	a*
Percent high: Catholicism Only Scale	69	60	45	35	a*
Percent high: Relativism Scale	34	37	41	41	26*
Percent high: Catholic Duty Scale	79	71	71	58	a*
Percent high: Empowerment of Women and Laity Scale	49	62	63	63	a

Behaviors

Percent who attended a Scripture study group in the last year	62	24	16	13	51*
Percent who attended a prayer group in the last year	74	29	24	9	54*
Percent who pray daily	85	67	52	28	64*
Percent who have 3 or more of their 5 closest friends in the same parish	44	32	30	17	a*
Percent who have made a retreat or a day of recollection in the last two years	46	22	11	3	a*
Percent who have gone for private confession in the last two years	77	53	34	9	a*

TABLE 4.3 (*continued*)

	I	II	III	IV	V
				Non-	Not
	Par. Inv.	Regular	Occasional	Attend	Cath.
Percent who have read the Bible					
at home in the last two years	74	65	50	41	a*
Percent who have heard of the					
Second Vatican Council	62	25	27	14	46*
Attitudes					
Percent who consider themselves					
a spiritual person	90	84	73	59	80*
Percent who agree: "I take					
seriously the pronouncements					
of the Pope on social, political,					
and moral issues."	85	75	53	48	a*
Percent who agree: "One can					
be a good Catholic without					
going to Mass."	39	53	77	83	a*

a Not asked; some questions were for Catholics only.

* Breakdown into types is significant at .05.

she is married, she married a Catholic man, and the two attend the same parish together now. Not only is she active in the parish, but she also goes to private confession, makes retreats or days of recollection, reads the Bible at home, and has a regular prayer life. She is likely to attend Scripture study groups or prayer groups.

Nobody should assume that all the Parish-Involved Catholics are key workers sustaining their parishes. Some participate in parish groups but take no leadership responsibility. For example, several sing in choirs or play on parish athletic teams. In addition, these people tend to have numerous close friends in the same parish. They like their parishes and give them high ratings, especially on how the parishes are welcoming. They disagree with the statement, "One can be a good

FIGURE 4.1

Attitudes of Five Types of Catholics

Traditional
Doctrine
Scale

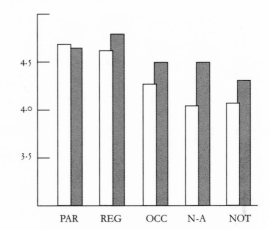

Catholicism
Only
Scale

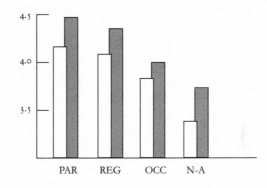

Catholic
Duty
Scale

PAR = Parish-Involved Catholics
REG = Regular Attending Catholics
OCC = Occasional Attenders
N-A = Not-Attending Catholics
NOT = Not Catholic

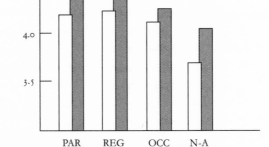

 Non-Latinos Latinos

Catholic without going to Mass." They are no different from others in their high approval of more lay participation, more women in leadership positions, and the duty to end racism and to close the rich-poor gap. In sum, these people are joiners who like their parishes, and they are personally religious persons with a strong, nourishing faith. Two good examples are Mary Mallozzi and Cecilia Coronado.

Mary Mallozzi: The Joy of a Nourishing Parish

Mary is thirty-one years old, employed as a social worker in an eastern city. She has been married for three years and is now expecting her second child. She spoke of her family:

> *Mary:* My parents were active Catholics; my father very much. Perhaps my earliest memory was when my father died when I was twelve. That experience had a life-long impact on me. I had a very strong, spiritual grandmother. She was the matriarch of the family. I will say that she had a tremendous impact on me, more so as an adult than as a child.
>
> *Interviewer:* Did you go to a Catholic high school?
>
> *Mary:* Yes, and for seventh and eighth grade I went to Catholic school too. I liked it. I was very happy, and it was a good experience, and I would do it all over again.
>
> *Interviewer:* How about your experience in college? Did that have any impact?
>
> *Mary:* I had started out at a small women's college in Pennsylvania, then I transferred to St. John's University. I went on a retreat my first year at St. John's, and I found that very rewarding. I kept up with my religion as an undergraduate. I went to church every Sunday. I was living at home, so it was kind of the thing to do, but I never minded doing it. . . . In college I dated someone for a really long time who one day said, "How do you even know God is there?" He started saying all these things, and I couldn't believe he was saying things like that! It really challenged my own faith and how I was supposed to respond to this. Still, I was really strong in my faith. I don't remember what I said, but the relationship didn't last.

Interviewer: Did you have a sense of having a Catholic agenda of some sort?

Mary: Yes. That was the whole reason I went to St. John's, when I was trying to figure out what it was I wanted to do with my life. I graduated as a political science student, then I was a paralegal in a law firm. I was trying to figure out how I could combine my interests in political science and my real desire to give something back which integrated my strong faith. . . . My grandmother had a big impact on me. I thought about going into the field of gerontology. I love my grandmother so much! I could devote my life to doing something like this. In giving back, my life will have purpose. Everything will have a lot of meaning. That is why I went to a Catholic college for social work.

Interviewer: So you see social work as an extension of your faith commitment? It's more than just a job?

Mary: That's right. That was part of the reason I resigned from my law job. I wanted to give more back.

Mary began attending Blessed Sacrament parish in the university town.

Mary: I think Blessed Sacrament had a tremendous impact on me and my faith. It was a significant point in my life. I met Jim [husband] there. He was also studying social work. He was very involved in Blessed Sacrament, and he had a very strong faith. He was a very good friend and then he expressed more of an interest. I got a spiritual director at Blessed Sacrament, and that was the first time I had ever done anything like that. They are very much in the Ignatian tradition. I loved it. I did a parish-directed retreat, and in it we had to use our Bibles and take certain passages. We had to take a passage a day and really try to put ourselves in that passage. That was the first time I really used the Bible. So that's where it started, and I have since wanted to know more about the Bible. What I do now, when my son sleeps, I have about two hours to myself. Most of the time I read the Acts of the Apostles to find out what happened after.

Mary got more and more involved in Blessed Sacrament.

Mary: We got so much out of Blessed Sacrament. Jim plays the guitar and sings, and so do I. So immediately the music was attractive. The spiritual direction I got from the parish director of the retreat was wonderful. I learned so much about my own spirituality, and it gave me the thirst to do more. . . . It's a very progressive parish. I wanted spiritual direction after I had gotten a little bit of it. I thought, "I am really learning a lot about my own spirituality; I need to get more." So I actually got a spiritual director and went to her once a month for about a year. Then I got involved and sang at Blessed Sacrament for two years with their folk group, and so did Jim. We were married there, so we went through marriage preparation there, which was fabulous.

The liturgies are very good. They are very planned out. The homilies—you always had food for thought. There was a series of lectures for adults after Mass while their kids are in C.C.D. Sometimes we would go to that. They were interesting and engaging. Another thing: confession has always been a hard thing for people my age. Blessed Sacrament began having Lenten services with mass confession. There were so many young people it was wonderful. To me it was a whole different experience, going to confession. I really liked it. It was collective, but then you could go by yourself to a priest. It wasn't mass absolution, but it was more than walking into a dark, quiet church and going into a booth. It was an hour to an hour-and-a-half-long celebration integrating different parts of the Mass. It wasn't a Mass, but it was in preparation for reconciliation. It was a way to feel welcome into the whole thing, calming you down before you go up to confession.

Mary and Joe liked the parish. They soon dived in and got very involved. They got to know lots of other parishioners and had good experiences. Then not long after the birth of their baby, they moved to a different part of the city for job-related reasons. They became active in a different parish and soon were facilitating a small faith community in it. The interviewer asked Mary her feelings about parishes.

Interviewer: Some people say it's possible to be a good Catholic without getting involved in churches. What is your view?

Mary: I'm not one to judge what a "good Catholic" is. However, I will say that I think Jesus wanted us to be in community with others and I think that you really need to be, in order to be a good Catholic. You can grow better when you are in community with other people who believe the same as you do.

Interviewer: As a Catholic do you have to go to Mass at least occasionally?

Mary: I hate rules, such as "you have to go to Mass." I hate it when people say, "Why does the Catholic Church say you have to go to Mass?" I try to reframe it and say, "It's part of our growth as religious people." During the week we try to strengthen our faith in what we do on an individual basis, but I think we all need to come together in community once a week. I think God asks us to do that, and we can grow so much more that way. We can share with each other. I think it's important. I would hate to say someone is not a better Catholic because they don't do something.

Interviewer: Do you think there are many young people like yourself who go to Mass regularly but are doing it only because they must?

Mary: Probably not so much in my age group now. Probably more when we were in high school. I think we are more aware now, and I think more people go because they want to raise their children Catholic and they don't want to set the example for the kids of not going to church. I think it's maybe a guilt thing. I think that there are a lot of people my age who don't know what good church is, and they're living back in the days when we were growing up. They are going because they want to raise their kids in the Catholic Church. They haven't experienced good liturgy, a sense of community, a sense of what "church" could really be.

Interviewer: Is your parish relevant to your spiritual formation?

Mary: Church is a very big thing to me. I need to belong to a parish that is going to nurture me along and offer me the tools in the areas that I need. I would seek to find that. This also has to do with my prayer life. Marian apparitions have a lot to say. Mary's life has a big impact on me. I put that in the same category as the saints. When I think of Mary taking all of this responsibility on without even knowing what was ahead, I think that was amazing. I find her to be a role model.

Interviewer: What is the most important element of church life that has meaning to you?

Mary: Liturgy. The Mass itself. But I would combine liturgy and community. I need more than just a good liturgy. I need to be able to go somewhere afterwards and get more.

Interviewer: What is your view of the role of the institutional church in your coming to a sense of what's ultimately true and morally true?

Mary: I guess in the end I go by what I've learned. I look at good and evil, yeah. I guess I pray about it, trying to find the right answer. I think I do have a discussion with myself about what is right and wrong. I think I can be a pretty good judge, but I'm not always right.

Interviewer: How do you weigh the Church's teachings in making decisions about right and wrong?

Mary: We're supposed to get everything from the Church's teachings. They can be wrong, I guess, but Vatican II changed a lot of things, so there could be more changes ahead. I weigh their teachings.

Interviewer: Do you weigh them against your own experience as a person?

Mary: Yeah, I guess I have to take my own experiences and then I can see sometimes where I am wrong.

Later the interviewer asked about issues facing the Church today. Mary said that for several years she firmly believed that priests should be married, and now she still believes it but she won't go out and protest or anything like that. She said she is not a feminist. The rules about birth control are a problem which she hasn't resolved. Her perception of the large number of gay priests also concerns her. But these problems aren't serious enough to threaten her loyalty to the Church:

Mary: I don't think there is anything that would drive me out of the Church. They are stuck with me! Those things [moral issues] are probably the things, though, that are difficult. They are things that I need to keep working on and think about. As I said, if I had to pick one side, I would go with what the Church wants.

Now Mary is active in a small faith community in her new parish, and she is hoping to put her children into the parish school in a few years.

Cecilia Coronado: For a Good Family

Cecilia is a thirty-four-year-old Latina of Mexican background, married with three children, living in the West. She had strong religious training as a girl, when her mother and father attended church every day. She attended Catholic grade school and high school. Her mother was a strong influence.

> *Cecilia:* When I was young I always obeyed her. My dad was, and he still is, very, very quiet. He never told us anything. My mom was the discipline. He'd tell her, and she'd tell us. My dad went to church. He was always there for functions for the church, but it was my mom who said, "We got to go to the church and pray for us; we got to go do a novena, we got to go and clean the church for the altar society." It was always my mom. But my dad was there at church too. My parents were real active, doing the festivals.
>
> *Interviewer:* Do you remember any types of religious devotion or piety at home?
>
> *Cecilia:* Just basic. If somebody died, we'd get together at their house and pray the novena. We never really read the Bible together as a family. We would say the rosary occasionally.
>
> *Interviewer:* Our Lady of Guadalupe?
>
> *Cecilia:* Oh yes, oh yes! There were pictures and statues and all that. There was a real strong belief in Our Lady of Guadalupe and the Sacred Heart. And my mom and dad are real devotional to the Sacred Heart. From my own experience I know that we need to do better, but I don't push things on my husband. He is not as devotional.
>
> *Interviewer:* Is it generally true among Latinos that religion is perceived as a more female or woman thing, and men are more distanced?

Cecilia: In the older generations it was. My husband is from that type of background. And from seeing the young kids at our parish now, I see more the girls involved than the boys. With the boys, I just don't see the interest.

Cecilia had been very sheltered as a girl, which she now regrets. She doesn't want her own daughters to be so sequestered from the outside world. Cecilia felt her mother wanted her to be a nurse, so she enrolled in nursing school. But her heart was not in it, and she never finished.

Interviewer: Were you still going to church at that time on a regular basis?

Cecilia: Yes. It was something I grew up with, that you have to go to church. That was something you had to do. My God, if I missed a Sunday Mass I thought that if I die tomorrow, I'm going to go to hell! That's the attitude I had. Then I rebelled. I ran for queen of our fiesta, met my husband, and rebelled. I never had boyfriends before, in my high school years. My first date was my senior year in high school. I was a naive little girl. I did not spend time with my friends having a nice time. I didn't even try to go out and party and drink all the while I was in high school. We just didn't do that. But then I met my husband and got pregnant.

Interviewer: Then did you pull away from church for a while?

Cecilia: No, then I was with my husband—well, he's my husband now. He lived with me for a while. My mother had no idea. I had moved out of the house and I lived in an apartment. I would go to church. I didn't always go to our church, I would go to another church.

Interviewer: Did you have a bad experience with any church official?

Cecilia: I was ashamed. The priest at the time really didn't say anything to me and I didn't go to him either. Of course, I had to deal with the family members and they were, "Oh, my God, you just don't do that! You just don't do that whether you're Catholic or not!" If you're Catholic you just don't get pregnant without being married.

Interviewer: Do you think the rules are harder for Catholics?

Cecilia: I don't know if it's for Catholics, but I know Hispanic people are just really, really strict. When I got pregnant I thought, "Oh

God, I'm really going to go to hell now!" (laugh) But I didn't stop going to church. I still went to church. I didn't receive communion or go to confession.

Interviewer: What turned things around? What brought you back or made you want to be more connected with the Church?

Cecilia: I guess being a parent. I told my husband we need to get married and go to church. Because he was not going to church then. The way he was brought up, both his parents are real strong Catholics who go to church. But he was a big rebel.

Cecilia and her husband were married two years after her daughter was born. She told him she wanted them to be active in the church.

Cecilia: The only thing I asked of him was that, now we have a daughter and in order to teach her right, you do need to start going back to church. It took him about six months and then he started. He still doesn't go much and I don't push him . . . He's a very hard person to get his feelings out, even to me. I'm always, "We need to talk." I'm a very open person and he's not. But he'll make a comment here and there.

Cecilia's children now attend the parish school. It's important to her that they are in the school of their own parish.

Cecilia: I think it is important to support our church and our school. . . . I want them to know their religion. To me it's real important to spend Sunday together as a family, to go to church as a family, to spend that time doing family things. I believe that our religion is strong but I think it is strong because of our family. There's a lot of times when we just got so much to do as a family. Usually everything we do is going to have something to do with the Church.

Interviewer: So, being Catholic is important to you?

Cecilia: Yes.

Interviewer: There's a perception that a lot of Latinos are becoming evangelicals and pentecostals and leaving the Catholic Church. Is that happening here?

Cecilia: Yes. I see it in our church because I call our church an "old religion" church. I think that we should move forward socially in our religion. I've been to other churches where you go and it just seems like the parishioners are so involved and just gung-ho. They do a children's liturgy where the children lead. In our parish we need to have more outreach. People talk about it. I'm the type of person that if you're going to suggest something to do, I'm going to see it through, but we have people that talk about something that would be a good idea and then nothing comes of it. Like right now, the whole problem in our church is we've been getting these instruments to play at the different Masses. Right now I think we have a lot of separation and segregation going on.

Interviewer: Between old and new Latino immigrants, that kind of thing?

Cecilia: Definitely. If I were to move to Mexico or if a small population of people from America would move to Mexico and join a church, I would not expect them to change things at their church for us. I myself would think I would need to fit in, go with the flow, do whatever their church is doing.

Interviewer: That's how it should be.

Cecilia: Right, but that's not what's going on right now. We have a small group of people that have moved here from Mexico. They speak Spanish. Some speak English, but yet we have to change our Masses around for them. And we're having to form another youth group for them. . . . I think it's up to us as parishioners to keep our Mass "alive" is what I call it, and to bring that about. I've also suggested to our priest that we should have a children's liturgy. I'd be willing to take the kids during that time. Because I see it with my own children. I tell them, "Now listen, because they're going to tell you a story." But there are so many words in it, and they have no concept of what's going on. But at times when Father uses the children's liturgy, I can see the kids say, "Oh, okay, I know what he's talking about."

Does Cecilia find anything about the Church to be problematic?

Cecilia: I do. I think that women are just as strong as men. I think it's wrong for these men, because they are men, they are the bishops, popes, deacons, or whatever. To me what they're telling me is that I cannot learn the same thing that they can learn, and I cannot be what they can be. I don't think Jesus intended all of his disciples to put us in a category, like "No, you cannot teach about my religion; you cannot teach my beliefs to other people."

Interviewer: But nothing prohibits women from doing that.

Cecilia: No, but they are limiting individuals when you can't be a priest because you're female. It's like, if you're a woman you have to be in this or that, but if you're a man you can be a brother or a priest, or a bishop or a deacon. But if you're a woman you cannot be a priest or a deacon.

Then she talked about birth control:

Cecilia: I would like my daughters not to have sex before they get married, before they meet the right man. What I'm talking about is like a married couple: for a married couple that's tough, that's tough. I took birth control pills and I knew if I didn't, I'd be pregnant every time. I'd be pregnant twice in one year. I knew that (laugh) because of my husband; he has no restraint. So I knew that if I didn't do something, I would be pregnant more than what we could financially afford. Not only that, but every time I did get pregnant, I would always have something go wrong. After the third time I told my husband I'd like to have more kids, but it wasn't going to happen to me the next time. The doctor even said, "You need to start thinking about not getting pregnant any more." I believe, on the birth control, if the couple decides after they've had children that they don't want more children, they can do that in good conscience. I think that the Lord is not going to hold that against them.

Interviewer: Do you think a person could be a good Catholic without being involved in the church in some way, or going to Mass?

Cecilia: I guess I've seen both sides of that. Myself, I like going to church for the fact that if I keep that in my schedule I have just that time to relax and reflect and think. I think if someone wants to be a Catholic, they should be connected. That's what they should do. Our parish leans toward being community, and this is also true of some of the other parishes around town. That's what we're shooting for. Not to be the St. Peters parish people exclusively, but the people should think that they are the same Catholic faith as others. . . . To me it's "They're Catholic too; what's the difference?" I was never brought up to think that "she's white, she's black, and you're Mexican." I never had a problem meeting white friends, black friends, non-Latinos.

Mary and Cecilia are good examples of parish-involved Catholics. Both find meaning in their parish activity, partly for their own nourishment and partly for their families and children. Both have some problems with the Church which they readily discuss, but the problems are not serious enough to cause them to leave.

II. REGULAR ATTENDING CATHOLICS

These persons attend church more or less regularly, and some are active in parish groups or committees. They are middle-of-the-road in their church participation and attitudes. Since they tend not to be very distinctive, we do not give an example here.

III. OCCASIONAL ATTENDERS

The only thing distinguishing occasional attenders (type III) from regular attenders (type II) is that they go to church much less regularly. None of them go more than once a month. They tend to be less committed to their faith and parish, and some have mixed feelings about being Catholic. We do not give an example.

IV. NON-ATTENDING CATHOLICS

Although the people in this category say they are Catholic, they are marginally so. Their upbringing included less parish involvement than average (though they attended Catholic elementary and high schools at the same rate as others). They are disproportionately male, and they tend not to have children living with them. They have much less personal devotional behavior such as going to private confession or reading the Bible at home, and they less often consider themselves spiritual persons.

In short: they are not very enthusiastic about Catholicism. They are a bit skeptical about ecclesiastical claims and about the pope, and in effect they are private persons who happen to be Catholic. An example is Sophia Langone.

Sophia Langone: A Lot I Don't Agree With

Sophia is a single woman college graduate, twenty-five years old, of Italian ancestry, in an eastern city. She has always been conscious of being Italian. She has attended both a Catholic high school and a Catholic college. She describes her family as "working class poor," partly because her parents divorced when she was small. Her father was not a Catholic. Sophia spoke warmly of her experiences in Catholic school, where she liked the religion classes.

> *Interviewer:* Do you remember some of the things you talked about in those classes?
>
> *Sophia:* I do. We went on a retreat, I remember that. Definitely. I remember the book we read, *The Road Less Traveled* . . . I think in my freshman year we started to do the Old Testament, which we never really did in junior high, so that was all new for us. And then in junior year we took a class on death and dying, and then senior year was a class on campus ministry. The teacher of my campus ministry class was a priest, and we talked about a lot of different things.
>
> *Interviewer:* How about college? You went to a Catholic college. Was there a religious dimension of the college?
>
> *Sophia:* Well. At college we went into a whole bunch of different issues. We learned about feminism and the Catholic Church and feminism and all different religions. That's one thing that we didn't really touch upon even in high school—different religions.

Interviewer: And did you like that?

Sophia: Oh, definitely, definitely! I think it opened me up to different areas that I don't know I'd have taken up if I went to a bigger university. I took four religion classes at my college. . . . I'm trying to remember what I took. I think I took a Women in Society religion class and I took an American Judaism class because I wanted to learn about a different religion, you know. We had a rabbi come in and teach the class, so that was extremely interesting. I got to learn about a different religion and see how close it was to Catholicism. And the feminist theory class was excellent.

Interviewer: I think you took graduate courses at a Catholic university.

Sophia: Right. It was interesting. I was in a sociology class, and on the first day of class we went around the class and had to introduce ourselves. What we were, what religion we were in. . . . A few people were Catholic, and they'd say "I was raised Catholic but I don't practice, but I'm not a Catholic now." So the teacher got to me and I said I'm Catholic, and she automatically said to me, "But you don't practice," and I said, "Yes, I do." I said I was raised, and I'm still, a Catholic. And everyone sort of just looked at me and said "Wow," you know, "You still practice, you are still Catholic!" And I said yes. I think it's very hard for a person to say you are raised Catholic and now all of a sudden, you know, you are not Catholic any more. I think if you were raised that, it's still in you somewhere. I may not go to Mass every day, you know, but I would still say I am definitely Catholic. I was raised Italian Catholic, so for me to say that I'm not Catholic, it's like saying I'm not Italian. You can't separate the two.

Sophia went on to say that she has now stopped attending Mass. She feels ambivalent.

Sophia: I can't say why. I don't know if it's just pure laziness or what. As far as the Church itself, there is a lot of stuff I don't agree with. I go back and forth on it a lot; I don't know, I'm kind of at the middle point, but for the big holidays, I'm there at church and have a feeling that you need to go. I'm at the point now where I don't think you need to actually go to church to pray or to go every Sunday and say that that makes me a Catholic.

Interviewer: When you say you disagree with some parts of the Church, what is it?

Sophia: Well, like the whole thing about divorce, and abortion. There were a lot of issues that were raised to me when I was in college. I think I came in with certain ideas when I came to college and after taking a number of classes like philosophy and sociology and religion, I started to question and say "I was taught this, but. . . ." I think I just took it as final, as that-was-that. But as I got older I said, "Oh wait, there are a lot of different aspects here, so. . . ."

Interviewer: Let's talk about these issues. Let's start with divorce.

Sophia: In C.C.D. we were taught divorce is wrong; you don't get divorced. You get married and that's that, no matter what. As far as my mother was concerned, it wasn't that she needed to be divorced, but that after she was, she did not go to church any more. I don't want to say that she did something wrong, but I think she felt a strain with the Church after she was divorced. For myself, I think deep down that my mother wasn't a bad person because she was divorced and we weren't bad people because we were the children of divorced parents. As I got to college I felt that there are some times when you need to be divorced, like in cases of abuse, and that the Church won't move with that and say, okay, maybe there are times when divorce can be an option.

Sophia also talked about the Church's position on birth control and stressed that today it is financially and emotionally impossible to raise a large family.

Interviewer: What about other issues?

Sophia: Those are the big ones. I think there's a lot of good to the Church, but there are issues like that. When I was raised we were taught of course not to have sex before you were married, birth control was wrong, and what-have-you, and my mother tried not to use birth control, but then she had four kids right way. And then my parents knew they could not do it any more, and so my mother had a choice. I found out later that my mother went to her priest and asked the priest if she could use birth control, and he told her no. My mother did not know what to do and she said, "Well, I already have four kids and I can't financially do this," so then she went to a younger priest who in turn told her yes. Then my mother said, "Okay, he said yes, so I'll go and do it." It's things like that just amaze me, that my mother actually went to a priest after having already four kids, where *I* would have made my own decision by then.

Interviewer: Back to your feelings about Mass. Why don't you go?

Sophia: I don't know. I asked myself that too. I'll go a few times maybe with a girlfriend. But for myself, I just don't know. I feel hypocritical going and thinking all of these things. I don't agree with things that we were taught and which supposedly are the beliefs now of Catholics. I don't feel right sitting there. . . . I've heard people say "You should go and receive the Eucharist. That's why you go." And I agree with that. For some people it's a community, and it is for a lot of people in my parish, but the parish has a lot of new people now, so as far as community there, it's not much. As far as the Mass itself, I don't think there is anything there that draws me to it.

Interviewer: Have you heard of people who shop around for parishes that fit them, either good music or good preaching or a sense of community?

Sophia: Not for me. No. I've attended Mass at different parishes, but I still associate my parish with that's where I received my sacraments, that's where all my friends went, that's where my family went. I think it's definitely a neighborhood thing. That's the parish you grew up in, and that's the one you stick with.

Interviewer: If the bishops and the pope came out tomorrow with a statement saying that they had changed their thinking on birth control and divorce and remarriage, would you go to Mass?

Sophia: I might. I don't know, but I might. But now I think I'm at a point where I think religion is more about spirituality and my own prayers and my own thoughts, and I don't necessarily have to actually go to Mass or be Catholic to be spiritual.

Interviewer: To you is there any place for any kind of group or community prayer? Any kind of group prayer experience?

Sophia: No. I haven't thought about that. No.

The conversation turned to Sophia's home and her mother's influence.

Sophia: Religion was always a big topic at home. We wouldn't necessarily talk about it, but I know my mother had different opinions than what we were supposed to be taught in C.C.D. or in church. I can't remember ever really being taught anything contrary, but like the divorce thing. My mother would say "Yes, but. . . ." I think my mother influenced me more than maybe the church did.

Sophia related how her sister was taught in a high school confirmation class that Protestants belonged to a cult. This infuriated Sophia, possibly since her own father was a Protestant. Why were they teaching that? She said that Catholics can be liberal on some issues while embarrassing on others.

Sophia: That's something I struggle with. We can be so liberal on some things and then there are so many other things that I think we are not liberal on. It's like you need to pick and choose what you want to believe or what you don't want to believe, or what you'll hold on to and say, "Yes, I'm Catholic and agree with policies on the poor and social justice, but then when it comes to these different issues like divorce, I don't agree with it." I don't think you can be 100 percent Catholic and believe every single thing that we were taught. It definitely is a balancing act. For me, I just dismiss everything I don't believe any more or I don't agree with.

The interviewer asked Sophia about various Church teachings on poverty, on social justice, on sexual behavior, and so on. Sophia said she appreciated many Catholic social teachings but disagreed with others. She talked about her problems on some of the women's issues like abortion and birth control.

Sophia is an example of a person caught between childhood religious training and her adult feelings on some moral issues. She will probably be a lifelong Catholic, but the conflicts have driven her away from Church. She will probably choose specific elements of the faith in the future.

V. Non-Catholics

About ten percent of our sample said they are not Catholics any more. Why not? What happened? We uncovered four facts about them. *First fact:* they are older than the other four types. This is largely the result of more years of life and more years of experience, which simply means more years in which to be influenced to change away from their home religion. In coming years we may expect more in our sample to switch to other churches, but not a large number. Past research shows that most conversions, switches, and dropping-out occur during the teens, twenties, and early thirties. Few occur after age forty, since life has a tendency to settle down after forty, with fewer changes of any kind—of residence, or jobs, or of churches (Hoge 1981:171).

Second fact: the majority say they have some other religion. This is true of 61 percent of the non-Latinos and 72 percent of the Latinos. Most of them are Protestants of various types.[4] The largest single movement is to nondenominational churches, and among Latinos a large group have also moved to pentecostal or evangelical churches.

Have they formally joined the other groups? Most, but not all. Fifty-one percent of the non-Latinos and 62 percent of the Latinos have formally joined another religion. We observed some hesitation when we asked the people in the interviews if they have formally joined another church or denomination, since the people's experiences were not always clear-cut. Some of the other churches do not seem to require formal joining, and some of the ex-Catholics were hesitant to undertake a formal act of joining, preferring instead to attend a new church and take part in its activities without making a formal commitment.

Third fact: As we have noted before, in religious beliefs and practices these people are not very different from Catholics. Most have the same faith in Jesus Christ and the same worldview even though they are now out of the Catholic Church.

Fourth fact: the majority of non-Catholics who are or were married tied the knot with non-Catholic spouses. Of the non-Latinos of type V, 85 percent of the ever-married had non-Catholic spouses, and of the Latinos the figure was 64 percent. These are high numbers. But no one should conclude that the act of marrying a non-Catholic by itself explains a religious change. This is because people who marry outside their faith have less commitment than average to their own faith (Hoge 1981: 75). Such people feel less loyalty to their faith than others, and when they subsequently marry outside the faith, the interfaith marriage is only part of the explanation for any later behavior. In the case of our sample members who married non-Catholics, on average they were less Catholic to start with.

Three Types of Non-Catholics

After scrutinizing the non-Catholics in our sample, we identified three types. They are persons who (1) lost faith or became disillusioned with the Church; (2) married a non-Catholic and joined the spouse's denomination; or (3) were evangelized by a friend or relative. We will describe each.

First: A definite group told us they had lost their faith or that they are disillusioned with religion and the Church. They comprise about 49 percent of the non-Latinos and 38 percent of the Latinos of type V. Some of these people said they no longer believed in the Church's teachings and were trying to be religious in their own personal terms; they seemed to have lost their religious commitment and were tired of the whole thing. But the main theme in this group was a feeling of alienation or anger at the Catholic Church. People told us stories about incidents in their lives which angered them. One woman complained that a Catholic priest would not give her and her fiance a church marriage because she was pregnant; another dropped out when she was single and became pregnant; another complained that the priest was living high while the parishioners were surviving on low incomes. Two of the women said that they were lesbians and believed that they could not be Catholics; one man was gay and said the same thing. Four or five persons seemed to have left the Church due to a divorce. Several appear to have rebelled more against their families than against the Catholic Church, but we lack enough detail to know for certain.

Our point here is simply that the people in this category had feelings about something that happened in the past, and the feelings are still present.

Second: Many of the ex-Catholics had married a non-Catholic spouse. This category includes marrying a non-religious person, which was the case for eight non-Latinos out of thirty-three in interfaith marriages and for three Latinos out of twenty-five in interfaith marriages. How many of the exits from Catholicism were directly due to these interfaith marriages? After reviewing the interviews we guess that it is about one-third of the non-Latinos and one-fourth of the Latinos. These figures aren't higher because some of the interfaith marriages obviously came later than when the persons switched denominations, and because a number of the interviewees convinced us that earlier incidents or disillusionments were more important in their decisions than their interfaith marriages.

Third: A portion of the non-Catholics told us that they were attracted to other churches, usually by friends or relatives. They told us that they switched because they found the new church more biblical, more filled with the Holy Spirit, more active, more friendly, or for various other reasons. They talked with feeling, often telling of an experience of healing or a burst of spiritual joy in the new-found faith. A few, by contrast, had non-dramatic stories, such as the person who had simply gone church-shopping and had found a good non-Catholic church.

What we said earlier about interfaith marriage needs to be said again here. Solid and happy members of any church, be it Catholic or Mormon or whatever, do not change churches. They are not candidates for being evangelized into a different church unless they are already ambivalent or dissatisfied with their own church. Therefore this third type of non-Catholic is not clearly distinguishable from the first type (persons who lost their faith or were disillusioned). Our only reason for distinguishing the two is to convey some sense of the relative importance of the influences on these persons.

Two good examples of non-Catholics are Joe Luis and Mary Landrum. Joe switched to an evangelical church due to his personal distress and the influence of friends, and Mary switched to a Presbyterian church after feeling uneasy as a Catholic and entering into an interfaith marriage.

Joe Luis: Needed a Complete Turnaround

Joe is a Latino salesman, thirty-eight, living in an eastern city. He was reared in a small town in the West where he was active in the Catholic

Church. His parents attended church every Sunday. He served as an altar boy and went to C.C.D. classes all through high school.

> *Interviewer:* Did you have religious images in your home? Statues, pictures, things like that?
>
> *Joe:* Yes, a cross. We had a plaque commemorating something about my mom and dad being Catholics. My grandmother had a large doll-like statue of the Virgin Mary in a little grotto above her bed. To all of us as kids, that was off limits. You could look at it but not touch it. And we had some paintings of Jesus.
>
> *Interviewer:* Was there anything distinctively Catholic about your religious education?
>
> *Joe:* I remember this: the Catholic Church was the true Church. It was the only true Church, and everything else was not a true church. This point was impressed on me. But I didn't really know much about my faith. It was more out of obedience to my parents. It didn't have much knowledge of history or culture.
>
> *Interviewer:* Did you make any retreats in high school?
>
> *Joe:* I did one, and it was great! It was called "Search," and it was real good. I felt "high" about that. Looking back, I wish I would have continued walking and growing in that faith.

Joe left home to go to the state university, where he studied math for four years but didn't complete a degree. He continued to attend Mass weekly.

> *Joe:* My sophomore year in college I was still drug-free. I had never done any drugs. But I did drink beer. And then, I remember in my sophomore year, I started reading the Bible. I thought I was making headway in how I was enjoying God's goodness in my life. Things were going well. I was getting good grades. I was on the honor roll, actually. I felt lonely, even though I was in a fraternity. I was away from home, and I just felt lonely. Someone gave me a Bible that was easy to read.

Joe was very active in his fraternity, and in his sophomore and junior years he turned into a party man.

Joe: Then I got into partying and into drugs. I just fell away and stayed that way for a long time. I got into a job situation. But I still went to church on Sunday. I had the belief that not going to church on Sunday was a sin, and I felt that I needed to do that just to cover myself through the weekdays. I felt guilty if I didn't go.

Joe experienced a traumatic week in which his life seemed to collapse.

Joe: I lost everything at once. I was seeing this girl, and we were going to live together in a house that she and her parents and I were going to buy, but it wasn't quite finished. I was managing a video store. And my car quit on me, and I had to take the bus to work. When I got in there, I was given the choice to be fired or to resign. When I came back to the apartment that I was renting until the townhouse was completed, I found out that I had to move. The landlady came and said, "Hey, I sold the house. You're going to have to move." In addition, my girlfriend found out that I was cheating on her. So she told her dad and I lost the house and the girl. And it all happened in about a week!

Interviewer: After all this did you become more reflective?

Joe: Well, I got angry, and I knew that God was souring, so I was angry with God for letting these things happen, and I knew that it was Him. So I went back to this church and figured that I needed to get right with God, and I walked in, and I started crying, and I just knew that it was *me*. I don't know, it was just the conviction I guess that the Holy Spirit was saying that it's your heart that's got to change.

Interviewer: Was this at your Catholic church?

Joe: Yeah. They had a renewal at that church. There was this priest, I would say he was a renegade. He invited everyone to come to a Wednesday night seminar for seven Wednesdays to learn about the life in the Holy Spirit. I wanted it, and I went. They talked about the indwelling of the Holy Spirit and the spiritual gifts. I started going.

Interviewer: Would you say you had a conversion experience?

Joe: Yes. From then, I just realized that I've got an obligation to follow Jesus.

Interviewer: Were you alienated from the Church or in disagreement with its basic teachings?

Joe: No, because I didn't know much about their basic teachings. Knowing what I do *now* about the Catholic Church, I do have some questions about some of their doctrines, but I didn't at that time. I was still going to Mass regularly.

Joe attended the charismatic group each Wednesday. After a time he came into contact with a group of members who met together separately.

Joe: There was this group, they called themselves "Children of Light," and we used to meet and have great teaching. These were lay people who were giving me great teachings about passages in the Bible—about the beatitudes or whatever. I was just tickled with it, I was okay with just staying there.

Interviewer: Did the priest come to that?

Joe: Yes, not regularly but he was there a few times. It was great teaching. I just loved it and everything about it, but I had about five couples come to me and say, "Joe, we love you. We love seeing you here. We just feel like the Lord would want you to be plugged in to a church where there are a lot of singles like yourself where you can get plugged in and serve and minister and be more active." So, I fought that for months, and then one of the other singles had said that he felt like he got a word from the Lord to go to this Covenant Life Church and there he would meet his future wife. So he went. That was the last time I saw him. . . . He did find a girl. They got married, and they moved to Springfield and that's where his law practice is. So I felt like, "Okay, I'm going to go there." And I went there and I just wanted to be by myself. It was great. What really got me right away was the worship. The first thing they do is sing a worship song. Maybe it was just that my heart was a lot softer at that time than it ever was, but the words of the song really grabbed me to the point that I started crying. I just started realizing that whatever I do, I'll always be God's precious child. I started thinking about that. I know how much my dad loves me, and yet this guy Jesus said he loves me more perfectly than my dad ever could.

And that just really floored me. Just the words really penetrated my heart and it was probably because I was really open to that at that particular moment. I really think it was the Holy Spirit working.

Interviewer: Did you feel welcomed at this congregation, or were you still a social isolate?

Joe: Just for two or three weeks I felt isolated, then I saw two guys there that knew me, and then they just started introducing me to other people and encouraged me to go to this home group that met on every other Tuesday night, and then before I knew it, I knew a hundred people in the church. It happened so quick. I just showed up at one of these meetings. I loved the worship, the music, the style. The teaching, the preaching, seemed really welcoming. It's all the same words, the same Bible. I was probably in a different spot to receive it, and it just came. Then in the application, they would give practical examples of how this could apply to our lives, and as I met other friends we would dialogue and talk about it, whether over lunch or dinner or a weekend or a volleyball game or something, we would talk about that. We would say, "Hey, that's a bad attitude, because you know what's really in the desire of your heart." It was just growth after that.

Interviewer: So there was a mutually supportive relationship between you and the other people.

Joe: Well, maybe just accountability. And encouragement. Because I hung around with some guys, and a lot of us were in the same boat. And I found out that even within that church there are a group of people who never normally partied together, but as they grew they were friends. There was a group of people that never really were party animals and then there were other guys that used to ski on a moment's notice, drop everything they were doing and head for the resort and party and go on road trips and stuff like that, you know, "hell raisers." Both groups were believers and both of the same body.

Interviewer: What was your relationship with Catholicism as you became more involved in this congregation? Did you stop going to Mass?

Joe: Yes, because Sunday service was held at this congregation, and I couldn't be in two places at once. The Sunday service was a couple of hours long at the minimum. Afterwards we would get together and do something, either go to lunch or something like that. I didn't give much thought to the Catholic Church after that. I just followed the way of Jesus Christ and the Bible. Christ is who I ultimately have to answer to. I always tell my mother this: I don't know how to become un-Catholic. So I don't know if I'm a nonpracticing Catholic or what.

Interviewer: How do your parents feel about your conversion experience?

Joe: At first they thought I was part of a cult or something, because they didn't understand. One of my brothers just thought I was having a drug relapse and burnout, but over time I said to my parents, "I don't hold anything against you for the way you raised me in regard to my religious beliefs. As a matter of fact, I thank you for what you did. You established the foundation. The foundation was always that Jesus Christ died on the cross for my sins and that we believed that." I've had brothers and sisters come and visit me at the church, and they can see that I'm not a drug user, I'm not an alcohol abuser, and I don't fight and quarrel with my siblings the way I used to. . . . I don't run around with girls. I was very known for that in the past, and I just went up to my dad and said, "Listen, it's not about sex, it's not about beautiful girls, matter of fact there are plenty of beautiful ladies out there that are going to live their lives purely and save themselves for their husbands and be every bit the woman my mom is, and I know that's what you really want." What woman would want a renegade? Who would want a man like that, who's not like-minded? So the big losers are the guys that don't turn their lives around.

Interviewer: So you attribute this turnaround in your life to this change? Were you knocked off a horse on the road to Damascus like Paul?

Joe: Yeah. I believe that I got knocked off a horse on the road to Damascus. Everything happened in one week; that was the horse event. But now I don't devote myself to the ways of the Lord like Paul did. I'm just trying to find out how Paul did that, because he said he worked for his living, you know, even though he had a right to live off of the Gospel, and all those missionary trips that he took just floor me. . . . Here's the other thing. How many of those other teachings did I hear about in a Catholic Church when I was growing up? It went in here [one ear] and out there [other ear]. But now, I have changed. I'm different so I can hear and say, "How can I apply this to my life?"

The interviewer asked Joe about his views of the Eucharist and the moral teachings of the different churches. Joe didn't think the differences were important.

Joe: As far as this particular congregation, I just feel I have a duty to find out what God's word says about that [moral teachings]. I think I'm like-minded with a lot of the people at this congregation about what is moral and ethical and pleasing to God. I believe it's very similar to the Catholic Church as far as abortion, premarital sex, the use of drugs or alcohol, or giving oneself to become a slave to anything.

Interviewer: What about non-Christian religions? Do you see Christianity as more true than any other religion?

Joe: Yes. I believe what makes it more true is: what are the other religions based on? Are the other religions based on other prophets? What is their basic belief? Is it founded on God or Jesus Christ? From what I understand, a lot of these other religions don't have a documented word of a coming Messiah, but we have Jesus that not only died on the cross but even more importantly was raised from the dead and actually walked on this earth. As far as I know, no other prophet has ever done that. So that's the basis for why I believe Christianity, that it is the way and the truth. I believe in the Bible.

Interviewer: Is this an area in which Catholicism is deficient, that it doesn't emphasize the Word enough?

Joe: From what I know, yeah, I think so. I don't know if I would call it a deficiency. It could be that I just wasn't hearing that particular part when they were encouraging us to read it. Maybe I just chose to ignore that. When I was at St. Edward's Catholic Church in the charismatic group, I thought it was just great and radical and a difference-making type of church. It was great. I met great people

there. I think in that group, if there had just been a Catholic elder
or a priest who would have said, "Hey, there's a void here for
young adults," it would have been different. That is a need. And
that is probably where most of the young people go astray or are
torn away. It's probably the crack in which I fell.

Joe met a women at the Covenant Life Church, and he will be getting married soon. He told about how the two of them have been
studying the Bible and preparing for their life together.

Mary Landrum: Fear of Being Oppressed

Mary is a married woman and recent mother, thirty-one, working as a
counselor at a university. She grew up in a large blue-collar Scotch-Irish
family in the Midwest, the youngest of seven children. Her parents
were very involved in their parish, and Mary attended Catholic elementary and high school. She was a very good student, but she felt restless.

Mary: My big turning point in Catholicism was when I was eighteen,
and I was a senior in high school in the religion class. I had a
teacher who said—I think for the first time I heard someone say
about Church leaders, "Well, okay, these folks are men, even
though we say they are infallible and all the rules are true rules
and you have to follow them. But, you know, the rules were made
by men." And I was going to an all-girls school, and I'm sitting
there thinking, "Wait a minute! You told me for twelve years that
I had to follow these things and that this came down from God.
And now you're telling me that it's just made up and it's our interpretation of the thing!" And I got really ticked off! I felt like I had
been misled. I felt like I had been lied to. I was just *really* angry,
and I decided I was not going to stand for this any more. I would
go to church every Sunday like my parents told me I had to, and I
would finish my schooling, but this wasn't for me. I wasn't going
to be doing this for the rest of my life.

Later, in college, I read some of the Rosemary Radford Ruether
stuff when I was writing a paper in a sociology course. I thought,
"Wait a minute!" She was good, and other people who agreed

with her, because they fought from within. And I kept thinking, "If I had the faith, I would fight from within," like she talks about. And I kept thinking, "I cannot fight from within, because there is no place for women to move up and make a difference, other than to serve people." Which, you know, would be a good thing. But I can serve people in other ways. So I chose to fight from without.

Mary attended a non-Catholic private college where she was happy to discover that she had the option of ignoring organized religion altogether. She attended Mass only when she came home on vacations. In the interview she talked about her mother's life.

Mary: When my mother had me, the seventh child in eleven years, she was just overwhelmed, losing her mind. And she finally found a priest who said, "This is crazy. Go on the pill. Get some kind of birth control for yourself." Because earlier we had an old parish priest who kept telling her, "No, you can't use birth control, you've got to take as many children as God gives you." And she was really careful and did what she could, but when she became pregnant again she was just miserable. And even with me, she was so unhappy! One of her doctors was telling her she could have an abortion and he would make sure it was okay. And she just felt like they were pushing her to do things that she didn't feel comfortable with.

Interviewer: It seems as if you started off as a happy Catholic girl, but something intervened.

Mary: (laugh) Well, here's what intervened. First there was a key moment in the class when they told me the pope was not infallible. And also every year we had retreats; that was part of a Catholic education. And retreats for a lot of people were this very meaningful, spiritual, life-changing event. And I would go and feel nothing! And feel manipulated and feel like I was told to do things and pushed to do things that didn't feel right to me. And one moment in my senior retreat, which is supposed to be this incredibly "send you off on a life of happy Catholicism" thing, I sat there when we had this moment of meditation—we were supposed to be writing a letter to God—and I just sat there and all I could do was write "I don't feel a relationship to you, God. I must not have the faith that they expect me to have." And all I could do was *cry* about that. Everybody else was crying tears of joy because they felt so happy! (laugh) And all I could do is sit there and think, "There's nothing here. They're telling me I have this faith, they're telling me that I was given this faith, and I don't feel it." And it was really frightening, because I felt alone and I felt like, you know, "What's wrong? Is it the Church? Is it me?" At the time I guess I decided that it was the Church.

During college she began dating the man she later married. He did not belong to a church and had never been baptized. His father was a professor and his mother was a television professional, and they were good people, but not churchgoers. Mary admired their lifestyle.

Mary: They were a model that you can still be a moral and good and caring person without having to be in an organized religion. And part of it for me at that time was, I don't want to have somebody in Rome, or somebody in Chicago, or the Bishop of Evansville, whatever, telling me what I have to believe and what I have to do! When I was nineteen, twenty years old I was feeling like I had to take a purposeful stand. I felt I had to be honest and say I believe in birth control, I believe in the woman's right to choose, and I believe that it's okay to be homosexual, so I'm not going to stay in this church which tells me I can't. Those were big issues for me. And the feminist stuff, the oppression of women, too.

Interviewer: Maybe your view then was that organized religion is silly, or unnecessary.

Mary: Well, I thought religion is *scary!* (laugh) I don't feel that any more; I've come past that. But at the time, it's like, it's scary! It takes over people, it tells you what you have to do and what you have to believe. And I didn't like that. I felt like, if I were given the chance to think things through myself, I'd probably come to where they are, but on my own. I had *never* been given a chance to think through things on my own. I was baptized when I was a month old, and I made my first communion when I was seven.

Interviewer: It sounds as if you were restless.

Mary: Restless, and wanting to get out of there. I mean, all of my siblings are still in Evansville now. I'm the only one out of seven who left. I was definitely restless. I didn't want to be like my friends in high school. I didn't want to be like my siblings. I wanted to be out of there and have a different lifestyle.

Interviewer: Where did this restlessness come from?

Mary: Well, I was the best student in grade school and high school. All the boys thought I was too smart for them. Or too frightening. (laugh) And in the area where I grew up, I'd look around, I'd think about the people around me and think, "Gosh, you're just not going anywhere." A lot of the people I was around in high school, and the guys I dated, I thought, "You're going to work in a minimum wage job for most of your life." And that was not for me.

Interviewer: What did your parents say about college? Did they push you to go?

Mary: Oh yeah. They said I had to go to college because I was so smart. I was the first sibling to get a four-year degree. And the first one to get a masters' degree. And a lot of my siblings are very bright. All four of my sisters are nurses, and they could have done more.

Interviewer: Why didn't they?

Mary: I always attribute it to the Catholic Church telling them that you need to have kids and just get a good job.

Interviewer: Where does that come from?

Mary: Um, I don't know. I think maybe since my parents had so many kids. I think my father probably underachieved too. Neither of my parents had college. Both finished high school and got jobs. So for them and for my extended family, getting a two-year degree was amazing, much less a four-year degree.

Interviewer: But just breaking out of the mold doesn't mean you'd no longer be Catholic. Plenty of people have broken out and remained good Catholics of a different type.

Mary: Right. I have friends who are of that kind. If I had gone through the kind of Catholic schools they did, I probably would be. Although I don't know. *They* can rationalize and are comfortable with it. You know, everybody talks about that the young Catholics today say birth control is okay with me even if the Church says it's not, and different stuff is okay with me even if the Church says it's not. But—that wasn't me, because I didn't have the faith and didn't have the peace. *Now* I go to a Presbyterian church, and I feel like this is a place that touches me spiritually and makes me think about things differently. But then I'd go to Mass and be in and out of there in twenty minutes, and it was just an exercise.

Interviewer: What was wrong with the Mass?

Mary: Mass was routine. It's peaceful in some ways because you know what to expect, and I loved the bells and whistles when they had the big High Mass and the midnight services at Easter. I *still* like those. I went to a Catholic wedding a month ago, and I thought, "Oh, this is beautiful!" But it's an intellectual exercise for me, as opposed to anything that touches me emotionally. Part of me felt like I should go to an Episcopal Church, and maybe it'll be the bells and whistles without the church in Rome.

Mary and Jim had a self-planned wedding in the outdoors, as a compromise between a church wedding and going to the justice of the peace. Even after marriage Mary said that she had a fear of being trapped by churches. A little later Jim brought up the idea of joining a church. She was hesitant.

Mary: I was like, why do we need an organized religion? Why can't we just every once in a while go hear a preacher? And, oh yeah, I guess it is a good thing to do. And Jim kept saying, "I think it would be really nice." And I said, "Okay, just as long as it's not one that's going to force me to do anything I don't want to do."

Interviewer: Did your mother give you the vibes that it's hard being a Catholic woman?

Mary: I heard those stories all the time, about how she would find out she was pregnant and come home and sob for days. My sister would know when she was going to have another baby, because Mother was so depressed! And the priest, Father Hart, would say, "Come on Bertha, that is what your life is about." And she felt like

"Well? Who says?" I think that came through very strongly. . . .
And our parish was really cliquey. There were the in-people, there
were the people who just went every Sunday, and there were
people who just had their kids in the school. My friends' parents
were in the in-clique, but my parents were busy working. My parents weren't close to the other people in the church, and I didn't
see the church reaching out and doing much for the people around
us or in the church.

Interviewer: I'm still puzzled about why you were so restless. You
were a success in high school, and everything seemed to be in
place.

Mary: I would have to say, I would also have gone through this restless
thing even if I had met a nice Catholic boy from Evansville and
gotten married. I would have probably gone back to the Church
and just done the rationalization thing: "Yeah, it's nice to have a
parish which is my social outlet." That's how my sisters think of
their parish—as their social outlet. They don't think of the church
as "Here's what I believe." They're not in the Right to Life movement. They both distance themselves from that. So I could see
myself as being like them if I had married a nice Catholic boy,
moved back, and had no reason to stay away. But I met Jim, met his
parents, and had lots of reasons not to return. Because here's these
role models of people who are intellectuals; I came into the family
and saw their life. (laugh) Saw a different way of being.

Mary and Jim started rethinking their life. Mary's parents hoped that
they would rejoin the Catholic Church, or at least *some* church. Jim's
parents saw no point to churchgoing. Mary was uneasy.

Mary: I started to feel sort of restless and sort of directionless. I
knew where I was going with my career, and I knew I was happy
with my husband. But on a larger picture, what was the point? It
is a problem! (laugh) And that's when I started to agree that Jim
and I should start checking out a church. And so we did.

Mary and Jim started shopping for churches. They agreed that they
would like to join a church together, not in separate denominations.

Jim was opposed to the Catholic Church, since he said its beliefs are contrary to his. They shopped for mainline Protestant churches and eventually joined a Presbyterian Church.

> *Mary:* The Presbyterian Church where we now go does give you a direction. It gives you a strong one and then lets you kind of choose within that whether you agree with some things. So I didn't feel the overwhelming sense of oppression that I did in the Catholic Church. But, I mean, some of the conflict we see in our Presbyterian church is really frightening! Some of the things the people say! They speak out! Some are angry. I mean, but in the Catholic church you go and you say yes, yes, and that's it.

The interviewer asked Mary about her siblings and Catholic friends. How are they adjusting to Catholicism?

> *Mary:* I have a lot of friends who are Catholic. Most of them are lapsed Catholics. If you ask them, they'll say they are Catholics. They go to church maybe once a year. They wouldn't say they left the church, but they aren't active. Their attitude is, either they can identify something that they really like about the Catholic Church, such as family life, or its social justice side, or the fact that the Mass is a very comforting thing. Or, it's something they don't think about. They just do, and they've always done it.

Mary expects to remain in some Protestant church or other, since that is what fits her and Jim.

REFLECTIONS

All these people began at the same place: all were confirmed Catholic as adolescents. But now, at an average age of thirty, they arrange themselves in a spectrum from being active in parish life at one end to having left Catholicism at the other end. As the examples teach us, these people vary widely in experiences and attitudes. Having parents who were active Catholics was important, but it did not ensure that they themselves would in turn be active. Some experienced alienating episodes during high school, others had their childhood teachings challenged at college, and still others entered into interfaith marriages. Some found parishes supportive, and others did not. Given our research method, we cannot describe precisely all the factors and influences which produced each outcome. All we can do is to depict the types and make an estimate of how many people fall into each.

CHAPTER 5

Latino Young Adults

. . . .

Our survey of young adult Catholics included a separate sample of Latinos so we could compare them with other Catholics. Research on young adult Latinos is urgently needed in view of the large wave of Latino immigrants coming to the United States each year. Due to rapid immigration and high fertility rates, the number of Latinos in the Catholic Church is booming, and in time the surge of Latinos will change everything. In Allan Figueroa Deck's words: "What the Irish have been to the Church in the twentieth century, the Hispanics will be in the next" (1995:6).

LATINO IMMIGRATION HISTORY

Although many Americans think of Latinos as an immigrant group, this is only partly accurate. The reality of Latino history is more complex. The oldest Christian institution in the region under the U.S. flag today is the Diocese (now Archdiocese) of San Juan, Puerto Rico, which was established in 1511, long before any English settlers arrived. The first Christian church in what are now the 50 states was at Saint Augustine, Florida, founded in 1565. Farther west, the cities of El Paso (now Texas) and Santa Fe (now New Mexico) were Catholic outposts in the seventeenth century in a northern province of Mexico. So the earliest Latinos in what is now the United States were not immigrants but rather were long-resident landholders who found themselves citizens of the United

States when the boundaries changed. The histories of Puerto Rico and New Mexico, especially, are of old Spanish and indigenous cultures later conquered by the English-speaking United States (Diaz-Stevens 1994).

The vast majority of Latinos in the U.S. today, however, are immigrants who arrived in the second half of the twentieth century. Large-scale immigration from Puerto Rico and Mexico began in the 1940s and 1950s. The history of Puerto Rico is unique because the island was a possession of the United States after 1898, but if we are speaking of the borders of today's fifty states, the statement is correct that Latino immigration is mainly a late twentieth-century story.

The growth of the Latino population in the U.S. (not including Puerto Rico) is shown in Figure 5.1. In 1990 it totaled 22.5 million, or 9.0 percent of the total population. By 2010 it is projected to reach 40.5 million, or 13.5 percent of the population. The Latino population will surpass the African-American population by the year 2010.

How many of the Catholics in the United States are Latinos? Nobody has precise numbers. Our best estimate is based on census data. It says that the U.S. had about 28.5 million Latinos in 1998, and if we assume that 65 percent were Catholic, which is a conservative figure (as we argue later in this chapter), we get 18.5 million Catholics, or about 30 percent of all Catholics.

Latinos readily intermarry with non-Latinos. By the third generation more than 33 percent of Latinas are married to non-Latino men, and this blurs the boundaries of exactly who is a Latino. By the third generation at least 33 percent of their descendants are part-Latinos.

From 1991 to 1995, 5.2 million legal immigrants arrived in the United States, of which about 45 percent were Latinos. The major countries of origin were Mexico (28 percent of the immigrants), Dominican Republic (4 percent), and El Salvador (2.5 percent). The entire continent of South America was the origin of 5 percent (*Statistical Abstracts* 1997:12). Outside of Latin America the number-one nation supplying immigrants was the Philippines (6 percent of the total). The estimated four to five million undocumented immigrants now living in the United States are not included in the census statistics cited here.[1] The vast majority are from Mexico (Portes and Rumbaut 1993:10).

We can expect immigration from Latin America to continue for decades to come because of the amazing economic advantages in the

FIGURE 5.1

Latinos in the U.S. Population

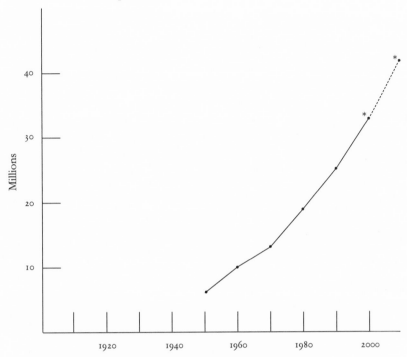

Sources: Cavis, Haub, and Willette (1988); *Statistical Abstracts* 1997.
* Estimated.

United States. Workers from poor Latin American nations can increase their income by fivefold or tenfold if they come to the United States—legally or illegally—and this excites the desire of many thousands to immigrate to the U.S. Efforts to immigrate are so energetic and intense that they are impossible for the U.S. government to control.

THE LATINO POPULATION TODAY

Latinos in the U.S. today are mainly native-born—about 62 percent. They are concentrated in certain areas, and five U.S. states contain the vast majority—California (9.9 million in 1998), Texas (5.7 million), New York (2.6 million), Florida (2.1 million), and Illinois (1.2 million). The states with the highest percentage of Latino residents in 1990 were New Mexico (40 percent), California (31 percent), Texas (29 percent), Arizona (22 percent), and Nevada (15 percent). The region of the U.S. with the fewest Latinos is the Midwest, whose population is only about three to four percent Latino. Also, Latinos today are disproportionately urban in their place of residence.

Latinos are younger than other Americans, and their rate of birth is higher. This predicts a growth in the Latino population even without any new immigration. In 1990 the birthrate for Latino women was 93.0 births per one thousand women, while for non-Latino women it was 64.4 per one thousand. For African Americans it was 78.4 births per one thousand (Moore 1994:37).

The level of family income for Latinos is much lower than the U.S. average. In 1992 the average income of non-Latino whites was $31,765, while for Latinos it was $20,054. The poverty rate for Latinos in 1995 was 27 percent, compared with 26 percent for African Americans and 8.5 percent for non-Latino whites (*Statistical Abstracts*:479).

OUR 1997 SAMPLE

The reader should recall that our sample of young adults was taken from parish confirmation lists and that not all Catholic adolescents in the 1970s and 1980s were confirmed. Experts estimated that among Latinos, about 30 to 40 percent of the youth were confirmed, and among all other Catholics, it was about 60 to 70 percent. This difference in rates of confirmation is important for us, since it introduces a bias affecting any comparison of our two samples. Put simply, the Latinos come from a smaller portion of the total population than is true in the non-Latino sample. We guess (but cannot prove) that the Latinos in our sample came from homes more church-involved, relative to average Latinos, than the homes of the non-Latinos in our sample. Since only 30 to 40 percent of the Latino youth were confirmed, probably our sample is more restricted to youth from church-involved families than is true in the non-Latino sample. In sum: the Latino sample is probably more committed to the Church today than is true for average young adult Latinos, and in addition this bias is probably greater in the Latino sample (due to the low confirmation rate) than in the non-Latino sample.

During the pretesting we became aware of the difficulties in interviewing some of the Latinos, especially persons who were less acquainted with sociological surveys and others who tended to be deferential toward anyone they perceived as being in authority. Our pretest interviewers reported that several respondents mentioned after the interview was finished that their attitudes were not really as favorable to the Church as they had indicated. Similar shows of obedience to authority have been found by other researchers (Marin and Marin 1991). Our advisors warned us that Latinos tend to be wary around interviewers, thus they often conceal their true feelings and give responses which they think are safe. To minimize these problems we needed to do everything possible. We needed to put the respondents at ease and to assure them that we were independent researchers assessing opinions, not church leaders checking up on anybody. Therefore we sent letters to all the target persons before phoning them, describing what we were doing and promising that all the information was confidential. We hired bilingual interviewers in each sampling area who spoke local Spanish and could offer to speak either Spanish or English, and we trained the interviewers to chat with the respondents so as to encourage them to be candid.

As the data collection progressed, we were surprised that very few of the Latino respondents preferred to speak Spanish. As we noted earlier, only four percent wanted to be interviewed in Spanish. Rapid acquisition of English was also displayed in a study by sociologist Gregory Rodriguez, which found that within ten years of arrival, 76.3 percent of immigrants speak English with high proficiency, and in the second and third generations almost all children of immigrants speak English proficiently (Sharry 1999). It is a finding common to research on immigrants: the second generation prefers to speak English when outside the home (Portes 1996:9–11).

Our Latino sample is composed mostly of second, third, and fourth generation descendants of immigrants. As we reported in chapter 3, only 12 percent were first generation, that is, born outside the U.S. (including those born in Puerto Rico).[2] We asked all the Latinos about which language they most often speak at home, and 63 percent said English, 13 percent said Spanish, and the other 24 percent said "both equally." The Latino sample we obtained includes persons better educated and with longer time in the U.S. than the average for Latinos.

DIFFERENCES BETWEEN NON-LATINOS AND LATINOS

When our findings came in, we were surprised that the differences between non-Latinos and Latinos were often small (a finding also in the study of D'Antonio et al. 1996). In earlier chapters we compared non-Latinos and Latinos on numerous measures. The principal differences can be summarized in five points.

(1) Latinos had greater participation in personal devotions of many kinds, including making the Stations of the Cross, saying the rosary, wearing medals and scapulars, keeping images of saints in the home, having altars in the home, having a car or home blessed, and carrying out *promesas* (promises) in return for divine favors. They are also more constant in prayer. Latinos, especially those over the age of thirty, took part in more prayer groups or faith sharing groups, more Novenas, and more spiritual healing groups.

(2) For Latinos, many more of their closest friends are also members of their parishes. The Latinos also make more positive evaluations of their parishes, and they are more hesitant about recommending more democracy in parish decision-making (59 percent in favor vs. 71 percent of others).

(3) Latinos much more often agree that "the Catholic Church is the one true Church" (64 percent vs. 48 percent of others). They also more often agree that "the only absolute Truth for humankind is in the teachings of Jesus Christ" (87 percent vs. 73 percent).

(4) Latinos agree more than others that Catholics have a duty to try to close the gap between the rich and the poor and to try to preserve the environment.

(5) Latinos are less informed about the institutional church, as indicated by the number who have heard of the Second Vatican Council (27 percent of the Latinos have heard of it, vs. 56 percent of the others).

On other measures the Latinos resembled the non-Latinos. The Latinos were *not* different in the percentage who have moved to other denominations, in their attitudes about empowerment of laity, and in their beliefs in core creedal statements.

Latino Catholics belong to different nationalities, and our sample included the different groups in correct proportions. But we are not able to talk with any precision about differences between nationality groups, for example, between Mexican Americans and Puerto Ricans or between Cubans and Puerto Ricans. Our sample was too small for that.

We do not wish to de-emphasize national differences within the Latino population. Latinos come from various nations and social classes, and the different strands see themselves as nationality groups, not as "Latinos" in a generic sense. They do not cooperate easily across nationalities. The major groups (Mexican Americans, Puerto Ricans, and Cuban Americans) are clearly dissimilar, and they have specific identities bound up with their own experiences. For example, Los Angeles's Mexican Americans have struggled long and hard to gain a minimal political recognition, but they are not yet ready to take the small, embattled, and isolated Central American community under their wing (Moore 1994: 35).

Five Questions Often Asked about Latino Catholics

(1) Are Young Latinos Less Church-Involved Than Other Catholics?

Past research indicates that Latino Catholics, and especially young Latino Catholics, are less involved in parish life than other Catholics, while at the same time they practice more personal and family devotions than others (for a review see Cadena 1995). Many authors have pointed out that Catholicism in much of Latin America in the past thrived in a situation of a severe shortage of parish priests, and therefore Catholic individuals and families developed a religious life largely independent of parishes. In time, traditional Latin American Catholicism centered more around the home and around personal religious devotions (e.g., Gonzalez and La Velle 1985; de la Garza et al. 1992).

Furthermore, many common people in Mexico, Puerto Rico, and Cuba held on to traditional religious beliefs and devotions, many of which were medieval and Pre-Tridentine, as a form of protest against what they saw as the elitist official Church. Latin American Catholicism gradually acquired a bifurcation between the official parishes on the one hand, and family-based and community-based devotions on the other, with a sense of distance from official parish Catholicism being felt by many laity. This two-track tendency is stronger in Latino Catholicism than elsewhere in American Catholicism. Allan Figueroa Deck summarizes the situation by saying that Latinos today "do not look first to the church or other institutions, but to themselves and to the family and local community" (1994:15).

How about today? Are young Latino Catholics less involved in the institutional church? We asked our 1997 sample about their commitments and involvements. In our sample it is not true that young Latinos are less involved in parish life than other young Catholics. As we saw in chapter 3, the Latinos reported the same level of Mass attendance as did the non-Latinos. They reported only a slightly lower amount of participation in parish groups, such as serving in a parish group or committee (15 percent of the Latinos vs. 19 percent of the non-Latinos).

Are these reports credible? In chapter 3 we discussed whether the survey responses are biased, and we concluded that there is a probable upward bias in our sample's report of Mass attendance. It is probable that the Latino report is biased upward more than the non-Latino report, so the true level of Latino Mass attendance may be lower. We believe, based on everything we know, that the true Latino church attendance rates are lower than for non-Latinos.

Young Latinas (women) have greater church involvement than young Latino men. See Table 5.1.

As the table shows, Latinas attend church more often and are more active in parish life. They evaluate their parishes more favorably than Latino men on two of the questions we asked. We also found that Latinos thirty to thirty-nine years old are much more involved in parishes than those twenty to twenty-nine years old. Thirty-nine percent of the older group reported weekly Mass attendance, compared with 25 percent of the younger group. Also 20 percent of the older group

TABLE 5.1

Latino Men and Women Catholics Compared on Church Involvement
and Evaluation of Parishes *(in percents)*

	Latinos *(Men)*	*Latinas* *(Women)*
Mass attendance in the last year:		
Once a week or more	26	36
In the last six months, have you been active in		
any group or committee in the parish? Yes	12	18
How well does your parish help you deal with		
important questions in your life? Very well	27	44
How well does it meet your need for help in		
personal and family life? Very well	35	49

reported being active in a parish group, compared with 12 percent of
the younger group.

When it comes to devotions, both personal devotions and in
groups, Latinos are much more involved than non-Latinos. (The data
are shown below in chapter 7.) Also Latinas are more involved than
men in most devotions. See Table 5.2.

Table 5.2 confirms that Latinos of both sexes are more likely to participate in personal devotions than in devotions taking place at parishes.
They practice home-based devotions more than non-Latinos—such as
saying the rosary, having home altars, having images of saints in the
home, and having a house or car blessed. Also Latinos are more
involved in prayer groups, faith sharing groups, and spiritual healing
groups than other Catholics (see chapter 7). We should explain that the
use of prayers and prayer groups as a healing technique is common in
the more traditional parts of the Latino community. Prayers and the use
of religious objects, such as rosaries and crucifixes, are commonly used
by traditional folk healers (in Spanish: *curanderos/as*) in the homes of
sick persons. Most folk healers are women. Women practice more devotions than men, though, as Table 5.2 shows, this varies from item to
item, and on many devotional practices men and women are similar.

TABLE 5.2

Latino Men and Women Catholics
Compared on Personal Devotions *(in percents)*

	Latinos (Men)	Latinas (Women)
In the last two years, have you: (percent yes)		
Gone for private confession	38	45
Made the Stations of the Cross	36	49
Said the rosary	58	70
Read the Bible at home	51	63
Attended novenas	14	23
Attended Eucharistic adoration, or benediction	19	29
Taken part in spiritual healing groups	11	20
Made a retreat or a day of recollection	17	19
Had your house or car blessed or consecrated	39	29
Promised God you would do something, in return for a favor granted to you	26	23
Prayer:		
About how many times would you say you prayed privately, in the last seven days? Daily or more	50	67
Spiritual Person:		
Do you consider yourself a spiritual person? Yes	73	81

Women are more constant in prayer (shown at the bottom of the table) and they more often see themselves as spiritual persons.

Among Latino Catholics, popular religion remains strong. Its contents vary, especially between the Caribbean-based popular religion and the Mexico-based version with its pre-eminent devotion to Our Lady of Guadalupe. An important issue regarding popular religion is whether it should be encouraged or discouraged by the official Church. For more than a century the American Catholic Church has looked askance at Latino popular religion and has even made some efforts to stamp it out. The prevailing argument was that it was filled with age-old devotions, superstitions, symbols, and semi-deities, and its influence impeded evangelization into the true Gospel of Jesus Christ. Recently more voices have been raised in its defense, saying that popular Catholicism is a genuine spiritual expression providing strength to often-oppressed people and that efforts to squelch it will merely alienate many of the faithful (Espin 1994, Rodriguez 1994, Elizondo 1998). The theological debate continues today. One noteworthy point in the debate is the assertion that the popularity of pentecostalism for Latinos today is partly because it embodies age-old elements of popular Catholicism which have been removed from the modern Catholic church (Espin 1994).

Regardless of the outcome of this debate, there is no doubt that popular devotions continue strong in Latino Catholicism and that future Latino immigrants will continue to be devoted to them. In Mexican communities today the herbal practices and faith healing of *curanderos/as* are thriving alongside modern medicine and official Catholicism. In Puerto Rico, the Dominican Republic, and Cuba a complex of beliefs called *santeria* and *espiritismo* blend Catholic beliefs with pre-Christian beliefs about communicating with spirits and local healing rituals. Gonzalez and La Velle, in their nationwide survey, found that foreign-born Latinos participated more in popular devotions than American-born Latinos, and among the foreign-born, Puerto Ricans and Mexicans were more involved than Cubans.

Our interviews included numerous accounts of the importance of popular religion during the people's upbringing. A thirty-seven-year-old Latina:

> My grandparents on my father's side had a statue of the Lady of Guadalupe in their house. Even if they don't go to church they still have the statue, knowing that she is there watching over them.

A twenty-six-year-old Latino:

> In every room in our house there was a religious symbol, whether it be the Virgen de Guadalupe—you've got to have one in every Mexican household and even in the bathroom—or whether it be rosaries.

In summary, our data indicate that young Latinos practice more devotions, especially personal and home-based devotions, than non-Latinos, as many others have observed. Whether young Latinos attend Mass less is not clear in our survey, though we guess that they do.

(2) Are Young Latinos More Traditional in Theology and Ecclesiology?

In the 1990s, numerous groups of American Catholics voiced doubts about some traditional church teachings, especially ecclesiological teachings about the nature of the institutional church. These groups formed action groups and coalitions, of which "Call to Action" is the best known nationally. But Latinos have not been active in these groups, leading many observers to say that Latino Catholics are traditional in their beliefs and in their views of the Church. Two important studies showed that Latinos are more committed than others to Catholic orthodox beliefs (Gonzalez and La Velle 1985; Archdiocese of New York 1982). Are young Latinos today more traditional in beliefs? Are they more devoted to pre-Vatican style parish life?

The comparisons of non-Latinos and Latinos in religious beliefs were shown in chapter 3. The overall pattern is that the two groups differ little on most attitudes. Yet two conclusions can safely be drawn, as noted earlier: First, young Latinos believe more than others that the Catholic Church is the one true Church and that the only absolute Truth for humankind is in the teachings of Jesus Christ. Second, young Latinos are less in favor of more lay involvement in church affairs at the local parish level. Are these differences due to the unequal educational levels rather than to ethnicity itself? We checked by controlling for educational level and found that the non-Latino vs. Latino differences remained strong, telling us that the higher level of education among non-Latinos does not explain the differences; the differences exist even apart from the effect of education.

We looked for differences on many other attitude topics but found none: on whether a person can be a good Catholic without going to Mass; on whether laypersons and women should be empowered more than they are now; on whether laity are just as important a part of the Church as priests are; on whether laity should be included in discussion of moral and doctrinal issues; and on whether in Mass the bread and wine actually become the body and blood of Christ. Our conclusion is that young Latino Catholics are more traditional in beliefs and more satisfied with parish life than others, but only slightly so and only on limited topics. They are a bit less ecumenical, a bit less relativistic, and a bit less ready for empowerment of laity.

(3) Are Latino Families Different from Others?

All past research on Latino family life agrees that the family, including the extended family, is more important to Latinos than to other Americans (Gonzales 1993, Sanchez 1993). Latino households often include three generations. Families are a source of emotional and material support, and their well-being takes priority over the ambitions of individuals. Latinas tend to marry early and to have many children; traditional norms stress wives' devotion to the family and militate against their working except in case of dire economic necessity. The Latino family has traditionally been patriarchal, with clearly defined gender roles and restrictions on the activities of daughters (Moore 1994).

An important element in traditional Latino family life is that religion was usually seen as the woman's domain. Women engaged in more devotions than men, and they were much more devoted to the religious education of children. The role of mothers, and especially of grandmothers, is a constant theme in analyses of Latino Catholicism, and it came out when our interviewees told about their childhoods. A thirty-year-old Latina:

> Our parents would send us to our grandparents' house in Mexico during the summer to learn Spanish. That was the only formal religious education training we had, because here we lived in an area where there were no Spanish-speaking churches. . . . The most important person is my grandmother. She would take the time to tell us stories about God and we would go with her to daily Mass. And we didn't know when Grandma would pull out that rosary. But you knew that when she said, "En el nombre del Padre, y del Hijo, y del Espiritu Santo" everything had to stop and it was time for the rosary. Right in the middle of everything.

A thirty-four-year-old Latina:

> I remember ever since I was little, we'd always say prayers before we
> go to bed. That, and before dinner, like on long trips, Mom would
> get out the rosary and we'd pray a rosary and different stuff like that.

A twenty-eight-year-old Latino:

> My early experiences are of my Grandmother's kitchen, having a
> shrine with a bunch of candles, pictures of Mary, and a lot of other
> religious articles.

For many Latino families the First Holy Communion of their children is a significant event, treated as a formal rite of passage. It is usually marked by a day of celebration, where family members and close
friends are invited to attend a specially prepared dinner, and the child
receives his or her first set of dress clothes. One of our interviewees
had very vivid memories of his First Holy Communion:

> When I had my first communion celebration, it was a very beautiful
> experience. All my family gathered for me, and we had never gath-
> ered for anything else, so it made me realize that it was something
> very beautiful and special.

How about our 1997 sample? The Latinos had a much lower rate of
interfaith marriage than others. Only 24 percent of the Latinos (of
those ever married) married non-Catholic spouses, compared with 50
percent of the non-Latinos. Also we found that the Latinos have
tended to remain closer to their places of upbringing. We asked, "Do
you live in the same area as you did during your junior high and high
school years?" Of the Latinos, 74 percent still live twenty miles or less
from their high school home; of the non-Latinos, 54 percent do. Even
when level of education is controlled, over half of the Latino vs. non-
Latino difference remains.

As we noted in chapter 3, Latinos told us that of their five closest
friends, more were members of their parish than was the case with
non-Latinos. Of the Latinos, 32 percent said that three or more of their

five closest friends belonged to the same parish; or the non-Latinos the figure was only 14 percent. This is a large difference, consistent with the finding that Latinos more often marry other Catholics and more often remain close to their hometowns. For Latinos, family life, community life, and parish life are more intertwined than is the case for other Catholics.

(4) Are Latinos Assimilating, Similar to Earlier Immigrants?

This question is constantly being asked today, yet it is difficult to answer with existing research. In addition the Latino community contains spokespersons for two distinct viewpoints on what the Latinos *should* do—which is a different question, yet a crucial one. One side argues that cultural assimilation, at least including acquisition of fluent English and completion of college degrees, is a necessary step toward economic and political empowerment. In this view, assimilation should not be feared, but it should be embraced as a necessary part of family betterment for immigrant families in the first two or three generations (Portes 1996). The opposite side argues that assimilation should be resisted at all cost, since it damages Latino identity (or more specifically, Puerto Rican or Mexican identity) and thus invites long-term co-optation and oppression from the dominant American culture (e.g., Diaz-Stevens and Stevens-Arroyo 1997). Our task here is not to take sides in this debate but rather to look at how research sheds light on the actual processes in today's Latino community. The most general conclusion from existing research is that assimilation is clearly taking place among Latinos in the second, third, and fourth generations. It is proceeding fastest among Cuban Americans, partly because they are the most educated and wealthiest national group (Portes 1996).

An issue widely discussed today is whether Latinos are proceeding on the same trajectory traveled by European immigrants during the first large wave of immigration (about 1860-1920). If the Latino processes resemble the earlier European history, we could use the European experience to help foresee the Latino future. The question is sometimes posed in another way: will Latinos find assimilation and upward mobility more difficult than was the case with the European immigrants? The literature is filled with arguments back and forth on these questions, but several points appear to be beyond serious dispute. Three of them are worth mentioning here.

First, the Latino immigration will be unlike the earlier European immigration in that it cannot be cut off by an act of Congress, as was done in the 1920s with the European immigrants. This time the southern border is too porous, and Congress is helpless to close it off even if it wanted to. So whereas the European immigration virtually ceased after 1925 and didn't resume for about forty years, the Latino immigration will not cease. In the case of the European immigration, the stoppage of immigration gave the nation a breathing space for incorporation of the millions of immigrants into all arenas of society, and it aided the economic progress of the immigrants. But the Latino immigration will not cease, so there will be no breathing space.

Second, the rise to the middle class will be more difficult for Latinos than it was for the Europeans. This is because the job market today has fewer openings for unskilled and blue-collar workers. Now to get a good job a person needs an array of skills. People without skills, or those unable to succeed in the job market for other reasons, cannot improve their lives. Thus it is probable that many of the less educated immigrants will find themselves trapped in a permanent underclass.

Third, recent changes in American culture make assimilation easier today. American culture at the end of the twentieth century is more pluralistic and tolerant than it was early in the century. Americans are more highly educated and more open-minded now. Therefore the new ethnic and religious traditions of immigrants are less frightening to other Americans, and Americans are less worried about their deleterious effects (McLemore and Romo 1985, Waters 1990).

Other non-parallels with the earlier European immigration are sometimes discussed, for example, the proximity of Mexico to the United States as opposed to the long distance between Europe and the United States, which suggests that Mexican immigrants today need to make less of a decisive break with their past and can envision going back home later. Thus they are less likely to cast their fate with America (Gonzales 1993:73). From the various arguments we conclude that assimilation, for better or for worse, will probably proceed more slowly for the new Latino immigration than it did for the Europeans. Economic progress will very likely be slower also, except for the most educated and best prepared persons. The European immigration history is not a plausible template for the Latino future.

(5) Are Young Latinos Leaving the Catholic Church?

We have seen dozens of stories in the media about how Latinos are leaving Catholicism and flocking to Protestant churches, especially evangelical and Pentecostal churches. No one disputes the truth in these stories. The question is the *extent* of the flow.

First we need to ask: How many Latinos today are Catholic? Estimates vary (see Cadena 1995). The National Survey of Families and Households in 1987–1988 found that 77 percent of Latinos were currently Catholic. The Cubans had the highest level—88 percent, and Puerto Ricans had the lowest—67 percent (Lee and Potvin 1992). Andrew Greeley, using National Opinion Research Center data, estimated that 67 percent of Americans of Hispanic origin are now Catholics (1997: 12). He concluded that the figure had dropped from 78 percent in the early 1970s. "If this hemorrhage should continue for the next twenty-five years, half of all American Hispanics will not be Catholic" (p. 12). The defections are not solely to fundamentalist and Pentecostal groups; almost half of the Latino Protestants in the 1990s now belong to moderate or even liberal Protestant denominations, such as Baptists and Methodists.

Barry Kosmin and Seymour Lachman, in their book *One Nation under God*, used nationwide poll data in estimating that in 1990 the Latinos were about 66 percent Catholic, 25 percent Protestant, 6 percent with no religion, and 3 percent in other religions (Kosmin and Lachman 1993:137). The Protestant denominational family with the most Hispanics was the Baptist. Cadena summarizes the available research: "Overall, the data shows approximately three-quarters of Latinos continue to remain Catholic. When specific groups are examined, Mexican-origin individuals have the highest Catholic affiliation, followed by Cuban-origin, with Puerto Rican–origin individuals having the lowest affiliation" (1995:48).

Clearly some Latino Catholics have left. But nobody should assume that the shift to Protestantism occurs after immigration to the U.S. and not before. Probably as much occurs in the country of origin as occurs in the United States. Protestantism, especially the Pentecostal variety, has experienced rapid growth throughout Latin America since the 1960s. In the middle 1980s the best estimates were Chile, 25 percent; Guatemala, 21 percent; Brazil, 18 percent; Mexico, 5 percent; and Venezuela, 3 percent (Stoll 1990: 333). In the 1990s the figures were much higher. For Guatemala the best estimate today is 35 percent Protestant (Smith 1999).

What do our own findings say about young Latinos leaving the Catholic Church? The main lesson, as we said in chapter 3, is that not many in our sample of confirmands have left, and no more Latinos have done so than non-Latinos. Of the total samples it was 9 percent of the Latinos and 11 percent of the non-Latinos who no longer call themselves Catholics. Of the persons thirty to thirty-nine years of age, it was 13 percent of the Latinos and 16 percent of the non-Latinos. Even though our data has some bias, we believe that young Latinos are not leaving the Catholic Church faster than non-Latinos.

Next, in chapters 6 and 7, we turn to two topics at the center of our research project—religious education and spirituality.

CHAPTER 6

Experiences with
Religious Education

· · · ·

Our study of young adult Catholics included questions about their religious education. We were interested because religious education programs are designed to transmit religious values from one generation to
the next, and we wanted to explore which values were being passed on
and how the young adults evaluated their religious education experience. This generation, unlike the one before it, received religious education that was far from monolithic. Also this generation lived in a
wider social world; it was formed by religious experiences that occurred outside the classroom as well as inside it, including experiences
in the family, in the parish, in the larger community, and in college.
Here we look at young adults' religious formation in broad terms.

Before the Second Vatican Council, Catholic religious education in
the United States was built on the foundation of the *Baltimore Catechism*.
Religion classes for Catholic school students and public school students generally involved the memorization of tenets of the catechism
in question and answer format. It is still possible to hear one of those
former students, now forty or fifty years later, recite key tenets of the
faith: "Why did God make you? God made me to know, love, and serve
Him in this world and to be happy with Him in the next."

Vatican II marked the end of the use of the *Baltimore Catechism* and the
beginning of a new journey in catechetical education with the publica-
tion of a *General Catechetical Directory*, promulgated in 1971, the *Catechism*

of the Catholic Church, promulgated in 1994, and a revised *General Direc-tory for Catechesis* of 1997.[1] These new documents depict the impor-tance of sound catechesis and the breadth and depth of catechetical education.

Our task here is not to debate the content of religious education pro-grams in the United States since the Council. Rather, it is to convey the voices of young adults who have come of age during the post-conciliar years and to report what they said about their religious education.

A few themes in our interviews were voiced constantly. The young adults between the ages of twenty and thirty-nine span a wide range of years, so our oldest respondents began religious education classes in the mid-1960s and the youngest completed religious education in the mid-1990s. Yet the telephone interviews, the face-to-face interviews, and the focus groups found no substantive differences by age. In other words, people in their twenties were remarkably similar to people in their thirties in their views about religious education. We found the same similarity between men and women, and, for the most part, be-tween Latinos and non-Latinos.

THE NATIONAL TELEPHONE SURVEY

In chapter 3 we introduced our telephone sample. Here we will review some of what they told us about their religious education.

Catholic School Attendance

As we saw earlier, many persons in our sample attended Catholic school. On the elementary school level, 50 percent of the non-Latinos had attended Catholic elementary school, as did 35 percent of the Lati-nos. On the secondary level, 28 percent of the non-Latinos and 15 per-cent of the Latinos attended Catholic high school—most of them for four years.

Smaller percentages attended Catholic college or university. Of all the persons who had attended some college, 14 percent of the non-Latinos and 10 percent of the Latinos attended an institution of Catholic higher education.

Attendance in Religious Education Programs

When we asked the young adults about receiving religious education at their parishes, such as C.C.D. classes, 68 percent of the non-Latinos told us that they had attended religious education classes, with 73 percent of them attending for four years or more during junior high and high school. Of the Latinos, 74 percent had attended religious education classes, with 59 percent attending for four years or more during junior high and high school.

We also asked about other kinds of religious programs. We asked both groups about involvement in Catholic youth ministry or youth programs while in high school. Sixteen percent said they were often involved in them, and 28 percent said they were involved occasionally. The rest were not involved. Of the Latinos, 20 percent were often involved and 22 percent were involved occasionally.

We asked those who had attended college for any length of time about campus ministry or Newman Center activities. Fourteen percent of the non-Latinos and eight percent of the Latinos had participated in such groups.

Vocations to the Religious Life and Priesthood

When we asked if they had ever been encouraged to become a sister, brother, or priest, 17 percent of the non-Latinos and 13 percent of the Latinos said yes. When we asked those who said yes who had encouraged them, 34 percent of the non-Latinos said parents or family, 20 percent said a priest, 12 percent said a teacher, 11 percent said a nun or sister, 7 percent said grandparents, 7 percent said other family members, 8 percent said other, and 1 percent said a member of the church. The men tended to say that priests had encouraged them, and the women more often said that Catholic sisters had encouraged them. Who encouraged the Latinos? Twenty-eight percent said a priest, 26 percent said parents or family, 16 percent said a teacher, 14 percent said a nun or sister, 7 percent said a member of the church, 2 percent said a family member other than a parent, and 7 percent said "other."

Young people are not receiving much encouragement to the religious life and priesthood. Are they receiving encouragement for other forms of apostolate, such as being lay ministers? Our survey did not ask, so we do not know. Young people, in our opinion, should be presented with the whole spectrum of available ministries and forms of service, for the sake of their spiritual development and for service to the Church.

Effects of Catholic School Education

In chapter 4 we analyzed the data to determine if education in a Catholic school predicted attitudes or behaviors. Does Catholic education predict if a person will be more likely or less likely to marry a non-Catholic spouse? The answer is no; we found no relationship. Does it predict attitudes about traditional Catholic doctrine, Catholic specialness over against other churches, relativism, the ethical duty of Catholics, or the urgency of empowering laity and women? No. We looked at five attitude scales and found only two relationships; both are weak and probably accidental. We did find among Latinos that having been involved in C.C.D. or youth ministry had a modest association with having a special loyalty to Catholicism (on the Catholic Only Scale). Among the non-Latinos we did not find this.

Does having Catholic education predict greater involvement in parishes today? Generally, no. The only association we found was with having been involved in youth ministry while in high school, and it was true only of non-Latinos; that is, the non-Latinos with a history of youth ministry are a bit more involved in their parishes than other young adults.

Is there a cumulative effect of a large amount of Catholic education which does not appear when we look separately at the effects of Catholic elementary school, Catholic high school, or Catholic college? It is a good question, but we had too few cases to test the idea and therefore do not know.

We did find one clear effect. Catholic elementary school, high school, and college clearly produced higher levels of knowledge and understanding of the Second Vatican Council. But beyond that, we could not discern any specific effects of this Catholic education, or indeed any clear effects of C.C.D. or youth ministry during high school.

Did a higher level of education in general (not specifically Catholic education) have any influence on these persons? Yes. Persons with more education were more informed about the Second Vatican Council, and among the non-Latinos they were slightly more informed about the 1986 statement about economic justice and the 1995 statement about the culture of death; the relationships are weak.

In-Depth Interviews

While a national survey can provide us with the big picture, intensive interviews and focus groups provide us with nuances of opinion and expressions of sentiments. When the respondents were asked to talk about their experience of religious education, their responses were negative and strikingly similar. Here are some of their words:

"The pedagogy was horrible"
"Teachers aren't prepared"
"Too rote, too mechanical"
"Nothing in depth, just Jesus is love"
"We got God loves you but not much else"
"No content; touchy-feely"
"Insufficient"
"Silly"
"I was confirmed and had no idea of what was going on"
"A baby-sitting session"
"More social than anything else"
"By and large my religious instruction was abysmal"
"Emphasis was on social issues"
"We played biblical trivial pursuit"

This list will alert the reader to the scope of the problem. The negative reaction of most of our respondents to their religious education points to a serious problem for religious educators and for the Church. We lacked the information to explain the source of these negative reactions. All we can do is to look at some structural and programmatic dimensions of the problem. We begin with the respondents' comments about religious education content.

The Content of Religious Education Programs

Faith in God was not problematic for our respondents. They are believers. Many of our respondents told us about their own faith. For example, a twenty-year-old college student:

> I think that when it comes down to it, if you don't have faith, you don't have very much. You can't see it, can't touch it, can't feel it, can't describe it, but you know it's there, the kind of thing that everybody depends on when they don't have anything else to depend on.

While the importance of faith was not considered a problem, the passing on of the specifics of Catholic faith was. The content of religious education programs was a sore spot. Some respondents reported that there was no content in their programs at all. Those who spoke in that vein describe their experience: "It was insufficient." "It was silly." "It was abysmal." "We got nothing in depth." "We got God loves you, but not much else."

One of the most cogent comments about the lack of content and its implications for her life was made by a college senior:

> It was too vague. I would hesitate to call it teaching or learning. I don't think much was taught, and I certainly don't think much was learned from my perspective. I think my lack of knowledge is what made me disinterested in the Catholic Church.

Others told us that while they would not say that their programs were devoid of content, the content was not substantive. Some used terms like "touchy-feely" to characterize their programs. Some remembered religious education as an arts and crafts exercise. The crucial point here is that while they remember making collages, banners, and other artifacts, and while some remember playing sports during class, they did not make any deeper connection to what those exercises meant. They describe those experiences as though they were disconnected from any religious meaning system. A twenty-six-year-old male:

> C.C.D. during grade school meant that you were taking sticks and gluing them together to make crosses and things. In eighth grade C.C.D. we played a lot of basketball.

A twenty-five-year-old female recalled: "I remember playing games or using coloring books. I remember we talked about the coloring books we had."

These comments stand in marked contrast to the following statement in which a twenty-year-old college student can recall today the lesson taught in one exercise:

> I really liked my second grade teacher, Sister Maria. I remember really enjoying her religion classes. She always did something unique. I remember once she told us all to pick our favorite things that we had in our desk and go and put it in a big pile in the middle of the room. We all did that, then she told us all that she was going to give it all away. But her whole point was having something that you really cherish taken away from you. The way she did things was so creative that I remember really enjoying her class.

The above recollection is the exception rather than the rule. Most young adults did not mention recalling any specific lesson or the link between any lesson and the value it imparted.

Pedagogy

While many respondents dwelt on issues of content, others talked at length about the teaching style and pedagogy. These comments were largely negative. Many persons said the methods used in the classroom were rote learning and memorization. Others described methods that were too loose and unstructured. A twenty-seven-year-old college graduate recalls his C.C.D. class:

We would have to stand up in class and recite things and then we were told what to say when the priest asked us questions. It was all very much by rote. I felt we were being rushed in for a two-hour "How to be a Christian" class and then we were rushed out. It wasn't that special or something we looked forward to.

One college student took another view of rote learning:

Memorizing wasn't a negative thing. I found out later when I worked with a confirmation class as a college student that many of the kids didn't know the Ten Commandments. You know, it doesn't mean you are a good person because you know them, but it's hard to go on to bigger questions if you don't know them.

While some respondents spoke about rote learning and memorization, others recalled the use of a textbook. They often could not remember the contents. A twenty-five-year-old had this to say about her confirmation text: "All I remember was the red book we had to read for confirmation. I can't remember what was in there, but I remember we had to do that for confirmation." Another respondent, a twenty-eight-year-old college graduate, remembers the use of a text as foundational to her C.C.D. program:

C.C.D. was worthwhile, not a waste of time. But for me a lot of the program was just out of the book, a chapter at a time. Fill out the exercises in the book and talk about it a little bit. It was taught probably by people who volunteered their time to teach. There was one very Catholic couple with very Catholic kids who had us in their house. But it was so unusual it was outside the norm. They seemed different to me, so different from my mom and dad that it seemed weird to me.

Her comment points to the problem of limited teacher training. Along with content and pedagogy, a great deal of criticism was directed at teacher preparation. It was not that the respondents denigrated their teachers. On the contrary, they often appreciated the teachers' commitment. However, many recognized that too often the teachers were volunteers without adequate preparation for classroom teaching. This comment was made by a young professional in his thirties:

> My religious education was generally a failure. There were occasional exemplary individual teachers who inspired me, but overall the quality of the experience was poor either because there was no content, or because there was too much of a touchy-feely orientation. Many young Catholics today do not know their faith. This is also because they were taught by lay people who, though well-intentioned, were inadequately prepared or untrained.

Some of the respondents interpreted the lack of support for qualified teachers of religious education as a reflection of the low value the Church places upon this ministry. An example is the view of a student in a secular university:

> We wouldn't send our kids to schools where the teachers aren't certified or accredited or weren't prepared. But in religious education, our Church settles for this a lot of the time. I know this is so because of certain circumstances, for example, few people have extra time to give. But we could do better than that. Once you get to the sixth or seventh grade, you can see that parents aren't ready to do this or aren't enthused about it.

Our conclusion, that the Church settles for less than the best in religious education, was echoed by other respondents. A thirty-three-year-old Mexican American woman spoke for herself and many others when she said: "In sum, junior high and high school religious education was mediocre at best. They weren't what they should have been. We are capable of something more."

Experiences in Youth Groups

Young adult Catholics varied widely in their religious education. Programs were diverse. A diocesan director of religious education told us that high school religious education is much less structured than elementary and junior high religious education. As an example, some respondents spoke of the option they had to attend a youth group instead of formal classes. According to our respondents who participated in youth groups, their primary purpose was social. This appealed to some but not others. A twenty-six-year-old male told us of his disappointment:

> After eighth grade, there is no C.C.D. You make a choice about whether or not you wanted to be in a youth group. At that time, the youth group wasn't much of anything. It was even less than the C.C.D. Quite frankly, I didn't see any value in the C.C.D. at all, so why would I want to go into the youth group? To me it was wasting time.

One twenty-year-old college student suggested that her high school C.C.D. class was like a youth group:

> Once you get into high school, they get creative with their C.C.D. programs. It was almost like youth group but in an organized fashion. Since I didn't know anyone that much because we had just switched parishes, I never really got into it. I did it for about a year and I didn't like it, so I stopped. It was more social than anything.

Community Service

A large part of the religious formation of many young adults was community service. While the service programs varied (including Christian outreach, community service, and Love in Action), the goal of the experiences was the same: to provide the students with an opportunity to offer direct service to a person or group in some kind of physical, emotional, or spiritual need, under the supervision of a teacher. Often a certain number of hours of service were required to fulfill the "service" obligations prior to the sacrament of confirmation.

While some of the comments about community service were positive, others were ambivalent and still others pointed to problems. A frequent criticism was that community service was not clearly related to deeper Christian values. This was voiced by two students at a Catholic university. One student remarked: "I did community service, but I never made a connection with being a Catholic." Another said, "I did community service, but there was no explanation of what this meant in relation to the faith." One college student told us, "I never got much out of religion class. Instead the emphasis was on doing community service, tutoring, summer day camp. My Catholicism was a hands-on type. It came through experience."

Retreats

The young adults had glowing stories about retreats. Some of their most positive memories were about retreat experiences. While the length of retreats varied—from a day to an overnight to a weekend— the responses to retreats were overwhelmingly positive. A woman college student:

> I went on this retreat when I was in the tenth grade. It was called Search. It was at the end of the year and I had been going through all these things with a couple of different boyfriends during the year. That was finally all behind me and it was, for me, a new start. It was a relaxing weekend. A lot of people were really influenced by that, people still talk about it. It was this "big click" kind of thing. My brother went on it last spring and he really liked it, too. I thought it was refreshing more than anything.

The "big click" that this student talks about was also described by others, often using other words, but the meaning is the same. The re-treats provided time and space for an experience of God that was pro-foundly meaningful. Most retreat experiences were quite simple, taking place at the school or parish or at a retreat house nearby.

Some retreats were more involved. A twenty-seven-year-old gradu-ate student had a powerful college retreat experience in Mexico:

> In sophomore year of college I did a two-week retreat in Mexico where we met with poor people, met with progressive pastors, and saw how the church was an active participant in people's lives. And through this experience I came to see this, in opposition to the kind

of church I had seen when I was growing up. We went to Latin Mass when I was growing up; it was very obscure, hard to understand. But here in Mexico, people participated in the church and in public life very naturally. In the church they discussed their lives. And I came to learn that there were alternative ideas about what church meant. And so this was my conversion, kind of, to what I think of as liberation theology generally.

Their experiences of retreats, whether it was one night at the local parish or two weeks in a third world nation, left a deep imprint on them, and their warm memories of the retreats are heartfelt.

The Family

For some of the respondents, the family and not the religious education program was their primary locus of faith development. One college student put it this way: "C.C.D. was a chore. I got most of my spiritual nurturance from my family." Another made a distinction about what came from the family versus what came from Catholic schools: "My spiritual development came from my family, not from school. I did a lot of community service in Catholic schools. This was good."

A young woman compared the role of the family with the role of the religious education program:

Personally, I think that family is the greatest denominator in that entire equation. I know people whose parents really didn't encourage them to understand, then they usually fall away either when they come to college or during high school. I have a really good friend who is Catholic and not practicing because her teachers encouraged her to question all of these things but never helped her to answer them. She basically wrote papers on why Catholics are stupid.

While the young adults praised significant people and events during their religious education, for the most part their words struck a note of alarm for the Church. Their experiences and attitudes demand a worthy response from the Church. Much needs to be done to strengthen Catholic religious education.

Young Adults Look Ahead

The young adults we spoke with gave us their views about future needs in religious education. The challenges seem to us to revolve around three needs: the need to prepare people for engagement in interfaith and ecumenical settings, the need for adult religious education, and the need to deal with the memory of Vatican II.

Interfaith and Ecumenical Settings

One of the most challenging topics in the interviews was the relationship of the respondents to people of other faith traditions. These young adults live in a shifting cultural and social reality which gives them daily contact with other religious groups. One result is a high rate of interfaith marriage. As we saw earlier, 50 percent of the non-Latinos and 24 percent of the Latinos who have ever been married wed a person of another faith or no faith tradition at all.

The religious consequences of living in an interfaith society became clear in the interviews. Our overriding impression was that while the respondents are comfortable working with, interacting with, and marrying people of other faith traditions, they are uncomfortable with what they perceive as Catholics' lack of knowledge of their own faith tradition. They sometimes contrasted themselves to other people who seemed to know their faith.

One person used the word "vulnerable" to describe herself in this regard: "I feel vulnerable in that I do not know enough about my faith to make an adequate articulation or defense of it in encounters with non-Catholics." A professional woman in her thirties expressed anger when she said: "I feel that the Church set me up by not giving me a firm foundation in Scripture, so I cannot respond to non-Catholics who are versed in the Bible."

Another respondent used the word "foolish." She said, "I feel foolish at work when non-Catholics ask me to explain certain positions of the Church which are in the news and I never learned them." Another: "In college, I remember being confronted in an elevator by a born-again Christian. I felt very insecure. He knew his faith but I could not articulate mine."

Many in this generation have experienced involvement in an inter-denominational faith community or group which offers personal support and Bible study. One woman told about her good experiences in Young Life and in the Campaigners group in her public high school. Both groups were mainly non-Catholic. She asked why the Catholic Church didn't have something like this.

Adult Religious Education

Many of the young adults feel the need for adult religious education now. This was put cogently by one respondent: "I want to be a Catholic. I want to know more about my faith. I want some substance." A twenty-six-year-old man with twelve years of C.C.D. lamented, "To this day I still don't know what it is to really be a Catholic." A thirty-year-old female who attended Catholic schools for twelve years told of her needs today:

> The Church doesn't have a captive audience when you're receptive and you're able to understand. But they have a captive audience earlier when you're in Catholic school and they have you five days a week for eight hours. And that's when they're teaching you "yes" and "no," when you are not capable of understanding the "whys" of these things. And if these lessons are taught, I think they are not retained. Now I am at a point in my life when the "whys" would be helpful, and there's nobody to teach you. You know, I can go to church on Sunday, but that's a definite hit-or-miss. I might get something every six months and I think, "Oh, there's an insight." The most intense church counseling I have had as an adult was my pre-Cana. It meant a lot to me because it explained a lot of things. I called recently to find out about those weekend Marriage Encounter programs. I need focus and guidance and structure.

A twenty-eight-year-old college graduate woman who attended C.C.D. classes earlier spoke along similar lines:

> I think in my Catholic training, as far as doctrine, or the whys, or the nuts and bolts, it was not there. I'm sure in my little C.C.D. programs

I was taught the really important things, like that the host is really Christ. But it wasn't until college that someone explained to me that the host is really Christ and we believe that, and I didn't seem to know that. Someday I hope to go through the RCIA program, because I don't know these things. Because I know there's a lot I don't know.

Another woman expressed a sentiment about the saints, a feeling which we heard in other interviews:

I would love to have been more educated about the saints. When my son was little and cried at night when he went to bed, I would say prayers to Saint James and Saint Andrew. I don't know anything about either of those saints, but I thought maybe they would look after him. So I think the saints are important. Yeah, they're comforting.

A twenty-five-year-old male student said this about religious education:

The education of young Catholics has to be revised and changed. Confirmation should be administered during college, or at that age. I was a high school sophomore when I was confirmed. The thing I remember most about it was I resented the fact that my parish made me attend two-hour classes on Tuesday nights, after I was going to a Catholic high school [during the day]. It was demanding enough that I didn't have a lot of time. It also conflicted with my track team meets. They were always on Tuesday nights. The class was pure review for me, nothing new. But I was forced to go to this class and just wanted to get it over with. The class lasted one semester. I felt it was kind of condescending. My confirmation meant very little to me. I resented it at the time. Now I understand confirmation better and I wish I had waited.

Finally, one respondent talked about the need to learn more about his faith in order to counter opinions held by others:

What always shakes me is when somebody says, "No Catholics use birth control because they don't believe in birth control." Or things like that. That seems like such old long-time-ago rules. But people that aren't Catholic think that all Catholics think the same. Stuff like that throws me off a little bit.

Our interviewees expressed a definite desire for religious education for their own children. As we noted earlier, ninety-five percent want their children to have religious education. Some of our respondents were explicit about what that should look like. A twenty-seven-year-old male graduate student told us his preference:

> I think, a lot of student involvement. A stress on critical thinking. It would be that being Catholic is being someone who critically engages the text, shares with other people, is committed to service to the poor, building community, these kinds of things.

After our interviews we have no doubt that young adults who have children of their own will have high expectations for children's religious education programs.

Knowledge of Vatican II

One of our findings will require a shift in thinking by Catholics of the last generation. We found a great lack of knowledge about the Second Vatican Council. These young adults are much different from the generation just before them, who were influenced personally by the Council.

As we noted earlier, our telephone survey revealed that 44 percent of the non-Latinos and 68 percent of the Latinos have never heard of the Council. Of those who had heard about it, 51 percent of the non-Latinos and 49 percent of the Latinos had actually read about or discussed ideas from the Council. Knowledge of what the Council was and what it meant for the Church is superficial at best. A twenty-eight-year-old woman college student is an example: "My understanding of the Vatican Council was, it made the Latin Mass become non-Latin. And it changed some of the words in prayers."

When we asked the telephone respondents about more recent pronouncements, the percentages who knew about them were even lower. We asked if they had ever heard about or read about the American bishops' 1986 statement on economic justice for all, and 16 percent of the non-Latinos and 12 percent of the Latinos said yes. When we asked if they had ever heard about or read about Pope John Paul II's statement criticizing the culture of death, 23 percent of the non-Latinos and 27 percent of the Latinos said yes. Somehow these teachings are not reaching young adults.

We looked further to see if attendance at Catholic school predicted a respondent's knowledge of Vatican II. Yes it had. As we noted earlier, having gone to Catholic elementary school, high school, or college all predicted that a person has heard of the Second Vatican Council. Also having gone to C.C.D. in junior high or senior high school (for non-Latinos) and having taken part in youth ministry in high school predicted knowledge of the Second Vatican Council. For example, for the non-Latinos, 62 percent of those who attended Catholic elementary school had heard of the Council, compared with 46 percent of all others; for the Latinos the figures were 36 and 25 percent. The impact of Catholic high school is even stronger: for the non-Latinos, 71 percent versus 48 percent, and for the Latinos, 55 percent versus 24 percent. The impact of youth ministry is 65 versus 46 percent for the non-Latinos, 39 versus 21 percent for the Latinos.

Does Catholic education predict knowledge of the American bishops' 1986 statement on economic justice for all, or knowledge of the pope's 1995 statement criticizing the culture of death? In general, the answer is no. But a higher level of education in general *does* predict knowledge of these two statements for the non-Latinos (not for the Latinos).

For religious education in the next generation, these three challenges—better education for interfaith settings, need for adult education, and need for stronger memory of Vatican II—demand action. More is needed, and better is needed. Again we ask, "Is this a high-priority value?"

To sum up: This chapter has reported the views of young adults about their religious education. Their views provide a challenge to the Church. We stated at the beginning that the intent of religious education is to transmit values from one generation to the next. We know that certain values have clearly been passed on to the young. For instance, our respondents are high on commitment to social justice (with the vast majority believing that Catholics have a duty to try to end racism, close the gap between the rich and the poor, and live more simply in order to preserve the environment). Did these convictions come from their religious education programs, their families, or the influence of social movements. We have no way to know.

The young adults, in general, gave a low grade to the Church for its efforts in religious education. While some of them gave us moving accounts of the powerful influence of an individual teacher, event, or retreat, they found the system on the whole to be wanting. There is much work ahead if the ideals of the *General Directory for Catechesis* are to become a reality in religious education programs across the nation. Ongoing formation of the young must be a priority for the sake of the mission of the Church. We return to this topic in more detail in our final chapter.

CHAPTER 7

Young Adult Catholic
Spirituality

·   ·   ·   ·

Spirituality is a major concern among young adult Catholics. To understand it one must recognize that Catholic spirituality has been changing dramatically over the past three decades.[1] This can be shown by an excursion through the spirituality of their parents' and grandparents' generations.

For many pre–Vatican II Catholics in the 1930s, 1940s, and 1950s, the "spiritual life" meant distinctive patterns of belief and behavior derived in large part from European Catholicism.[2] Sin loomed large in Catholic consciousness, as did the importance of reparation for sin, the need for self-mortification, and the need to control the passions. Pre-conciliar Catholic spirituality was distinctly otherworldly, emphasizing that Christ's kingdom was not of this world, that death was an ever-present reality, and that the greater glories lay in the world to come (Dolan 1977). Asceticism, penance, and self-discipline were prerequisites of the true spiritual life (Chinnici 1996) as symbolized by the widespread Catholic practice of "giving up" something during Lent. In addition, clerical and monastic ideals dominated institutional norms of Catholic spirituality. Catholics learned that taking vows of poverty, chastity, and obedience meant a higher striving for spiritual perfection, and an intrinsically higher spiritual state and holier calling than available to those in the lay state.

Pre-conciliar Catholic spirituality was also heavily imbued with a sense of the miraculous. This was especially true regarding healing and cures by saints and the Virgin Mary—where most of the devotions were in the vernacular rather than Latin and, therefore, more accessible to the laity. And while the "Holy Sacrifice of the Mass" stood at the official core of the Catholic experience of the miraculous, the liturgy was often overshadowed in importance by devotional practices tied to ethnic and cultural identity (Taves 1986).

Pre–Vatican II Catholic spirituality also followed regular ritual patterns that included special days ("First Fridays") or months (May, the "month of Mary"), certain prayers (morning prayers, the Angelus), Forty-Hours devotions, Novenas, benedictions, and various rituals, processions, pilgrimages, and devotions to patron saints. These activities were typically rooted in the local parish or around parish-based organizations such as the St. Vincent de Paul Society, the Altar and Rosary Society, or the Sodality (Lescher 1997).

Another feature of pre-conciliar Catholic spirituality was its highly sentimental character, especially in relation to the "communion of saints," that is, the faithful on earth, in purgatory, and in heaven (Taves 1986). Emotional bonds of the living with the dead were expressed and reinforced by a distinct Catholic material culture that included statues, pictures, scapulars, medals, prayer books, candles, rosaries, holy cards, ashes, and relics.

Catholic spirituality prior to Vatican II had a quasi-scientific character in which the pursuit of holiness included states of prayer, levels of perfection, steps of self-examination, and disciplinary qualities necessary for attaining holiness (Chinnici 1979, 1996, Wittberg 1997:251). The terms were precise and scientific. Virtues and vices were broken down into various subcategories. Sins were catalogued and classified in step-by-step procedures known to generations of Catholics standing in Saturday afternoon confessional lines.

With the improvement of education and the spread of mass publishing in the later nineteenth century, spirituality among non-Latino Catholics became increasingly standardized under the direction of the hierarchy (Taves 1986). This standardization promoted Church unity in the pluralistic situation in the United States and contributed to the creation of a united Catholic front in the face of nativist animosity.

However, throughout much of the twentieth century, assimilation generated a gradual decline in "devotional Catholicism" among non-Latino Catholics. Shifts in Catholic theology and the growing influence of a small group of liturgical reformers added to the decline. Nevertheless, non-Latino Catholic spirituality remained primarily a parish-based form of devotionalism well into the 1950s. Earlier in the century, a eucharistic movement promoted parish-based frequent communion, attendance at benediction, and visits to the blessed sacrament. Parishes also acted as focal points for retreats or missions, in addition to serving as centers for Catholic social and cultural life. And in spite of the decline in ethnic-based forms of Catholic spirituality through the mid-twentieth century (Orsi 1985), Marian devotion among Latinos and non-Latinos alike remained strong. This devotion included saying the rosary and promoting the Immaculate Conception, the miraculous medal, apparitions, and Marian confraternities, sodalities, and *Guadalupanas*. Throughout the Cold War years, the Virgin Mary provided solace for individuals and interceded for the sins of the world. Mary also became linked symbolically with the war against "atheistic communism," thereby adding a distinctive Catholic supernatural dimension to the political anxieties of the age (Kselman and Avella 1986).

Catholic Spirituality in the Post-Conciliar Era

By the 1960s, spirituality among American Catholics began to change more dramatically. After Vatican II, many of the traditional and ethnic-based forms of piety, penance, and devotionalism continued to decline. Long-standing Catholic practices such as Friday abstinence and the Eucharistic fast were no longer mandatory. Catholic theologians and liturgical reformers placed greater emphasis on word and sacrament in a quest to rein in much of the subjective piety of the older devotionalism.[3] With the Vatican II promulgation of *Sacrosanctum Concilium* (Constitution on the Sacred Liturgy), Catholic laity were encouraged to embrace the official prayer life of the Church by taking "full, active, and conscious participation" (II.14) in the liturgy. Furthermore, the Council's endorsement of ecumenism and its acknowledgment of the spiritual authenticity of non-Christian traditions and of religious liberty in *Unitatis Redintegratio* and *Dignitatis Humanae* lent new legitimacy to Catholic experimentation with alternative forms of spirituality, including those of Eastern religions. Three other developments also had significant effect.

First, the documents of Vatican II signaled a more positive affirmation of the material world and the human body, thereby encouraging more this-worldly engagement. Emphasis on the salvation of the world received further legitimation with liberation theology, the call for the "preferential option for the poor," and the focus on peace and justice issues and community service in Catholic religious education. Peace and justice priorities were also encouraged by the media visibility of Catholic activists such as the Berrigan Brothers, Dorothy Day, and others who tied spirituality to the call to service.

A second development centered around Catholic Charismatic Renewal in the latter 1960s. The Charismatic Movement spawned new modes of spirituality that were small-group centered, highly affective, and focused around discernment and various charisms of the Holy Spirit (Fichter 1975). For middle-class Euro-American Catholics, charismatic spirituality gave expression to an encounter with the divine more akin to what was characteristic of American evangelicalism. Collaterally, and in keeping with Vatican II, charismatics gave new emphasis to Scripture as a source of Catholic spiritual edification.

Third, the concept of "inculturation"—the process by which the gospel is adapted to a particular culture—gained legitimation. This development contributed to a proliferation of ethnic and alternative Catholic spiritualities including Latino/a, African American, Asian, and Native American spirituality, spirituality of the laity and married couples, and Catholic feminist spirituality.

This is the setting for the later 1990s, when we gathered new data on young adults. We now turn to our sample.

THE SPIRITUALITY OF YOUNG ADULT CATHOLICS

Our sample data lead to four conclusions. First of all, spirituality in the 1990s is strong. There is no evidence that young adult Catholics today are a generation of irreligious scoffers. While our data support other studies (D'Antonio et al. 1996, Davidson et al. 1997, Hoge et al. 1994) showing that young adults are less religious in institutional attachments than other age cohorts in the Church, there is no evidence that they are any less spiritual. See Table 7.1.

Eighty percent of non-Latinos and 77 percent of Latinos consider themselves "spiritual persons." An even larger percentage (96 percent of non-Latinos; 98 percent of Latinos) pray to God, with the majority doing so "once a day" or "several times this week." In addition, as we saw in chapters 3 and 4, only 10 percent of our sample have left Catholicism entirely. Sixty-three percent of non-Latinos and 59 percent of Latinos self-identify as "active Catholics." Ninety-five percent want a child of theirs to receive religious instruction. Ninety-three percent believe that Jesus Christ was God or the son of God. Eighty-one percent believe in a divine judgement after death.

It is not only the churchgoing Catholics who told us they are spiritual persons. Many others did also. As we saw in chapter 4, even the majority of *non-churchgoing* Catholics told us they considered themselves spiritual persons, telling us that churchgoing and being spiritual are commonly separated in their minds.

We compared Catholics and non-Catholics on the questions in Table 7.1. The non-Catholics and Catholics were similar with regard to how many saw themselves as spiritual persons, but the non-Catholics were more constant in prayer. That is, 60 percent of the non-Catholics said they prayed daily or more, compared with 48 percent of the Catholic non-Latinos and 53 percent of the Catholic Latinos. Here is further evidence that although people in our sample who no longer call themselves Catholic have left the Catholic Church, they have not stopped being religious. The majority are still people of Christian faith and self-described spiritual persons, but now they take part in other Christian groups.

Second, we found few significant differences in spiritual practices along gender lines—other than reinforcement for the widely noted fact that women have higher rates of devotionalism and church involvement than men. More of the women than men in our sample attend church regularly and practice private devotions. Women make Stations of the Cross, say the rosary, and read the Bible at home more frequently than men. Women are higher than men in frequency of prayer, including prayer with friends or household members. Gender differences in participating in spiritual groups are small, although

TABLE 7.1

Current Catholics: Spirituality and Prayer (*in percents*)

	Non-Latinos	Latinos
Do you consider yourself a spiritual person?		
Yes	80	77
No	12	14
Don't know	8	9
Do you ever pray to God?		
Yes	96	99
(Of those who said yes:)		
How many times did you pray privately during the last seven days, not counting mealtimes or church services?		
Twice a day or more	16	25
About once a day	32	33
Several times a week or less, or don't know	52	42

Latino women (but not non-Latinos) are higher than men in having taken part in spiritual healing groups.

Third, we found few significant differences on measures of spirituality between our twenty to twenty-nine and thirty to thirty-nine age cohorts other than the fact that the former were generally less active in such practices (and in religion in general) than the latter—in keeping with well-established life cycle patterns associated with religious behavior.

Finally, differences between our non-Latino and Latino samples on items relating to spirituality were also negligible with the exception of devotional practices and reports of religious experiences. As noted in other studies (Dolan and Deck 1994), Latinos were generally higher in devotional practices than others. However, in regard to frequency of prayer, Mass attendance, and general religious beliefs, differences between Latinos and others were not pronounced.

Participation in Religious and Spiritual Groups

We asked the interviewees about their participation in religious or spiritual groups. See Table 7.2.

These young adults are infrequent attenders of Scripture study groups, Scripture discussion classes, prayer groups, faith sharing groups, or social justice groups, but we should remember that Catholics of *all* ages have low rates of participation in such groups. Davidson and his colleagues found that only 14 percent of Catholics of all ages said they attended prayer groups or faith sharing groups at least once a month (1997:46). In a 1996 nationwide survey of Catholics done by the University of Maryland, the respondents were asked, "In the last two years have you made a retreat or a day of recollection?" and 18 percent said yes. Also, "In the last two years have you attended a meeting of a Catholic social justice group or organization?" and 13 percent said yes.[4] Our findings are similar.

The last item in Table 7.2 has higher numbers than the others. Our respondents reported a comparatively high level of doing meditation—either in groups or on one's own.

These young adults have modest levels of participation in Catholic spiritual or devotional groups. Attendance was near zero at meetings or prayer groups associated with Marian apparitions and at non-Christian spiritual groups. We emphasize one conclusion: These young Catholics are not turning to any non-Christian religions, Eastern spiritual movements, or New Age groups in significant numbers. Most spiritual searching and experimenting is done *within* the Catholic or Christian tradition.

When we compared the participation levels of the twenty to twenty-nine and thirty to thirty-nine samples we found definite age differences among the Latinos but not the others. Latinos thirty and older had much higher levels of participation in Scripture studies and prayer groups. Sixteen percent of the younger group have participated in Scripture study or Scripture discussion groups in the last year, and 33 percent of the thirty and older group have done so. Twenty-four percent of the younger group have participated in a prayer group or faith sharing group in the last year, and 33 percent of the older group have done so. Why the young and old groups of Latinos are so different is unclear.

TABLE 7.2

Current Catholics: Participation in Groups *(in percents)*

	Non-Latinos	Latinos
In the past year, have you done the following?		
Taken part in a Scripture study or Scripture discussion class. Yes	19	24
Attended a prayer group or faith sharing group. Yes	20	28
In the past two years, have you?		
Attended any charismatic prayer service. Yes	13	17
Attended any meeting or prayer group associated with Marian apparitions, such as at Medjurgorie. Yes	2	5
Made a retreat or a day of recollection. Yes	18	18
Attended Novenas. Yes	6	19
Attended Eucharistic adoration or Benediction. Yes	26	25
Attended a meeting of a Catholic social justice group or organization. Yes	7	9
Taken part in spiritual healing groups, either church-related or any other. Yes	10	16
Attended any spiritual group or prayer group in a Christian denomination different from your own. Yes	18	13
Attended a spiritual group of a non-Christian religion. Yes	3	4
Participated in meditation groups or done meditation on your own. Yes.	32	35

Personal Religious Practices

A variety of personal devotions are practiced by young adult Catholics. The majority report reading the Bible at home, saying the rosary, wearing medals, crucifixes, scapulars, or rosaries, and keeping images of saints in their homes. Latinos engage in these practices more often than non-Latinos, and this is especially true of having a house or car blessed and keeping images of saints in homes. The last three items in Table 7.3 are commonly identified with Latino Catholicism but not European, African American, or Asian American Catholicism; in our sample Latinos practice them much more often.

For comparison, the 1996 University of Maryland survey asked all Catholics how often in the last year they had listened to any religious programming on the radio or television, and 73 percent said that they had done so at least once. It asked them if they had made the Stations of the Cross in the last two years, and 45 percent said yes. It asked if they had said the rosary or attended a novena in the last two years, and 56 percent said yes. Our sample has slightly lower rates than Catholics of all ages in general.

Our survey confirms use of personal religious practices among young adults, and it corroborates the common observation that Latinos are higher in devotional practices than others. In our survey the Latino respondents were higher than non-Latinos on all forms of personal devotional practice, not only those typical among Latino Catholics.

In light of the above, how do young adult Catholics construct and express their spiritual life? What connection do they make between spirituality, Catholic identity, and the religious currents of American society? We will address these questions under nine headings: Family and Parental Influence; Traditional Devotionalism; the Mass; the Bible; Saints; the Virgin Mary; Material Culture; Faith and Parish Communities; and Social Justice and Community Service.

Family and Parental Influence

Our data have several measures relating parental factors to outcomes of church involvement among grown children. Parental factors are also indirectly related to the formation of young adult spirituality.

TABLE 7.3

Current Catholics: Personal Religious Practices (*in percents*)

	Non-Latinos	Latinos
In the past year, have you:		
Listened to religious programming on radio or television? Yes	55	59
In the past two years, have you:		
Gone for private confession? Yes	37	42
Made the Stations of the Cross? Yes	29	44
Said the rosary? Yes	46	64
Read the Bible at home? Yes	53	58
Worn medals, crucifixes, scapulars, or rosaries? Yes	51	70
Kept images of saints in your home? Yes	61	83
Had your house or car blessed or consecrated to God, the Virgin Mary, or a saint? Yes	9	33
Kept an altar in your home? Yes	3	18
Promised God that you would do something extraordinary, such as taking a trip to a shrine, in return for a favor granted to you? Yes	10	24

Generally speaking, our findings substantiate the common assumption that when individuals come from stable families in which both parents were practicing Catholics and committed Church members, they tend to remain Catholics as adults, even when they have periods of church inactivity in late adolescence, or when they reject doctrines and forms of piety and devotionalism practiced by their parents. A higher percentage of the core Catholics in our sample lived with both parents during their high school years and had parents who attended church weekly.

An attendant issue concerns the impact on young adult Catholic spirituality of baby boomer parents (born between 1946 and 1964) who experienced the conflict and turmoil over Vatican II and the negative reaction to *Humanae Vitae* in 1968 (Seidler and Meyer 1989). Some researchers have speculated that baby boomer Catholics are more alienated from the Church than previous generations. We believe there is some truth to this observation. Some of the young adults we are studying, like their parents, had to unlearn an old Catholic identity and relearn a new one during a formative period of their lives. This sometimes meant rejecting as outdated the rituals and symbols that were once normative to Catholic identity. As Philibert (1999) has noted, baby boomer Catholic parents were also the first generation of Catholics to let their children choose for themselves, and the first generation whose Catholicism often meant freedom from demands of the Church rather than a sense of obedience and affiliation with it. Baby boomer Catholics are also more likely to have married non-Catholics. Certainly these developments influenced the religious and spiritual socialization of the next generation.

Since our sample of young adults are all confirmed Catholics, it is likely that their parents were more committed and less alienated than the above profile depicts. However, we observed that in one-on-one interviews, young adults occasionally noted that the most influential norm of spirituality in their life was a grandparent rather than a parent. This, too, lends credence to Philibert's observation that some young adult Catholics today need to look back to a time before the Council (or to an immigrant expression of Catholicism) to find inspiring models of commitment to the gospel of Christ.

Traditional Devotionalism

When we asked young adults in our sample about their participation in traditional modes of piety and devotionalism, they showed less interest than previous generations of Catholics in these traditions. Fewer than half of all respondents made a retreat or a day of recollection, went to private confession, made stations of the cross, or attended novenas, eucharistic adoration, or Benediction in the last two years. As noted previously, although the general direction is one of decline, there is a higher level of popular devotionalism among Latinos.

Where young adults do engage in these traditional practices, it should not be assumed that such activities signal a rebound effect or a conservative Catholic reaction against Vatican II liturgical reforms. For Latino Catholics, such practices have overtones of ethnic and cultural identity and relate to unique aspects of popular religiosity. For many non-Latinos, the question today is not what these practices meant previously, but what they mean today in American culture with respect to the need for credible symbols, religious boundaries, the quest for supernatural experience, and for spiritual sustenance. This is an issue that needs further exploration. It is also one that can serve as a bridge to engagement with young adults.

The passing of traditional devotionalism stems from assimilation, the post-conciliar emphasis on the liturgical and scriptural foundations of Catholic spirituality, and the wider global spiritual options available to young adult Catholics. This is true within the Church (e.g., Charismatic Movement; cursillos; marriage encounter; contemplative groups, etc.) and in American culture at large (e.g., non-Christian spiritual traditions; feminist, African American, and creation spirituality). It also expresses a weaker institutional commitment to the doctrinal and disciplinary message of the Church. And as we noted at the beginning of the chapter, shifts have occurred in contemporary spirituality away from sacred/profane and spirit/matter dichotomies, from an emphasis on self-denial, otherworldliness, and from traditional forms of disciplined asceticism and formulaic moralism. Spirituality today incorporates many contemporary psychological and therapeutic criteria emphasizing authenticity and a more holistic and integrated understanding of the human person (Downey 1994), along with a growing emphasis on practice (Wuthnow 1998).

The Mass

Young adult Catholics have a lower level of regular Mass attendance than thirty years ago (Stark and Glock 1968:83–87). As noted in chapter 3, 31 percent of non-Latinos and 31 percent of Latinos reported attending

Mass weekly. Regarding the distinctive Catholic understanding of the Mass, our sample have a stronger belief in the Real Presence than indicated in other polls. Eighty-seven percent of the non-Latinos and 96 percent of the Latinos agreed with the statement that "In the Mass the bread and wine actually become the body and blood of Christ." And, in our Princeton Research Associates poll, a 1997 national random sample of 701 young adult Catholics, we asked how important certain beliefs were to the individual's vision of what was essential to Catholicism. The belief that "Christ is really present in the Eucharist" was ranked one of the highest of nineteen indicators (we return to this in chapter 9).

We heard from young adults that the experience of the liturgy, when attended by good homilies and good music, and by a strong and vibrant sense of community, keeps them connected to the Church and facilitates their return to it. It reinforces Catholicism's communal character and highlights the Eucharist as a sacramental source of spiritual life. This occurs even where connections to other aspects of the Church are rejected, as with a male interviewee who observed that while he "could [sic] care less about the pope and the bureaucracy," he had "the deepest regard for the Eucharist."

Conversely, where parish liturgy is experienced as "boring," "mechanical," and "unwelcoming," the effect is detrimental. An ex-Catholic Latina who now considers herself a "non-denominational Christian with a Catholic background," and who attends a non-denominational evangelical Church, speaks for many when she complained of the poor homilies, passiveness, and "blank expressions" she often saw while attending Mass. This contrasted dramatically with her experience in an evangelical church:

> The experience of going to that [evangelical] church was not like anything Catholic that I had ever been to. . . . I always knew who Jesus was . . . I knew he was the son of God. But that was it. I just knew the facts. So, it was really like a black and white movie. But when I started going to this other [non-denominational] church and started to learn about who Jesus was, his background and where he came from and the culture of that time and what was going on . . . all of a sudden it

was like the Wizard of Oz where it just turns into color. . . . And, I had never been to a church where people went early to get a seat. I had never been to a church where people stayed even up to a half hour after church was over.

The Bible

The Bible played a peripheral role in pre–Vatican II Catholic spirituality but in the post-conciliar Church it has become more important. Our interviewees often expressed an interest in knowing more about the Bible. They view the Bible as revealed truth, and they incorporate Bible reading into their prayer life. They reject literal or "fundamentalist" hermeneutics in theory, if not always in practice. However, while slightly better than half (53 percent of non-Latinos; 57 percent of Latinos) indicated that they had "read the Bible at home" in the last two years, the overwhelming majority (80 percent of non-Latinos; 74 percent of Latinos) have never taken part in a scripture study or scripture discussion class.

Many interviewees reported feelings of inadequacy when confronted by fundamentalist and evangelical Christians who challenged their faith and who were better versed in Bible knowledge than they were. We also heard that disaffection with institutional Catholicism is connected to Bible-related issues. For example, of the reasons given for switching to non-Catholic denominations, the second most important (next to the influence of a spouse) was that these churches placed more emphasis on the Bible and had better Bible teaching (16 percent non-Latinos; 34 percent Latinos).

Saints

Saints have been traditional role models in the Church, as Catholicism's virtuosi who inspired previous generations in their spiritual journey. Saints have been drawn overwhelmingly from the Church's clerical and religious ranks.

In our telephone surveys, 61 percent of non-Latinos and 83 percent of Latinos indicated that they had kept images of saints in their home.

However, in our focus groups and one-on-one interviews, few non-Latinos mentioned saints as important or formative in their own spiritual life. Latinos, in contrast, more frequently mentioned saints as sources of inspiration or as prayer intercessors. In our Princeton Research Associates poll, respondents ranked "devotion to saints" twelfth out of nineteen categories relating to what they believed was essential to the Catholic faith.[5]

While there is still vibrance and interest in saints in some Catholic quarters and especially among Latinos, our data suggest that the cult of the saints has diminished as a marker of Catholic identity and personal inspiration. This is due, in part, to the shift toward equating authentic human development and spiritual development, noted previously. Not infrequently our non-Latino interviewees remarked that the lives of the saints (insofar as they were aware of them) are out of keeping with contemporary psychology or too "different" or "strange" from their own lives—in no small part because of preeminence of virginity, celibacy, and austerity. One interviewee noted, "As a married woman, there is not a lot out there." Remarked another:

> Saints don't impress me at all . . . . They are nice stories and all, but I don't pray to saints and I don't hold any stock in that in my own life. . . . Holiness is what I need to do to be whole, to be complete.

We also found few initiatives on the part of our interviewees to reappropriate the lives of the saints as models for their own lives, or to connect the virtues of saints with values and practices relevant to the contemporary world. For example, nobody linked austerity and asceticism with environmental concerns about materialism and overconsumption.

Young adult Catholics are like many other individuals in America's free-market religious economy; they seek spiritual substance from an array of cultural sources—which may or may not be "Catholic." We found that while the spiritual writings of Catholic authors such as Henri Nouwen and Thomas Merton received occasional mention, our non-Latino interviewees were just as likely to refer to popular writers and spiritual authors as diverse as M. Scott Peck, Joseph Campbell, Laura Schlesinger, and James Dobson.

The Virgin Mary

It is widely recognized that the cult of the Virgin Mary endures in Catholic social and cultural settings. In our Princeton Research Associates poll, "devotion to the Mother of God" was listed as the third most essential component of Catholic identity. In addition, 46 percent of non-Latinos and 64 percent of Latinos indicated that they had said the rosary in the last two years. However, in one-on-one interviews and in focus group settings, non-Latino young adults made few references to the importance of the Virgin Mary in their spiritual life, other than as a symbol or cultural icon of Catholic identity. And as noted earlier, very few of our interviewees (non-Latino and Latino) had ever attended meetings or prayer groups associated with Marian apparitions.

Material Culture

We pointed out that pre-conciliar Catholicism included a dizzying array of material objects associated with devotional piety. This material culture is less visible today, although there are significant differences between Latino and non-Latino Catholics in this regard. As noted in Table 7.3, 51 percent of non-Latinos but 70 percent of Latinos indicated that they had worn medals, crucifixes, scapulars, or rosaries. Sixty-one percent of non-Latinos but 83 percent of Latinos had kept images of saints in their homes. A much smaller percentage (3 percent of non-Latinos; 18 percent of Latinos) had kept an altar in their home. What remains unclear, however, is the relationship between the use or display of these items and a specifically Catholic spirituality. Material culture and spirituality can have an ambiguous relationship because the display of religious symbols may be a matter of asserting ethnic and cultural identity independent of doctrinal or institutional commitments, or it may simply derive from conformity to pop culture stylistic trends.

Faith and Parish Communities

How do young adult Catholics rate their parish experience as a factor in their spiritual life? Twenty-five percent of non-Latinos and 28 percent of Latinos indicated they were not on the registry list of any parish. Those who are perceive their parishes in positive terms in regard to their spiritual significance, welcoming nature, and in helping them with important questions in their life (see chapter 3).

However, although parishes receive favorable ratings in our sample, there are few indications that the spirituality of young adult Catholics remains parish-formed or parish-bound. This is obvious in regard to the low levels of Mass attendance and the waning involvement in parish-based modes of devotionalism (Stations of the Cross, Benediction) mentioned earlier. It is also suggested by the fact that nearly half of our sample (47 percent) reported that *none* of their five closest friends were members of their parish.

In addition, nearly three-fourths of our sample (77 percent of non-Latinos and 70 percent of Latinos) have never participated in a prayer group or faith sharing group—parish-based or otherwise. Only 19 percent of non-Latinos and 15 percent of Latinos have been active in any group or committee in the parish or in another Catholic group in the last six months. And only a small number have taken part in charismatic prayer services, spiritual healing groups, groups associated with Marian apparitions, non-Christian spiritual groups, or twelve-step or recovery groups.

The number of young adult Catholics who cross over to other Christian denominations to meet spiritual needs is suggested by the fact that 18 percent of the non-Latinos and 13 percent of Latinos said that they had attended a spiritual group or prayer group in a different Christian denomination in the last two years. An even larger number (34 percent of non-Latinos and 39 percent of Latinos) reported that they listened to religious programming on radio or television "weekly or more" or "occasionally."

Social Justice and Community Service

As noted previously, commitment to the poor and emphasis on social justice were important elements of post-conciliar Catholic identity. How strong is this call to serve among this "Mother Teresa generation" of young adults?

In our 1997 Princeton Research Associates poll, the conviction about "charitable efforts toward helping the poor," and the belief that

"God is present in a special way in the poor," ranked second and fifth respectively as essential to Catholic faith. In addition, as Table 3.2 in chapter 3 indicates, the vast majority of our confirmands agree with statements relating the application of faith to the improvement of society. Yet only 7 percent of the non-Latinos and 9 percent of the Latinos in our sample had attended a meeting of a Catholic social justice group or organization over the last two years. Fifty-three percent strongly agree or agree with the statement that "the Church should stick to religion and not be involved in economic or political issues." And only 16 percent of our non-Latinos and 12 percent of our Latinos had ever heard about or read about the American bishops' 1985 statement on economic justice for all. (A slightly higher percentage [23 percent non-Latinos; 28 percent Latinos] had heard about or read John Paul II's more recent statement criticizing the culture of death.) We conclude that social justice is perceived by most young adult Catholics as a necessary part of their faith, even though few are involved and few have knowledge or understanding of the tradition in this regard.

Summary of the Findings

Our findings can be summarized in eight points: First, young adult Catholics remain overwhelmingly spiritual even where their commitment to institutional Catholicism is loose and tenuous. Where they have fallen away and then returned to active practice as Catholics, the majority do so precisely because of perceived spiritual needs ("felt empty," "lack spiritual life"). And the persons now non-Catholic have not fallen away from the Christian faith; they have *switched churches* or kept a personal spirituality while rejecting churchgoing. This finding differs significantly from studies pointing to a more fundamental loss of faith and a relativistic worldview among persons disaffiliating from mainline Protestantism (Hoge et al. 1994).

Second, although less true for Latinos than for non-Latinos, traditional forms of devotional piety continue to decline. These forms are weak ritual and symbolic venues for shaping Catholic spirituality or for defining Catholic identity. And, although appealing to some segments of the young adult Catholic population, we did not find—as the Davidson study (1997) did not find—a significant rebound effect signaling a widespread movement back to these traditional forms among our interviewees. And, as noted earlier, where this interest does exist, it cannot be assumed to be an expression of conservative Catholicism; it may as well be an expression of the need for demonstrative boundaries, personal conversion, and public witness.

Third, the Virgin Mary endures as a cultural icon of Catholic identity. Yet her utility in the actual construction and expression of young adult Catholic spirituality is limited. This is less true for Latino Catholics for whom the cult of the Virgin Mary, such as Our Lady of Guadalupe, serves as a symbol both of religious and cultural identity and of liberation from unjust social structures (Vidal 1997:637).

Overall the disassociation of many young adult Catholics from traditional forms of Catholic devotionalism and from the saints is having important effects. The norms and patterns of this older spirituality promoted a distinct Catholic ethos and mythos. They fostered a distinct Catholic identity and set Catholics apart from non-Catholics in unequivocal ways. They also facilitated lay linkage to the institutional Church and built community.

Fourth, and related to the above, young adult Catholic connections to parish life are weaker today. Beyond Mass attendance, many young adults have limited connections to parishes that might contribute in distinct ways to their spiritual formation as Catholics. This is slightly less true for older Catholics in our sample who are at a life cycle phase (married and with children) traditionally associated with higher church attendance and parish involvement. It is also significant that so few young adults indicated that their closest friends were members of their parish. Sociological research has shown that friends are important in maintaining the plausibility of a worldview, anchoring spirituality in a particular place, and in the importance attached to following church teachings (Wuthnow 1988:211).

Fifth, the Mass remains a primary source of institutional-based spiritual nurturance for young Catholics, even while attendance rates have declined in recent decades. Our Princeton Research Associates data suggest that Mass attendance has an important and indirect impact on Catholic spirituality because it is associated with a higher level of attachment *to all components of Catholicism*, even where the direction of causality remains unclear.[6] In relation to the disconnectedness from parish life noted above, a heavier burden has been placed on the community-building capacity of the liturgy—which may explain, in part, why young adult Catholics often describe a "good liturgy" by its ability to draw the community together. The Mass also expresses and reinforces a Catholic sacramental imagination, a distinct sensitivity to the reality of the divine in the concrete and visible (Greeley 1990). Whether this sacramental imagination can be sustained with more sporadic Mass attendance by young adult Catholics remains unclear.

Sixth, research on religion today points to the uncoupling of religion from spirituality, to organized religion's waning monopoly over the sacred, and to spiritual seeking outside the parameters of institutional religion (Roof 1993, Wuthnow 1998). While young adult Catholics are exposed to a multitude of spiritual wares, our research suggests that widespread assumption that young adults today are a "generation of seekers" needs revision. The level of spiritual seeking by young adult Catholics as measured by actual participation in other traditions or by spiritual experimentation is low. As noted earlier, attendance was near zero at meetings of prayer groups associated with Marian apparitions, at non-Christian spiritual groups, and at twelve-step or recovery groups. We found no evidence that Catholics or non-Catholics in our sample are turning to any non-Christian religions, Eastern spiritual movements, or New Age groups in any significant numbers. Insofar as they take part in any religious or spiritual groups at all, these groups are Christian and typically Catholic. And, although non-Catholics were somewhat higher in involvement in some of these groups, the patterns were weak, mixed, and not easily summarized.

Seventh, an emerging evangelical-like spirituality can be found among young adult Catholics. The most obvious aspect of this trend is the emphasis on a "personal relationship with the Lord," rather than on traditional Catholic sacramentalism, communalism, or on the mediational role of the Church. While individual Catholics so disposed are likely to have previous experiences with Protestantism or a Protestant spouse, we believe this evangelical orientation is growing. It derives from the influence of the Cursillo and Charismatic Movements, the new ecumenism, participation in Protestant-organized Bible study groups, and the waning of evangelicalism's historical anti-Catholicism. It is also linked to the broader cultural tendency to diminish the significance of denominational identity. Among our interviewees, however, this evangelical orientation appears not to be associated with a strong and exclusive biblical orientation, with a "Jesus only" mentality, with being "born again," per se, or with strong commitment to proselytizing as with many Protestant evangelicals (Smith 1998). Rather it expresses a more individualistic religious identity that minimizes institutional affiliation or community commitment.[7]

Eighth, our data show that many young adult Catholics link spirituality with social justice initiatives and service to the poor. In this respect, their spirituality is not a me-centered one. It is a spirituality with important implications for the transformation of society. Yet it often lacks connection with specific Church teachings or with contemporary Catholic theology. The tendency to emphasize charitable rather than structural approaches to social problems is one indication of this missing connection. Nor is it clear that social justice concerns among young adult Catholics derive from the experience of the Mass, as liturgical reformers had hoped.

The dominance of personal freedom, autonomy, and self-sufficiency in contemporary American society and the privatizing of religion is widely discussed today. On the debit side, these developments have been associated with removing faith and spirituality from a community and institutional basis, weakening denominational loyalties, and evaporating a common moral vocabulary (Bellah et al. 1985, Roof and McKinney 1987, Roof 1993, Hoge et al. 1994). Is this privatizing trend influencing Catholic spirituality? Do young adult Catholics have a mediated and communal spiritual sensibility symbolized by the Communion of Saints, the Mystical Body of Christ, and some level of commitment to the Church's teaching authority? Or are they spiritual "Lone Rangers" in keeping with the cultural ethos of autonomy and individualism? In our research we found evidence of both. Here we identify two spiritual types of young adult Catholics.[8]

TWO SPIRITUAL TYPES

Church-as-Choice Catholics

The tendencies toward "Lone Ranger" spiritual individualism are most pronounced among the young adults we identify as church-as-choice Catholics. These individuals are not concerned about a specific denominational identity. As one person put it, the Church is "just another human institution . . . that was constructed by people." While Catholicism has more "bells and whistles than Protestantism," it is essentially the same. These young adults see little importance in the distinctiveness of Catholic institutional identity. To them Catholicism is one choice or preference among others. Church-as-choice Catholics also see little necessary connection between religion and spirituality. The particulars of Catholic doctrine and Church life are not as important to them as the broader human quest to find spiritual fulfillment. "Religion" is about doctrine and institutions; "spirituality" is about a higher power and personal faith. These are "two separate things." Individuals with these views are weakly connected to Catholicism's sacramental and symbolic tradition or to its institutional character. They are a large part of the 64 percent of young adults who believe that one can be a good Catholic without going to Mass. Nor do they view other elements of the Church's sacramental life as essential. As one twenty-four-year-old Latino said about of confession:

> Why would I want to speak with a priest and ask for confession to a man? Maybe the priest is a good person, but for something very personal and spiritual, God is here with me and he's the only person who understands.

Another commented that "When I do something bad, I tell God right now I'm sorry and I don't think I need another person there." And regarding saints, another observed: "I believe we can go directly to the Father though Jesus's name. I don't think it is necessary to go through his saints."

Other church-as-choice Catholics differentiate between Catholicism as a religious tradition into which they were born, and the priority in their lives of spiritual sources extraneous to it. A twenty-six-year-old African American Catholic male who recently embraced a new biblical perspective brought to him by a Protestant minister commented:

> I still consider myself 'Catholic.' I practice Catholicism but, again, the Catholic piece of me is not as important—or does not play as much a role—as the spiritual side of me ... which was opened up by this woman.

Church-as-choice Catholics tend to conflate religion and spirituality with ethical behavior. They exemplify a subtype of Ammerman's "Golden Rule" Christians (1994). Like their Protestant counterparts, "Golden Rule" Catholics view spirituality primarily in terms of being a "good person" or having compassion for those in need—rather than a function of anything derivative of or distinctive to Catholicism as a living faith tradition. Noted one respondent: "I just feel as long as you live a life without harming others or yourself and ... you are just really living a good, decent life, then you really are living the way God intended you to live." A twenty-year-old inactive male said that he believed you could be a "good Catholic" just by "praying and just being, or trying to be, a good person." Another twenty-eight-year-old male responded to the question as to whether or not a person could be a good Catholic without going to Mass by emphasizing the priority of "lived spirituality":

> Jesus never said that you had to come to the temple to pray. [He said] that whenever two or more of you are gathered in my name, I am there. ... I think that even if you didn't attend a Mass. ... but yet you went to a soup kitchen and you lived spiritually, you did what Christ taught you do, [which] is to help your fellow man. Aren't you living that scripture?

Church-as-choice Catholics are also more likely to follow a spiritual path in which they seek sources of inspiration that, as one woman put it, "help reinforce the choices I've made in my life, the values I have" rather than conforming to the doctrinal and disciplinary traditions of the Church.

Core Catholics

Core Catholics (an estimated 10 percent of our sample) are much less individualistic in their spirituality and in their relation to the institutional Church. They are spiritual church attenders. They take seriously the teachings of the pope (even where they may disagree with particulars), view Catholicism as the one true Church (while acknowledging the truths of other traditions), pray daily, and reject the idea that one can be a "good Catholic" without going to Mass. Core Catholics do not separate spirituality from religion or see the two as antithetical. And they do not believe that the spiritual life can be lived as a "solo project." As one thirty-five-year-old male noted, religion and spirituality "flow back and forth from each other, we're put here to praise God and serve others and you can't do that on an individual basis." Accordingly, an individual needs to be connected to a religious institution in order to have his or her spiritual life strengthened and directed by the tradition's collective wisdom. For core Catholics, spirituality is also perceived as having an objective basis in the Church's sacramentalism. When a person is disconnected too long from that tradition, his or her spirituality will be adversely impacted. As one thirty-year-old male told us, "If you stop sacramental life, you are a dead Catholic." While this emphasis on sacramentalism does not preclude the use of other spiritual resources, for core Catholics those derived from the tradition are the more foundational and formative. This is true regarding the Virgin Mary and, to a lesser degree, the saints.

CONCLUSION

A core of young adult Catholics practice a spirituality rooted in the symbols and disciplines of their tradition, while the majority are less connected to the tradition. The issue is simple enough. Young adult Catholics, like most other individuals, seek spiritual meaning in their life experiences. They draw symbols and inspiration from a variety of material and personal sources (nature, music, childbirth, marriage) suggestive of the Catholic sacramental imagination. They also draw inspiration from the American spiritual marketplace even when, as our data show, their actual spiritual experimenting remains primarily within the broad parameters of the Christian tradition. Their spirituality is also pragmatic and praxis-oriented. However, feelings, emotions, and personal experience count more than theology and doctrines in all of these respects. In a radically relativistic and individualistic culture, the authority of personal experience has become one of the few certain norms for authenticity—spiritual and otherwise.

Young adult Catholics construct their spiritual life by testing personal experience with a variety of sources. These sources must be accessible, plausible, and culturally relevant to them. Institutional Catholicism with its panoply of spiritual models, practices, and critical theological traditions, has lost considerable normative authority in this regard. This loss stems from the lack of knowledge of the spiritual tradition on the part of many young adults, from Catholicism's internal turmoil since Vatican II, and from the free-market nature of the American spiritual economy. It also derives from the loss of plausibility of elements of Catholicism's traditional spirituality in a changed historical and cultural context. In our postmodern world of pluralism, ecumenism, relativism, suspicion of institutions, and the cultural uncoupling of spirituality and religion, the spiritual narratives of many young adult Catholics often resemble generic "faith journeys" with limited connection to their tradition. Many young adults drift toward a religionless spirituality.[9] While it is true that the Church's traditional forms of spirituality remain viable among certain Catholic subgroups—even where they lack awareness of the real valences or historical diversity of these forms—we find meager evidence of a sustained interest among young adult Catholics today in such traditions or practices beyond their relevance to a generic quest for personal spirituality. Nor are the emergent, post–Vatican II norms of a credible and distinct Catholic spiritual life familiar or obvious to many of them.

CHAPTER 8

Catholic Identity of Young Adults

. . . .

The 1990s have been filled with talk about Catholic identity. People ask, "Will today's young adult Catholics have as firm a Catholic identity as their parents or grandparents? Do young people today *feel* Catholic in their bones?"

Before we can address these questions we need to make two clarifications about identity. First, the Catholic identity of institutions is different from the Catholic identity of individual people. The "Catholicness" of a college or hospital must be analyzed differently from the Catholic self-concept of an individual. Our interest here is limited to the Catholic identity of individuals.[1] The most important research has been done by social psychologists, and they treat the concepts "identity" and "self-concept" interchangeably.

Second, Catholic identity involves both the identity felt by an *individual* and the identity-related characteristics of the Catholic *tradition* as it exists today. The topic can be approached from both directions, and we will do so in this chapter and the next. Here we begin with the study of Catholicism as a part of individual identity. Chapter 9 starts with an analysis of Catholic tradition. Both provide important lessons, as we shall see.

Social psychologists have studied identity and self-concept of persons in hundreds of empirical studies. Investigators agree that the self-concept is composed of numerous elements and that each person needs to coordinate or integrate them in some way in order to achieve a sense of unity. To illustrate the elements, let us look at typical results from the "Twenty Statements Test," in which college students were asked to give twenty answers to the question "Who am I?" Here is a sample list written by a college freshman in 1966:

1. Clarie M. (name, implying gender)
2. Five feet five inches tall.
3. A Negro.
4. Catholic.
5. One hundred forty-eight (weight).
6. Interested in sports.
7. Not conceited.
8. Honest with people.
9. Not one who always criticizes.
10. Interested in all types of music.
11. One who likes to dance.
12. Sometimes easy to get angry.
13. Considered attractive.
14. Easy to talk with strangers.
15. Quick to respond to some emotions (Gordon 1968:121).

Clarie listed her objective social characteristics first and her personal attributes later. She mentioned "Catholic" fourth in the list, and apparently she sees it as a social attribute which positions her in social space. Whether or not her self-concept included exactly fifteen elements is unimportant, since they subside in importance after the first five or ten.

Researchers have used this test as a way to map the self-concept. They have found that respondents tend to exhaust all their "consensual" references (public and agreed-upon) first, then switch to describing themselves in "subconsensual" references (such as "too thin" or "trying to do better in school"). The former are unchangeable reference points, while the latter are open to change. Religious identity, such as "Catholic," is normally considered a consensual response not open to change (Gordon 1968:124).

ARRANGEMENT OF ELEMENTS

The self-concept, in summary, is a construct built out of elements such as these. How are the elements arranged? Morris Rosenberg (1979) has demonstrated that the self-concept is more or less organized, and it has the shape of a hierarchy. A small set of elements constitute a "master identity" which organizes the other parts. To exemplify the hierarchy, listen to how Lyndon Johnson described himself in a speech:

> I am a free man, an American, a United States Senator, and a Democrat, in that order. I am also a liberal, a conservative, a Texan, a taxpayer, a rancher, a businessman, a consumer, a parent, a voter, and not as young as I used to be nor as old as I expect to be—and I am all those things in no fixed order. (Quoted in Gordon 1968:123)

The question of Catholic identity asks, where does being Catholic fit into the total self-concept? The higher it is positioned in the hierarchy, the more important it will be in organizing other elements and influencing life decisions. This varies. For one young person, being Catholic is very important and very influential in arranging the rest of his or her life; the person not only *says* this, but all of his or her *behavior* proves it. For another young person, being Catholic is only incidental, probably a by-product of other elements of self-concept such as family, ethnicity, or friendships.

Given that the self-concept is a construct of elements arranged in hierarchical order, how did they come to be arranged in this way? Here the psychologists agree: the importance of any element is a result of how *valuable* it has been in the person's life. The development of the self takes place gradually, and the centrality of any element is a result of its effect on overall spiritual development. It is a question, for example, of how does being Catholic (in its various aspects), being active in the Knights of Columbus, being a parent, being a business manager, or being a member of the Junior Chamber of Commerce contribute to one's basic sense of well-being and authenticity? Also, how does it contribute to the coherence of the whole? Let us be clear that we are not talking about pop psychology's common use of the word "self-esteem" as being synonymous with gratification, self-display, or feeling good.

Spiritual development is slower and deeper. It is more constitutive of the person, and it involves self-renunciation and discipline as well as self-promotion and expression.

With this broad sense of "self-development" or "spiritual development," we can say that the importance of any element of the self will rise or fall, over time, depending on its contribution to the total package. Self-esteem (understood in its broadest sense) is centrally important to all humans, and all feel a constant drive to strengthen it. All people want a positive basic self-esteem and will make great exertions to achieve it. This is axiomatic in identity theory.[2] Psychologists tend to use Darwinian language of variation and selection to describe how individuals experiment with variations in their self-concept. The elements which serve overall self-esteem are gradually selected for greater investment, and they move higher in the hierarchy. In time they influence the importance of other elements.

As Morris Schwartz said in the book *Tuesdays with Morrie*, "If the culture doesn't work, don't use it" (Albom 1997:34). This is an oversimplification, but it shows the logic. Rosenberg illustrates how people emphasize one or other element of the self, depending on how the elements contribute to enhancing basic self-esteem:

> To the extent that individuals focus their sense of worth on *different* self-components, the success of one person is not necessarily achieved at the expense of another. It is thus entirely possible for each person to judge himself favorably by virtue of selecting his own criteria for judgment. Take four boys. One is a good scholar, the second a good athlete, the third very handsome, and the fourth a good musician. So long as each focuses on the quality at which he excels, each is superior to the rest. At the same time each may blithely acknowledge the superiority of the others with regard to qualities to which he himself is relatively indifferent. It is thus possible for each to emerge with a high level of self-respect and, indeed, mutual respect. (Rosenberg 1979:74)

An individual is not totally free to form his or her self-concept, because external forces impose limits. For example, in a caste society or a racist society, one's caste or race is inescapable, and it forms a fixed portion of the self-concept around which the individual can make choices in building the total structure.

We can now make several statements clarifying Catholic identity. A person's self-concept is an organized structure of elements, one of which for Catholics is "I am Catholic." The first query about Catholic identity is where this elements fits in the total construct and how it relates to other elements. If it is central, it will be more important than many other elements (such as occupation, ethnicity, family role, and club membership) and will have the power of organizing and rearranging others toward greater consistency and unity. This is the situation idealized in the Catholic tradition, as it is in all religions, and might be seen as the "ideal Catholic identity" or "intrinsic Catholicism." We return to this topic below.

Different elements of self-concept exist side by side and compete with one another. Since time and energy are limited, a person cannot consider all of his or her self-concept elements as equally crucial. As one element rises in importance, another must recede. There is (to a great extent) a fixed-sum quality to the parts of self-concept, and the only escape from the fixedness of the sum is to arrange the elements in some degree of unity, so they resemble horses all pulling in the same direction, not in opposite directions. A unified self-concept (or unified "identity") generates more energy and more spiritual gifts for its owner.

The self-concept grows over time, and the process is partly rational and partly nonrational, just like the process of choosing an occupation or spouse is partly rational and partly not. The process is more like falling in love than like making a business decision. That is to say, all levels of one's personality and identity are involved, and the process takes time. The most important question is whether the person feels a spiritual benefit.

Religious identity, ethnic identity, or family identity will grow strong or weak depending on their benefit to the totality, consciously and unconsciously.[3] Take ethnic identity, for example. It can be emphasized, or it can be deemphasized, within limits, by an individual. One Mexican-American person may stress Mexicanness because it has proved gratifying. Another person of the same ancestry and history may take the opposite policy because ethnic identity has proved baneful, and that person will feel and act as if it is unimportant. It all depends on personal experiences. And it is limited by things like personal appearance, language, and social attitudes.

All of us know college alumni who are gung-ho about their colleges and find their identity as Stanford alumni (or Notre Dame or Penn State or whatever) important in their lives. It is usually because this facet of identity has been beneficial in some way. For some, the personal growth and fulfillment of the college years was a pearl of great price, and they are eternally thankful; for others it has been the friendships and business connections provided by membership in their graduating class. It all depends on how the elements of self-concept have contributed to their lives.

James Whitehead, a psychologist who has probed Catholic identity, said in a personal interview that the heightened concern over Catholic identity today arises from recent changes in Catholicism which have modified laypersons' understanding of the faith. A half century ago most American Catholics thought it was a matter of obeying the pope, maintaining devotional practices, and eating fish on Friday. But recently these behaviors have fallen away as the marks of Catholic identity, and now people inquire more about what is really the core of the faith. Whitehead said that young people ask him in conference after conference, "What does it *really* mean to be Catholic? We don't know any more. What is the essence?" In Whitehead's view, people are looking to the New Testament core, since the earlier behavioral marks (he calls them "peripherals") are no longer compelling.

Elements within Elements

Some elements of self-concept may be arranged in a nesting configuration, so that specific elements exist within general ones, or local within regional. This is common with group memberships. All people belong to groups-within-groups and must make decisions, consciously or unconsciously, about levels of investment. Allen, Wilder, and Atkinson give examples:

> Political divisions provide a clear-cut example that illustrates the principle: the city, the county, state, nation—each lower level entity is contained within the higher one. Religion also offers many examples:

there are subsystems of sects within the more inclusive group of Protestants, but the Protestant and Catholic groupings are part or subsystems of a more inclusive category. . . . A person is at the same time a member of each of the groups that exist at different levels of the complex system. (Allen et al. 1983:100)

The question arises, to which level do I *really* belong and *really* give my allegiance? Am I more committed to my department than to the company as a whole? Am I more committed to my city than to the United States as a whole? Am I more committed to my denomination than to Christianity as a whole—or, in the reverse direction, more committed to Catholicism than to my specific parish or religious community? How do we know what God really wants? This brings us to the theological issue of ecumenism, to which we return in the next chapter.

The Role of the Outgroup

Psychologists studying group identity have found that it is strengthened when an outgroup is visible. The presence of a threatening outgroup enhances the feelings of group members that their membership is important, and groups facing dangerous outgroups achieve commitment and unity more easily. In such a situation the ingroup members tend to perceive increased similarity among themselves (Allen et al. 1983:99–108).

The nature of the outgroup is important. If it is nonthreatening, it has less effect. Outgroups are often misperceived, and the main error is in seeing them as more unified and homogeneous than they really are. Research has found that members of a religious or ethnic group tend to see outgroups as more unified and threatening than the situation warrants as judged by observers (Allen et al. 1983:101).

THREE TYPES OF CATHOLIC IDENTITY

In our telephone interviews and personal interviews we talked at length about Catholic identity, and as a result we identified three types. (The persons who said they are no longer Catholic are ignored here.)

First are persons whose Catholic identity is important and central, and it clearly includes parish life, the sacraments, and institutional authority. We call these people "parish Catholics." Their distinguishing feature is that they go to church and find meaning in parish life, including sacraments, celebration of holy days, and taking part in parish groups. Second are persons whose Catholic identity is important and central, but it does not include taking part in the institutional church. They do not attend Mass except on a few special occasions. We call them "spiritual Catholics," as used in the widely heard statement "I am spiritual but not religious." Their commitment is to some of the Catholic teachings, spirituality, and traditions, but not to the institutional church. Someone has suggested the name "Christmas and Easter Catholics" for them. Third are persons whose Catholic identity is an extension of family or ethnic identity. We call them "contingent Catholics," since their Catholicism is contingent on other central elements in their identity. They are neither churchgoing Catholics nor spiritual Catholics, yet they see themselves as Catholics and expect to remain so. (Another apt name has been suggested: "derivative Catholics.")

This threefold categorization is different from the types of church involvement we presented in chapter 4. This one is a typology of commitments, and it is unavoidably imprecise. The first type (parish Catholics) includes commitment to the Catholic faith and the institutional church, the second type (spiritual Catholics) is committed only to the faith, and the third type (contingent Catholics) has little commitment to either, since its motivation is dependent on other things. Because commitments are difficult to discern in standard phone interviews, we are unable to measure how many people fit into each type.

In chapter 4 we saw examples of two of the commitment types. Mary Mallozzi is a clear case of a parish Catholic. Her Catholic faith is central to her life, and she is committed to the Mass, the pope, and Mary. Cecilia Coronado is another parish Catholic, but not as clearly, since her interest in parish involvement derives partly from her concerns to have good family life and to rear her daughter in the right way.

Sophia Langone is a spiritual Catholic. She loves the tradition and sees it as part of her total being, but she has stopped going to church and is now looking for a way to be Catholic without the institutional church.

Here we present three more persons as examples. Diana Suarez is a parish Catholic, Robert Wilkes is a spiritual Catholic, and Vivian Lopez is a contingent Catholic.

Diana Suarez: Parish Catholic

Diana is a thirty-seven-year-old Latina, married with three children. She grew up in Texas and now lives in the Midwest. Her upbringing wasn't especially religious, but her husband came from a very religious family. Soon she had three children, and now the family attends church regularly. The interviewer asked if her marriage had an effect on her religious life.

> *Diana:* Definitely. It was like a stepping-stone to getting me there. God calls us all at different times. I think my calling started there. It really kicked into gear when my kids turned teenagers.

The interviewer asked Diana if she had ever had an experience of some kind of sacred reality.

> *Diana:* Yes. A couple of years ago, I was asleep and I had a dream about the Virgin Mary. I was in a big house, I had no idea where. There were kids everywhere, little kids, two, three, four, five years old going in and out. I was thinking "Where am I?" I saw the silhouette of the shoulders and head of Mary coming down, just as bright as they could be, her face was like porcelain, white. She had this blue cape. She was looking at me and talking to me, but not moving her lips, telling me that I needed to pray no matter what happened in my life, whatever I was going through, not to give up the faith, but to pray. Waking up, I didn't know whether it was just a dream or was kicked off by something. But she came to me and told me to pray. I told my husband about it and I said, "It was real. If she appeared to other people, why couldn't she come to me in my dream?"
>
> *Interviewer:* What's special to you about Mary? Is it that Mary is an intercessor?

Diana: Intercessor, yes. I do a lot of my praying to Mary. She was a mother who had the worst thing that I could ever think of: watching her son be crucified, knowing that he had the power to say he didn't want to do it. And knowing that she was pregnant by the Holy Spirit. Back then, they stoned you to death. But she had the faith that God would keep her safe because it was His will. If it was His will that she was stoned, then it was His will. She put that complete faith in Him. I relate to her as a woman. She had a child and suffered. The will of God will never take you where the grace of God cannot keep you.

Interviewer: What nourishes your spiritual life? Do you find the Mass meaningful?

Diana: Yes. It's amazing how sometimes the stories relate, especially the Old Testament. Or, even the homilies, with the priests. Sometimes it's like he's talking specifically to me.

Interviewer: What's the most significant part of the Mass to you?

Diana: The priest's homily. Well, there are times when the homily doesn't speak to me personally. That's okay. I enjoy going and receiving communion.

Interviewer: What about the sense of community? Is that important in how you experience liturgy?

Diana: No, I don't think it's a big part. I think it's how the Mass affects me personally or how it relates to what is going on in my life.

Interviewer: So you don't go to Mass to have a community experience.

Diana: No. I like to see the people there and it's probably becoming more communal since I started sponsoring someone, because that person looks to me for added support. To me religion has always been personal.

Interviewer: What aspect of the Church is most important to you?

Diana: I think it's a toss-up between the actual Mass and the fact that we have adoration chapel here, knowing that the chapel is there twenty-four hours a day, seven days a week, the fact that it allows me the opportunity to go pray whenever I want. There is someone there all the time. People sign up for different times. I do my chapel hours each weekend, which I find really comforting.

Diana went on to talk about problems with her children, one of whom was a delinquent for a while and another of whom has an alcohol problem. She stressed how religious education and churchgoing helps youth establish lasting values in their lives.

> *Interviewer:* How important is it to you to be Catholic and to remain Catholic?
> *Diana:* It's what I live for. It's all I've known. It's all I really want to know. Maybe I need to learn about other religions, so I can know more. . . . I was baptized into the Catholic Church, therefore I consider myself Catholic. I'm committed to that.

Robert Wilkes: Spiritual Catholic

Robert is a twenty-seven-year-old graduate student in the Midwest, studying Latin American liberation movements. He is newly married. He recently returned from two years working in Mexico in a church-related program bringing American students to Mexico. Robert is committed to Catholic social action. In the interview he contrasted the vital Catholic group he belonged to in Mexico with the depressing state of parishes in his college town.

> *Robert:* In Mexico people participated in the church and in public life very naturally and discussed politics, discussed *everything*. In the church they discussed parts of their moral lives. And that wasn't something they just did on Sunday. They met during the week through their church to do local activities. And I came to learn that there were alternative ideas about what church meant.
> In Mexico we had a church and pastor committed to the participation of the people, to discussing the real problems of the people. It was important for the people to participate in church life in a real active way, via music, via giving reflections on readings from the Gospel. And I came to see that the church was committed to speak to where people were at and to participate with them in their liberation and their own development.
> *Interviewer:* Was this a big church in Mexico, or a small group?

Robert: It was a parish of fifty to seventy-five people. . . . So if the president of Mexico would, let us say, cut funding to the poor, people would say "Is this a Christian thing to do? Of course not. How can we repeal this? Well, we need to organize a petition and organize a strike. How do we do this? Well, we need to reach out to the labor unions. We need to reach out to these groups." And they said, "In order to be good Christians, we need to go out and do these things." And it was a community concern and a community issue. . . . People were motivated out of their faith to act in Christian, loving ways. And I felt like they cared about me, and they didn't know me from Adam! And I didn't know them either prior to this experience. And yet here we were, part of a common community, trying to build a better world. And that didn't sound or seem ludicrous there; it seemed like a real feasible goal that we were doing.

Interviewer: That seems to have been quite an experience. Did it change your views about the faith, or about the Church, or anything?

Robert: It's hard to know . . . But I think that 99 percent of the Americans who came through in groups had a real transformative experience through the programs I worked on . . . I think that seeing these visitors realize that their lives were interconnected with others and that together they should be working for a better world with social justice, that this was doing God's work, that encouraged me. At the same time seeing the Church hierarchy in the Vatican and in Mexico crack down on this aspect of the Church was very disheartening to me!

Robert told about how he became involved in the Mexico program—through the campus ministry of his undergraduate college. He found the campus priests and the programs inspiring, and his first trip to Mexico was a two-week retreat put on by the campus ministry. The interviewer then asked Robert about his experiences in parishes in the United States since returning.

Robert: I've had a hard time finding a parish that I feel comfortable with. . . . For example, there was a parish here at the university that I kind of liked. We had a lot of lay participation, singing of songs, there was a social justice component, the sermons were often about current events and how we have to think about the moral dilemmas we face every day and how we could find sources in the Bible for these concerns. And then the local bishop ended this kind of experiment. He said it was acting outside of canon law, and so women were not permitted to participate in the Mass and lay people were not permitted to participate in the same ways. It left a sour taste in my mouth. It felt like something was going good for a while. We had the wheels turning, and things were in motion, and then this kind of experiment was cut short. . . . I tried to find somewhere else to go, but it seems easier to do something else, to read a book or something, than to try to hunt down something.

Interviewer: Is there a Catholic faith community available here? A real faith community?

Robert: I don't feel like it's available. The things here just don't appeal!

Robert has stopped going to Mass. The interviewer asked about his interest in other kinds of churches, and Robert said he had no interest, since he is so Catholic. He thought other churches were authentic and were doing they best they can, and if mergers of denominations involving the Catholic Church took place in the future, it would be okay with him. Institutional church structures have little meaning in themselves, and anyway they will change in the course of time. Robert is critical of many things about the Church, and he would like to deflate the role of the pope, to remove the requirement that priests be celibate males, to redefine the priesthood, and to reorganize church life along different lines.

Interviewer: It sounds as if you will be a lifelong Catholic.

Robert: Definitely.

Interviewer: But you're not a lifelong parish participant.

Robert: Not now. I don't have any plan for that. But it's a dilemma. I know I need a faith community, because I valued that in the past. And I know that's the right way. But the experiences I've had since haven't lived up to that, and it's easier just to stop searching and stop shopping around. I don't know. Maybe later.

Vivian Lopez: Contingent Catholic

Vivian is a twenty-two-year-old single college student of mixed Puerto Rican-European ancestry, living in the eastern U.S. She sees herself as a Latina more than anything else. Her parents are now separated. Vivian attended C.C.D. during high school, then stopped, and soon she stopped Mass attendance except for major holidays. She is not very interested in churchgoing.

> *Vivian:* I don't foresee myself going to church regularly now or in the near future. If I happen to get involved with someone or marry someone who is Catholic, I could foresee myself going to church regularly if he does. If I have children I would like to raise them Catholic, so I probably might go to church regularly because of them.

Vivian's parents wanted their two daughters to go to religion classes and get confirmed, but after that they let the daughters make their own decisions about religion. Vivian said that if she had children someday, she would like them to have religious education.

> *Interviewer:* If you have children, what is the preferred solution for their religion?
>
> *Vivian:* I would like to give them some religious background or education up till maybe junior high. And then after that I'll let them decide if religion is important to them.
>
> *Interviewer:* What is a good age for letting them decide what they want?
>
> *Vivian:* Um, maybe fourteen, fifteen.
>
> *Interviewer:* So, it would be nice if the children knew they were Catholic and also knew what it meant, right? Would you like them to be people of faith, or are you interested in just giving them an exposure to what it is all about?
>
> *Vivian:* The second. Exposure. I think that Catholicism, even though it is a religious identity, has a lot that goes with it that is cultural as well. Not necessarily religious, but different attitudes than other religions have, or just family celebrations and family traditions. I think a lot of the holidays we celebrate are religious,

and there is also a large portion of it that is family tradition or is family-related. I guess I sort of divorce the religious aspect of it from the rest. The religious is there, but I don't think Christmas or Easter are totally religious holidays. It is a big part. But when I think of Easter I don't really think of Christ rising.

Interviewer: As you see family life, it should have these rituals in it, right?

Vivian: Yes. And they are part of the tradition. I think a lot of the holidays have sort of become commercialized and the religious aspect of them has been lost. I think I would like a balance of both, and have children knowing that it's more than just the Easter Bunny but also a part of the culture and family traditions as well. And a time for families to be together.

Interviewer: So you're also emphasizing family and that a family should have this dimension to it.

Vivian: Yes. I think a family should have some traditions that they practice together. Generally most traditions are tied to religious aspects, and most people get together around the holidays. Families could have other things as well that they do together, things that have no religious component. . . . I think it would be important for us to celebrate Christmas and Easter, and one of the reasons I would prefer to marry someone who is Catholic—I don't have to, but I would prefer—is, then I would be able to celebrate Christmas with my whole family instead of celebrating holidays separately. I would like the family to celebrate Christmas and Easter. Also it makes for less complications.

Interviewer: Would you prefer an active Catholic, or a nominal Catholic, or wouldn't it matter?

Vivian: Um, I wouldn't want someone who is to the point that they would make me do things I wouldn't want to do. If I did not want to go to church, he would have to be comfortable with that. If he were extremely involved, I wouldn't want that to be a source of tension.

Interviewer: Summing up: you believe in religious education for children, at least for exposure and for identity, and you emphasize family and rituals. How about the doctrines, learning abut the catechism, the sacraments, or the Bible?

Vivian: I don't really know what I would want, because I personally don't know anything about the Bible. And I don't know too much about the sacraments.

Interviewer: I have heard some people say that they wished they knew more about the faith. Do you have those feelings?

Vivian: Well, it comes up sometimes, like with my grandmother. She's very religious. She was telling me that she was going to a novena, and I didn't know what a novena was! Or, another example, she says the rosary. I think I might have said, 'I don't know if I have ever said the rosary.' And she was shocked that I didn't know what you're supposed to do. . . . Since I do identify myself as being Catholic, I think it's sort of unfair sometimes for me to say that, if I don't know what a novena is. How could I consider myself a Catholic, even though I do, when there are so many things I just don't know? I feel a sort of responsibility that I should know.

Interviewer: Do you feel inadequate?

Vivian: Sort of. Well, not *inadequate,* but maybe in some respects I'm a pseudo-Catholic. Like I take the parts of the religion I like and then don't accept the other parts that I don't. . . . I'm probably more of a *questioning* Catholic. I'm still a Catholic, but yet there are so many things I have problems with.

Interviewer: Do you ever think you might leave the Catholic community?

Vivian: I don't think so, since as I was saying, there are cultural ties to it as well. . . . Well, it's more just for identity. Usually people identify with the religion of their parents, and it was something almost "passed down" to us.

Vivian told how her mother had recently moved to the South and had decided to join a Protestant church there. This amazed Vivian, and it resulted in complications in family life at holiday time. At Christmas time Vivian was hoping that the whole family would go to church together, but her mother didn't want to go to the Catholic service, and also her sister, who has stopped churchgoing, didn't want to either. Vivian went with her grandmother and her great aunt and uncle.

Vivian: I wanted my mom to come so we could all go together, but she didn't want to, because she goes to *her* church. . . . And I wanted my sister to come with me. I would have liked her to be there. It would have been nice. But she didn't want to go, so I said, "Well, it's your decision." I guess I missed having my mom there, because I just sort of always expected that she will be going. It was sort of a custom that we'd always go to Mass on Christmas.

Vivian then gave her views as to why she has lost interest in the Catholic Church. She saw it as antiquated and unrealistic in the modern world. She mentioned the pope's position against birth control and abortion. She opposes the Church's condemnation of homosexual acts and of suicide. She talked about the influence her college has had on her. She attended an elite private college, not Catholic.

Vivian: I think a lot of people there are sort of anti established religions. They are in favor of spirituality and in favor of religion, but their own sort of religion. And against more structured doctrines, like moralistic attitudes saying that people are unable to decide for themselves.

Vivian sees herself as a Catholic, but for her it is mainly for maintaining family traditions and for locating herself in American society. If her family situation changed, she might reconsider her commitment to the Catholic faith and Catholic Church, since this commitment is contingent on family influences.

JEWISH STUDIES OF IDENTITY

It is instructive to listen in on American Jews as they discuss identity, since many of their concerns have parallels in American Catholicism. The Jewish community has carried out important research which has lessons for all of us.

The Jewish discussion usually begins with alarm that the interfaith marriage rate among Jewish young people has become frightfully high. In the 1990 National Jewish Population Survey the rate for recently married persons was 57 percent (Kosmin et al. 1991, Goldstein 1993). All Jewish writers agree that interfaith marriage is a threat, since it produces offspring with less Jewish identity.[4] An old Jewish quip asks, "What do you call the grandchildren of intermarried Jews? Christians." (Actually, not all will be Christians, since some will withdraw from *all* religious identification.)

The people most concerned about Jewish identity are leaders of Jewish institutions worrying about their institutions' futures. To them the most important facet is that the person feels a sense of kinship with the Jewish *community* and is committed to supporting it. Daniel Gordis explains:

> The huge synagogues that American Jews built in the 1950s and 1960s often search desperately for members and lack worshipers. National organizations like the American Jewish Committee, American Jewish Congress, B'nai B'rith, and Hadassah now struggle to survive. And they worry that younger generations of American Jews do not join them as their parents and grandparents once did. (1997:85)

Jews in America have some similarities to Catholics. Both have a history of immigration to a predominantly Protestant country, so both have had long experience as outsiders. Both came at about the same time, and the international diversity of both groups was similar. Today both communities have integrated into American life so fully that members of neither feel like outsiders; certainly Catholics do not. Some Jews continue to worry about anti-Semitism, even though it has greatly subsided in America during the twentieth century. Anti-Catholicism in America abated after the 1950s and 1960s, and today it is rarely heard.

Jewish history included much more discontinuity during the past two centuries than Catholic history. In Europe prior to the time of Napoleon, Jews in countries like Germany, Poland, and France were forced to live separate from other citizens, and they were usually seen by the rulers as separate nations, not just minority enclaves. Jews were prohibited from living in many sections of cities, from entering the majority of occupations, from studying in universities, from getting government jobs, and on and on. Thus when the events of nineteenth-century Europe offered Jews "emancipation," it was life-changing (Cohen 1983:18ff). And when in addition they had an opportunity to come to the United States, where they were treated as citizens with rights and privileges like anyone else, it was doubly life-changing.

Jews in Europe had been defined and regulated by outsiders, and as a result they grew to have strong Jewish identity. Everyone knew who was in, who was out, and what it meant to be a Jew. But not in America. Here Jews had plenty of opportunities, and in time they made incredible gains in wealth, status, and political power. In the American setting it is no wonder that young Jews ask "What is a Jew?" and "Why be a Jew?" Earlier, Jewish identity was externally imposed and unavoidable. But in America all the external limits and identifiers are absent. Today Jewish identity is no longer imposed from outside; every young person must choose it. Someone has commented that this gives new meaning to the notion of the "chosen people." In this respect the Jewish experience of the loss of externally imposed identity is similar to the Catholic experience.

Today the rate of interfaith marriage for Catholics is about the same as for Jews. The loss to the Catholic community via intermarriage is probably smaller (though we lack precise data) because Catholics work harder at evangelization and at welcoming non-Catholic spouses who are thinking about converting. Jewish rabbis, by contrast, are not much interested in converting non-Jewish spouses (Tobin 1999).

An important difference between Jews and Catholics is that the former have divided into separate denominations, while the latter have not. The principal Jewish denominations in the U.S. today are the Orthodox (about 6 percent of all Jews), the Conservative synagogues (about 40 percent), the Reformed synagogues (about 39 percent), and the Reconstructionists (about 2 percent). In addition, about 15 percent of American Jews have no denominational preference (Lazerwitz et al. 1998:40). The divisions into denominations resulted from the influence of modern American culture on the Jewish community. The overriding issue was the competing claims of the law of the Torah and traditional Jewish texts versus the norms of Western, liberal society. The Orthodox resolve such disputes in favor of Jewish law, the Conservative adopt a middle position, the Reform give precedence to the norms of liberal society and see the Jewish law as non-binding, and the Reconstructionists de-emphasize the supernatural in Judaism (Lazerwitz et al. 8ff).

Intermarriage varies greatly by denomination. In a large 1990 study of American Jews, intermarriage rates were 3 percent for Orthodox Jews, 37 percent for Conservatives, 53 percent for Reforms, and 72 percent for secular Jews who have no denominational affiliation (Kosmin et al. 1991). The more Americanized and assimilated the Jewish sub-group, the higher is the intermarriage. It is no mystery why the Orthodox intermarriage rate is so low. The Hasidic Jews (the most orthodox and sectarian group) have the lowest rate of all. This is because they live in their own neighborhoods; they teach their children Yiddish and Hebrew rather than English; they prohibit all use of television, radio, movies, newspapers, and computers; they do not let their girls work outside the home; they do not allow their children to attend college; they teach their children to be suspicious of gentiles and of non-Orthodox Jews; and they arrange marriages for their children by the time they are seventeen. The policy works. It also creates strong Hasidic identity among the children. But nobody recommends this as a guide for all Jews, since it would be impossible. Only a small minority of American Jews today would stand for these defensive strategies, and all the others would protest loudly and go their separate ways. Today the only viable option for mainstream Jews to encourage in-marriage is to make a U-turn from defensive to affirmative methods. Alan Dershowitz:

> The only way to maximize the likelihood of a Jewish marriage is to make Judaism and Jewish identity so central to the lives of Jewish children that it becomes unthinkable to give up something so important. Threats, guilt, and other traditional mechanisms for discouraging intermarriage and assimilation do not work. Indeed, they tend to backfire and turn the children away from Judaism. Intermarriage will continue; it will probably increase. We must learn how to deal with that reality in the most constructive manner possible. (1997:323)

How is this to be done? By education. Effective Jewish education is needed which displays all that is precious and inspiring in Jewish tradition.

Secular Jews

An important distinction in the Jewish discussion is between Judaism as a religion and Jewishness as ethnicity. Some Jews are believers in the religion and loyal practitioners of its rituals, while others are nonbelievers whose commitment is mainly to the tradition and the ethnic group. The latter group has grown and the former has shrunk in America in the last two decades (Wilder 1996:116). Persons committed only to ethics and tradition are commonly called "secular Jews." They typically argue that agnostically inclined Jews should feel no obligation to believe biblical teachings about God and God's law. Other Jews disagree, notably the Orthodox, who consider that anyone not keeping the laws, rituals, and dietary rules of the Torah out of faith in God is not a "real" Jew.

Is there a Catholic counterpart to a secular Jew? The closest thing is an "ethnic Catholic," that is, a person whose loyalty to Catholicism is a by-product of commitment to the ethnic group. In our study we found many of them, and we called them "contingent Catholics." Such people typically know little about church teachings, they have little faith in God, and they are not very interested in religion. Yet, as good Italian Americans or Mexican Americans or whatever, they say they are Catholic and they occasionally go to church as part of the total package. Our threefold typology of Catholics, outlined above, has a counterpart among Jews. Parish Catholics are similar to synagogue-active Jews, spiritual Catholics are similar to synagogue-inactive Jews, and contingent Catholics are similar to secular Jews.

Catholics have much to learn from the Jewish cacophony. Pressures on the Jewish community resemble pressures on American Catholics, and the twofold commitment of religion and ethnicity is similar. Probably most important is the Jewish debate over affirmative vs. negative efforts to maintain Jewish identity.

CHAPTER 9

Catholic Identity and Tradition

In chapter 8 we analyzed Catholic identity beginning with the individual. Here we work in the other direction—beginning with the Catholic tradition. This chapter has two main parts, first on core versus periphery and second on boundaries.

CORE VERSUS PERIPHERY

To this point we have talked about "Catholic" without further specification. Now we look more closely. If a young adult says he or she is Catholic, *what about* Catholicism? Here we look at the question of *what aspects* of Catholicism within its vast collection of teachings, rituals, devotions, and practices are the most important to him or her.

Catholicism includes an amazing collection of teachings, symbols, rituals, devotions, and practices which has grown up over the centuries. Some parts of the tradition are inspiring and life-giving, some are inscrutable, and some are obviously specific to some past epoch. All old religious traditions have this character. They all have their mystics, ascetics, seers, liberators, moralists, and scholars. A living tradition needs living interpreters to convey its vital teachings to today's devotees, and the devotees must somehow determine *to what* in the tradition they are most devoted. Catholic identity, like all aspects of identity, is the product of a constant process of experimentation, negotiation, and transformation.

In sum, all religious persons, including Catholics, must distinguish a core of their faith from its periphery. In Catholic theology this is labeled "the hierarchy of truths," which upholds some teachings as authoritative and central, and downplays others as less important.

Let us look at the situation in Judaism. Scholars have been faced endlessly with the question of what is really important:

> When Hillel was asked to transmit the core of the Torah to a skeptic in the time he could stand on one foot, the great scholar replied: "What is hateful to you, do not do to your neighbor; this is the whole Torah. The rest is commentary; go and study." Micah summarized God's demand of Jews thus: "Only to do justice, to love goodness, and to walk modestly with your God." Jeremiah quoted God as asking for "earnest devotion to Me," who delights in "kindness, justice and equity in the world." Akavya Ben Mahalalel, a first-century sage, had only three entries on his list: Torah; work; charity. (Dershowitz 1997:256)

New spiritual movements in any religion gain their power if they make new interpretations of tradition which are meaningful and empowering. Again, Judaism:

> All modernist Jewish social movements have sought to reconstruct Judaism so that it may comport with modern thought, culture, and social conditions. They all shared a "husk-and-kernel" imagery of traditional Judaism which divided traditional Jewish life into two spheres. One was defined as central, contemporary, and essential; the other was peripheral, outdated, and unnecessary. The husk was to be abandoned; the kernel was to be retained and recast. (Cohen 1983:27)

No one should see innovation and reformulation of the age-old Catholic tradition as something negative, as a product of compromise, surrender, or accommodation to the culture. This assumption has been held by some sociologists of religion, who interpreted any religious change as a response to modern society and who thus saw twentieth-century religious change as a rear-guard action to halt the decline of faith (Smith 1998:100). This interpretation is wrong. On the contrary, living religious traditions are constantly reformulating their teachings and identities. The apostle Paul labored to cast his Jewish-derived message in categories and in a language his Hellenistic world could understand. Thomas Aquinas recast the whole of Christian doctrine within the framework of Aristotelian philosophy, which was being rediscovered in his time. The task of rethinking religious tradition so as to give it new meaning and nourishing power is a requirement for its vitality.

Sociologist Michele Dillon stressed revitalization of tradition in her study of Catholics:

> It is evident that if the vibrancy of the tradition is to be sustained, each generation of Catholics must discover Catholicism by experiencing the rituals and knowing the multifaceted doctrine. (1999:253)

Pope John XXIII made a distinction between timeless truth and changing modes of thinking in his 1962 opening speech to the Second Vatican Council:

> It is necessary first of all that the Church should never depart from the sacred patrimony of truth received from the Fathers. But at the same time she must ever look to the present, to the new conditions and new forms of life introduced into the modern world which have opened new avenues to the Catholic apostolate. (*Documents* 1966:714)

A Catholic today finds it necessary to make choices: he or she must search for the essential core. The process, in reality, is the same as with assessing any other element of one's identity. The person will try out this and that, then will increase devotion to whatever proves to be nourishing and in turn ignore the rest. A young adult Catholic named Anna shared her feelings about the problem:

> A big problem for young Catholics is knowing what to accept and what to ignore. Nowhere in our education are there guidelines for

this! Nobody teaches us how to do this. We are on our own, and many people drop out of Church due to confusion or guilt—guilt for birth control, guilt for cohabitation, or guilt for homosexual acts. Why doesn't the Church teach us [what is core and what isn't]? The Church merely says that we need to follow all the rules. But we can't, and many people are alienated.

Anna went on to say that young Catholics today need guidance in weighing how essential various Church teachings are, for example, teachings about birth control. She believes that to obey all the teachings is impossible today. In our experience the majority of young adult Catholics agree with Anna that some Church teachings are in fact not workable and that Catholics today need guidance on what is essential and nonessential.

Anna has no qualms about being a "cafeteria Catholic." To her there is no alternative. We can sympathize with her feelings and we agree that some young Catholics feel undue guilt when they are criticized as being "cafeteria Catholics." We believe the term "cafeteria Catholic" should be removed from the research lexicon as being unduly freighted with theological assumptions. We are all, to some degree, cafeteria Catholics. All of us, willy-nilly, make choices, sometimes due to influences from family and friends, sometimes on our own.

Sophia Langone, whom we met in chapter 4, has the same feelings. She was opposed to Church teachings about birth control, divorce, and abortion, and she found no way of distinguishing these teachings from the rest of Catholic doctrine. She felt that if she dissented from these moral teachings, she could no longer attend Mass.

For myself, I feel hypocritical going to church and thinking all of these things I don't agree with, that we were taught or what supposedly are the beliefs now of the Catholics. I don't know how I would feel sitting there in the church. . . . My friends feel the same thing. If you go and you sit there, but then you don't agree with some of this, and then if you go with your family, you are like, "Oh boy, why am I here?"

Our interviews taught us that many young adults today have not learned to distinguish core and periphery, even though the generations growing up in the 1960s and 1970s knew how to do it and felt free to do so. To simplify a bit, the earlier generation found a way to dissent and stay. But the young today are not clear about how to think about essentials and nonessentials. They also talk differently about the Church. It is revealing that our interviewees did not use the concept "people of God" in reference to the Church.

At the present time the role of personal choices in American Catholicism in actual life is probably more important than at any time in the past. The feeling of entitlement to personal choice has entered Catholic life, as it were, by osmosis from modern American culture, and young Americans today feel an entitlement to follow their personal choices in life's big decisions. Christian Smith summarizes:

> For moderns—perhaps especially modern Americans—the ultimate criterion of identity and lifestyle validity is individual choice. It is by choosing a product, a mate, a lifestyle, or an identity that one makes it one's very own, personal, special, and meaningful—not "merely" something one inherits or assumes. (Smith 1998: 103)

The 1997 Survey on What Is Essential in Catholicism

What do young Catholics say about essentials versus unessentials in the faith? We commissioned a telephone survey of a national random sample of young adult Catholics to see what their choices would be. In October 1997 we hired Princeton Survey Research Associates to interview 701 self-described Catholics twenty to thirty-nine years old. Of them, 94 percent were raised Catholic, five percent were converted as adults, and one percent didn't know. Of the persons raised Catholic, 86 percent had been confirmed. Twenty-seven percent were Hispanic and 4 percent were black.

The survey asked, "I have some questions about different elements of the Catholic faith. Some of these elements of the faith may be more important to you than others. How essential is each element to YOUR vision of what the Catholic faith is?" The interviewer then read the first item and asked, "In your opinion is this essential to the faith, important but not essential, or not important to the faith today? If you are unaware that this is an element of the Catholic faith, please say so." Then the interview went through the total list of nineteen. To ensure fairness, the sequence of presentation of the elements was varied. Table 9.1 shows the results, and Figure 9.1 graphs the percent saying "essential."

The highest-ranked elements were the sacraments and special attention to helping the poor. They comprise four of the top five elements. The other one was devotion to Mary the Mother of God, which was ranked fourth. As expected, theologically central topics were ranked higher than topics related to the institutional church.[1]

What ranked low? The five lowest-ranked elements had to do with (1) specific moral teachings—the right of workers to unionize, teachings about the death penalty, and teachings about abortion, and (2) specific institutional rules—that only men can be priests and only celibate persons can be priests. Our research team did not include a question about birth control, since the official Church teachings about birth control are so widely ignored by young Catholics that we expected it would be ranked very low, and including it in the survey would be pointless.

To summarize Table 9.1: the elements seen as most essential to Catholicism are the sacraments and special attention to the poor of the world; moderately essential elements are the Church's present institutional arrangements; and least important are specific moral teachings and specific rules about the priesthood. The top-ranked elements are quite specific to Catholicism; of the top five, two pertain to the sacraments and one is on devotion to Mary the Mother of God (specific to Catholicism), while the other two are about serving the poor (found throughout Judaism and Christianity). If we look at the bottom-ranked elements, we see that all are elements specific to Catholicism and mostly to the institutional Catholic Church.[2]

Are young adults aware that all of these are parts of the Catholic faith? Not entirely. Two of the elements in the interview took a number of the respondents by surprise. Eighteen percent said they were unaware that the Church's support of the right of workers to unionize was part of Catholic social teachings. Nine percent said they were unaware that the teaching that Christ established the authority of bishops by choosing Peter was part of the faith.

TABLE 9.1

Nineteen Elements: How Essential (*in percents*)

	Essential to faith	Important but not essential	Not important to faith	Unaware is part of faith
Belief that God is present in the sacraments	65	27	3	2
Charitable efforts toward helping the poor	58	35	3	3
Belief that Christ is really present in the Eucharist	58	28	6	5
Devotion to Mary the Mother of God	53	33	7	4
Belief that God is present in a special way in the poor	52	33	7	5
Having religious orders of priests, sisters, brothers, and monks	48	38	9	3
Necessity of having a pope	48	34	11	5
Being a universal church throughout the world	45	33	13	5
Efforts toward eliminating social causes of poverty, such as unequal wages and discrimination	42	39	10	6
Teaching that Christ established the authority of bishops by choosing Peter to head the Church	42	33	12	9
Having a regular daily prayer life	41	43	11	3
Devotion to saints	41	42	10	4
Obligation to attend Mass once a week	37	45	14	2
Private confession to a priest	32	39	25	1
Teachings opposing abortion	31	34	25	6
Belief that priests must be celibate	27	25	39	5
Teachings opposing the death penalty	22	37	30	7
Belief that only men can be priests	17	25	47	7
Church's traditional support of the right of workers to unionize	14	33	30	18

Note: "No opinion" is not shown.

In Table 9.1 two items provide an important comparison—the second and the ninth. The second mentioned charity: "Charitable efforts toward helping the poor," and the ninth mentioned social action aimed at the structures of poverty: "Efforts toward eliminating the social causes of poverty, such as unequal wages and discrimination." As in all earlier research studies which compared charity with social reform efforts, the respondents here gave more support to charity. It is, to be sure, easier and less divisive.

Our research team expected that various subgroups of young Catholics would have distinctive views about what is essential to the faith, but our attempts to identify them largely failed. Not many differences appeared. The persons who were confirmed Catholic were no different from the others; men and women were not different; and educated and uneducated Catholics were not different. But we found that frequency of Mass attendance *was* a predictor of attitudes about what is essential. This occurred in an unexpected way: the regular Mass attenders rated *everything* more essential than the non-regular Mass attenders. It was not that they had some favorite elements which non-attenders ignored; it was merely that they considered everything as more essential. Why was this? Perhaps they felt a tinge of guilt at the prospect of rating some elements nonessential. Perhaps they were so committed to parish involvement that they felt little need to make distinctions. We are uncertain.

Latino Catholics differed from non-Latino Catholics on three items. The Latinos rated two items lower: "Belief that Christ is really present in the Eucharist" (48 percent essential vs. 63 percent) and "Belief that God is present in the sacraments" (54 percent essential vs. 70 percent). They rated one item higher: "Private confession to a priest" (42 percent vs. 26 percent). We checked to see if the Latino vs. non-Latino differences were explainable by the lower educational level of the Latinos. When we controlled for education we found that the relationships weakened but did not disappear, showing that education is a partial explanation.

We have never seen research on Catholics which asked questions like these. The results contain an important lesson for Church leadership about core and periphery. The perceived core is vital to know. Sociologists since Emile Durkheim have shown that objects, ideas, or symbols in which people are heavily committed, and in which they

FIGURE 9.1

How essential is each of these elements to *your* vision of what the Catholic faith is? (percent saying "essential to the faith") Catholics 20–39.

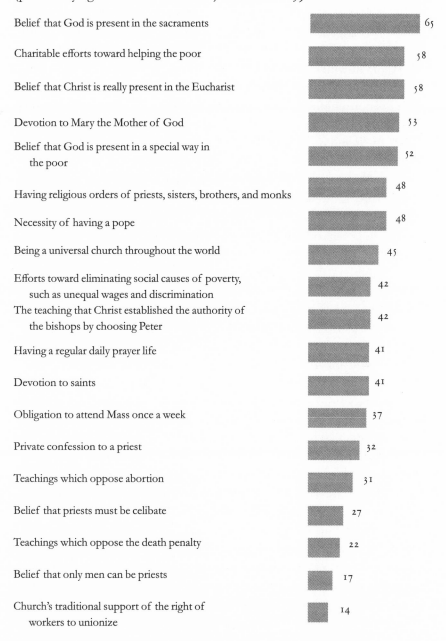

Belief that God is present in the sacraments	65
Charitable efforts toward helping the poor	58
Belief that Christ is really present in the Eucharist	58
Devotion to Mary the Mother of God	53
Belief that God is present in a special way in the poor	52
Having religious orders of priests, sisters, brothers, and monks	48
Necessity of having a pope	48
Being a universal church throughout the world	45
Efforts toward eliminating social causes of poverty, such as unequal wages and discrimination	42
The teaching that Christ established the authority of the bishops by choosing Peter	42
Having a regular daily prayer life	41
Devotion to saints	41
Obligation to attend Mass once a week	37
Private confession to a priest	32
Teachings which oppose abortion	31
Belief that priests must be celibate	27
Teachings which oppose the death penalty	22
Belief that only men can be priests	17
Church's traditional support of the right of workers to unionize	14

have personal investment, serve as fixed points anchoring their lives. These objects are sacred and untouchable. Nobody would even *think* about changing them—even while the interpretation of the object's significance may be in process of being recast. If due to some calamity, such as, for example, conquest by an invading army, the core sacred entities *are* changed, this is destructive of the people's morale, vision, and health. Supremely sacred objects are the core of identity. By contrast, elements in which people have no investment can be changed, especially if by making the change the central commitments are somehow defended, strengthened, or solidified. In short: in the opinion of young adults, the items at the top of Figure 9.1 must be maintained inviolate, while the items at the bottom may be adjusted with little consequence if there is reason to do so.

Here is an example which explains the principle, albeit on a topic a bit dated. A parish we know had a music committee which proposed using guitars in worship. Choice of musical instruments in worship would appear to be a good example of a peripheral element in Catholicism. It is an issue which one would think should be decided solely on factors such as local musical taste. But it was not peripheral for all the members. A faction of the laity was offended and angered, since to them having guitars represented a loss of something spiritual and sacred. To them, organ music was traditional and essential, not at all peripheral. This instance alerts us that what the theological leaders say about core and periphery may not equal what various lay persons say. Empirical research is needed so that the leadership is informed about people's thinking.

The 1997 Princeton survey allows us to take stock of what young laity think is the core of the Catholic faith and what is not. How can we interpret the pattern in Table 9.1? Do they make a distinction in their rankings between elements specific to Catholicism and other elements belonging to Christianity generally? Not really. Do they make a distinction between the Catholic faith and the institutional Catholic Church? Again, not really. Many specific rules of the Church (concerning, for example, priests) are deemed to be peripheral more than core, but one crucial part of institutional church life—the sacraments—is unquestionably core. Do they make a distinction between personal religion and religion as a part of life in a community? Not very clearly. The findings are not easily interpreted, and more research is needed.

This research has an implication regarding diversity in religious life. One should expect, in normal life, that individuals will vary somewhat in their views about the Catholic faith. Also one should expect that encouraging members to exert some choice in their Catholicism will result in a better fit for everyone, in the aggregate, and thus in an overall strengthening of Catholic commitment. It follows that diversity and choice is salutary for religious commitment, and this includes choices of devotions, groups, and parishes.[3]

CATHOLIC BOUNDARIES

All groups need boundaries. Boundaries strengthen collective identity by creating distinctions between members and nonmembers. Members of any group know who they are partly by knowing who they are not.[4] Collective identities depend heavily on contrast and negation, that is, on definitions contrasting "us" and "not-us," and they require symbolic markers separating those who belong from those who do not. Constructing and maintaining the definitions and boundaries is called "identity work" by social psychologists (Hogg 1992). It is one of the tasks of leadership.

The Function of Boundaries

A subjective sense of boundary is needed to define a group's identity. This is a sociological axiom clearly demonstrated in anthropological studies of primitive societies. All such societies have a strong group boundary which defines "us" versus "not-us." Primitive societies always define outsiders as somehow inferior, subhuman, even bordering on the animal (Schreiter 1985:64ff). Also, political wisdom has it that every nation or alliance of nations needs an external enemy to maintain unity. A group without boundaries will find that its members are troubled by questions about how they are different from outsiders and whether maintenance of the group really matters.[5]

Without doubt Catholic boundaries are important. A Catholicism without boundaries would have a character of "everything is included" or "anything goes," which does not provide identity at all; it leads to weakened faith. Let us look at a different religious denomination. In the United Methodist Church a recent task force studying its "identity crisis" said "One of the most serious problems for United Methodism is the perception that there are no theological norms, no bounds beyond which it is impossible to go and still be a Methodist" (Campbell 1995).

Group boundaries are difficult to maintain in modern industrial society, since both official boundaries and subjective boundaries are weakening. Today a European or American person may live anywhere he or she wishes, may marry anyone or not marry at all, and may freely experiment with groups and religions other than his or her own. The person carries no tribal identity, and in the United States a large portion of the population carry little ethnic identity either. The tendency in American popular discourse since the 1960s has been to assail boundaries within the society as being too confining and oppressive. The values of modern higher education promote cross-cultural study and travel in hopes that the experiences will increase tolerance, understanding, and goodwill. Today middle-class parents shell out thousands of dollars so that their children can travel overseas. Every self-respecting university promotes foreign and cross-cultural studies. The opposite values are opposed by our cultural leaders—such as living within group boundaries, making no contact with outsiders, and keeping up negative evaluation of the outer world.

A basic change occurred in American attitudes in the direction of ecumenical goodwill during the latter twentieth century. Polemics of Protestants against Catholics virtually ceased after the 1960s (Coalter et al. 1996:9).[6] External pressures on Catholicism, which fortified Catholic subjective boundaries earlier in the century, fell away. Today the sense of boundaries needs to be consciously taught.

The formation of Catholic identity, or for that matter any religious identity, today is partly a task of strengthening subjective boundaries. The problem for religious communities is that sociological boundaries and definitions have weakened. Few groups are defined externally through social barriers, as, for example, Jews were in premodern Europe. Now each group needs to strengthen the identity of its members through education, training, and personal experiences.

Two Kinds of Boundaries

Group boundaries are of two kinds: official and subjective. Official boundaries are dictated by legislators and leaders, while subjective boundaries are those understood and accepted by members. The two may or may not match. Two denominations or two tribes may establish an official delimiter between them, but some of the members may not take the delimiter seriously and may even derogate it as an annoyance. Interfaith or interracial couples in the dating stage can be totally aware that a boundary separates them, but if they don't accept the boundary's rationale, they will ignore it or even attack it.

The distinction between official and subjective boundaries is one example of a common sociological distinction between official rules and popular attitudes.[7] A government may proclaim a rule or law, but if popular sentiment does not accept it, the rule becomes unenforceable, irrelevant, and, in the course of time, a scandal. As scholars of jurisprudence know, a law has no chance of being enforceable unless the majority of the persons affected by the law accept it as legitimate and reasonable. The experience of lawlessness in the United States during prohibition demonstrates what happens when this is absent. The situation is the same with setting group boundaries: if a proclaimed boundary diverges too far from the current commitments of members, it will soon prove to be unworkable and even damaging.

Catholicism, like other communities, has both official and subjective boundaries. It has official boundaries, written by the Magisterium and set forth in canon law and other documents, between it and other religions. They exist officially, but are they accepted subjectively? This is an empirical question. Catholics have varying views. At one extreme, some Catholics are devoutly committed to the Catholic Church and reject all other religions, while at the other extreme a portion say that a dozen Christian denominations including Catholicism are basically all the same, and the boundaries are mere irritants.

Attitudes about Boundaries

Some empirical research has been done. Surveys have asked how many Catholics accept various boundary markers defining what is a "good

TABLE 9.2
Percent of Catholics Saying That You
Can Be a Good Catholic Without:

	Percent "Yes"
Without going to church every Sunday	77
Without obeying the Church hierarchy's teaching regarding birth control	72
Without their marriage being approved by the Catholic Church	68
Without obeying the Church hierarchy's teaching regarding divorce and remarriage	65
Without donating time or money to help the parish	60
Without donating time or money to help the poor	56
Without obeying the Church hierarchy's teaching regarding abortion	53
Without believing that in the Mass, the bread and wine actually become the body and blood of Jesus	38
Without believing that Jesus physically rose from the dead	23

Source: Hoge 1999: 12.

Catholic." A 1999 Gallup survey asked a national sample of self-described Catholics if a person could be a good Catholic *without* engaging in a variety of behaviors required or enjoined by the Church. Table 9.2 shows the percentages saying "yes."

These questions measure lay feelings about the boundaries around what is a "good Catholic." The majority of Catholics rejected all the boundary definitions except the last two, which were about doctrinal beliefs. This indicates that Catholics take doctrinal boundaries more seriously than boundaries defined by specific moral teachings or obligations to the institutional church. The 1999 survey included all Catholics, but when we looked solely at young adult Catholics the pattern was similar, except that the percent saying "yes" was always a bit higher. This poll is only partly pertinent to our discussion of Catholic boundaries, since it asked about "good Catholics," not "Catholics" in any juridical sense, and it does not include assessment of feelings about other religions. But it gives us good information about how Catholics feel about boundaries.

In our 1997 nationwide poll of Catholics twenty to thirty-nine we asked whether in their opinion two boundary-defining Catholic rules could be changed. See Table 9.3.

These two rules constitute official boundaries around the Catholic Mass and sacraments. The young adults had diverse opinions about how unchangeable the rules are, yet the majority accepted them. The first rule in the table (about non-Catholics participating in Eucharist) was considered the more crucial of the two. These two are a sample of dozens of rules forming the official boundary around Catholicism.

TABLE 9.3

Today there are some people calling for changes in some Catholic rules. Please tell me if you think each is a rule that could be changed, or is this something that the Catholic Church should never change. If you have never heard of the rule, please say so. (*in percents*)

	Should never be changed	*Could be changed*	*Never heard of rule*	*Don't know*
The rule that non-Catholics should not be allowed to partake in the Eucharist.	45	36	13	6
The rule that lay persons and non-Catholics are not allowed to preach the homily or sermon during Mass.	39	37	18	6

Our survey also asked about what distinguished Catholics from Protestants. See Table 9.4.

Again we found very mixed attitudes among the young adults. Almost half found few differences between Catholics and Protestants. The greatest level of agreement in the table (and a very small majority) is where 55 percent said that the Catholic Church demands more of its members than other Christian churches do. The only conclusion we can draw is that about half of the young adult Catholics today find the Catholic-Protestant boundary to be unimportant.

Tolerance Zone and Personal Comfort Zone

To understand subjective boundaries between religions, we need to make another distinction. Hoge, Johnson, and Luidens, in their analysis of how Protestants define religious boundaries, found it necessary to distinguish two zones which exist consciously in everyone's mind—the "tolerance zone" and the "personal comfort zone." The tolerance zone is broad. It includes any religion considered by a person to be acceptable for *anyone* to choose. The personal comfort zone (which is much smaller) contains only the ones people might consider *for themselves* (Hoge et al. 1994: 120). These researchers found that for most mainline Protestants, the tolerance zone contains all religious groups seen as morally responsible, including Judaism, all Christian groups except cults, and the major portions of other world religions. The only groups outside of the tolerance zone are cults which deny freedoms to their members and religious movements suspected of criminal behavior, oppression, fraud, or violence.

The personal comfort zone for most mainline Protestants includes the major denominations, such as Methodists, Presbyterians, Episcopalians, and Lutherans. Most of the Protestants Hoge and his colleagues interviewed thought that distinctions among these mainline denominations were unimportant. An example is the view expressed by a forty-one-year-old Presbyterian professional man:

When I was growing up in the fifties and sixties, I don't think there was a dime's worth of difference among Presbyterians, Methodists, or Episcopalians in terms of the way theology impacted on the

TABLE 9.4

Here are three statements about the Catholic religion. Please tell me if you strongly agree, moderately agree, moderately disagree, or strongly disagree. (*in percents*)

	Strongly or mod. agree	Don't know	Strongly or mod. disagree
The Catholic Church is more faithful to the will of Christ than other Christian churches.	43	7	50
In their main beliefs, Catholics today are essentially no different than Protestants.	48	12	40
The Catholic Church demands more of its members than do other Christian churches.	55	6	39

people. If you get the ministers and priests together, they could have World War III arguing about issues that nobody cares about. But as far as most people are concerned, they're really interchangeable. And I don't think there is any particular value in having a Presbyterian heritage or ethos or way of doing things. (Hoge et al.: 120)

Most of the persons interviewed in the Protestant study saw the mainline denominations as being essentially the same, but they believed in a boundary *around* the group of denominations. For these persons, religious groups outside the personal comfort zone were (among others) the Baptists, fundamentalists, Pentecostals, and Catholics. They said that they would not feel comfortable in those churches. Of course there was wide variation in these attitudes. The researchers concluded from the Protestant interviews that tolerance and respect for other religions are growing among young adults—thus enlarging the tolerance zone. The personal comfort zone does not seem to be changing.

The distinction between tolerance zone and personal comfort zone clarifies a research finding which several investigators have found baffling. These researchers found that Americans express great tolerance for many religious groups and a remarkable degree of relativism in their beliefs as to whether groups other than their own also possess truth, yet these attitudes do not seem to affect their commitment to their own churches. A belief in religious relativism does not seem to lead, as the researchers expected, to an opinion that differences between denominations or churches do not matter. That is, a respect for others (a wider tolerance zone) does not diminish one's commitment to one's own church.

This finding calls into question the earlier theory propounded by Peter Berger (1967), saying that inherited religious traditions are inherently precarious and subject to destruction by the corrosive forces accompanying modernization: mainly cultural pluralism, means-ends rationality, mass media communications, a sense of moral relativity, and the rise of the secular state. In Berger's view, religious faith cannot be sustained in a social situation in which the traditional communities are bombarded by points of view which challenge the received faith and lead to attitudes of relativity both in truth and morals. Berger argued that the experience of cultural pluralism, when introduced into any traditional community by mass media, extensive travel, college education in secular schools, and sustained contact with members of other religions, would corrode their faith and lead them to relativism.

Yet sociological studies testing Berger's theory in America have not found what was expected. On the contrary, religious faith has thrived in modern American society, and not just in secluded enclaves such as mountain villages, but in the midst of the most pluralistic, secular cultural centers. One explanation is that the situation in modern America emphasizes personal choice rather than obedience to received tradition, and hence believers do not feel dependent on broad cultural support as they form their own religious commitments. For example, the fundamentalists studied by Nancy Ammerman (1987) were well aware of cultural pluralism and the assumptions of the secular portions of American culture, yet this did not weaken their faith. Whereas some intellectuals may expect that the pluralism of modern America would neutralize traditional religious faith, in reality it is not happening.

Americans, even the most cosmopolitan, are accustomed to cultural pluralism and develop their own religious commitments as a response to it; their religious faith does not depend on a belief that the faith is given and natural in the nature of things. Christian Smith concludes, based on a major study of evangelicals: "There is little reason to believe, therefore, that the modern necessity of having to choose one's own religion makes that religion any less real, powerful, or meaningful to modern believers" (1998:104).

Michele Dillon says the same, based on her study of Catholics: "As other studies have documented, the availability of religious and other options does not undercut the conviction with which individual choices are made" (1999:244).

In our survey of confirmands we found no noteworthy relationship between the belief in religious relativism and belief in Catholic doctrines, as discussed in chapter 4. Also the belief in religious relativism was not associated with frequency of church attendance. Our findings, added to those of other investigators, call into question the assumption that a belief in religious relativism endangers Christian faith. Logically it would appear to do so, but the reality of American life seems to be that it does not.

The Principal Boundaries of Catholic Identity

Catholicism today has clear official boundaries, stated in terms of sacraments of initiation, ordination, excommunication, and rules of discipline. How about subjective boundaries perceived by members? With a little simplification we can say that Catholicism has four subjective boundaries—the boundary with mainline Protestantism, the boundary with evangelical Protestantism, the boundary with secularism, and the boundary with popular religion. Anyone concerned with Catholic identity today must analyze each of the four.

The boundary with mainline Protestantism is a low barrier, and it is gradually sinking lower. Subjectively it is felt by many Catholics as unimportant. The reason is that Catholicism as practiced in America is not much different from some Protestant denominations such as Lutherans and Episcopalians. In our interviews, persons who crossed this boundary typically said something like this: "Well, the churches are different, but the differences aren't that great when you get down to it, and after all, we're all worshiping the same God, just in different ways. So denomination really doesn't matter." This boundary is most likely to be crossed by middle-class Catholics and by non-Latinos more than Latinos. Mainline Protestantism is in Catholics' tolerance zone but not in the personal comfort zone of the majority.

The boundary with evangelical Protestantism is a higher barrier for most Catholics, but not all. Due to the similarity of Protestant Pentecostals to Catholic Charismatics, devotees of both groups find it easy to traverse the boundary in either direction. We have read dozens of articles about the loss of Catholic Latinos to Latino Protestant Pentecostal groups, and our own sample contains a number of such persons. Evangelical Protestantism is in most Catholics' tolerance zone, and it is in the personal comfort zone of a small number.

The boundary with secularism is different. It is a matter of religious authority more generally, and it is basically a boundary between a life of faith versus a life based on science and skepticism. The boundary with secularism is also a problem for mainline Protestants and other religious groups in close contact with the secular culture. Secularists in America tend to be individualistic about religious truth, saying that religion is (usually) worthwhile, but no claims about church authority or scriptural authority can be taken seriously. Secularists are typically tolerant of religious differences, and they are first and foremost intent on maintaining religious freedom in the society. It is uncommon that secularists are opposed to any of the Christian churches, but they are strongly opposed to any government action which even so much as implies favoritism of religion over non-religion. Rather, they see religion as a private matter governed by personal choice and preference, to be treated by government and industry the same as clubs for preservation of cultural heritage. Secularists can readily be church members, especially in churches having no claims to doctrinal authority, such as Unitarians or Ethical Culturists. To them religious commitments and religious choices are okay; there is no problem unless the commitments impinge on other people or claim universal obligation.

The boundary with popular religion is a different kind, almost the opposite of the boundary with secularism. It distinguishes Catholicism from "pre-Catholic" beliefs and rituals which have hung on for years in spite of official church rejection. Lippy, in his book on popular religion, defines it:

> There is a central zone of religious symbols, values, and beliefs . . . that comprises the totality of religion in a culture. But what is held in common may not receive systematic articulation or even rational justification by the religious elite of any one tradition, let alone by the ordinary people of a culture. As individuals draw on this central zone and on subsidiary zones, they erect for themselves worlds of meaning, they create identities for themselves, they engage in the age-old task of religion by finding a way to make sense out of their lives. (1994:10)

Popular religion, in one form or other, is widespread in America, and its pervasiveness presents a problem to religious leaders as to whether they should accept or reject it. But there is no escaping it. Religion as actually lived out in any culture is a mixture of the official and the unofficial. In middle-class America today, popular religion is found in the beliefs in angels, the hundreds of spiritual therapies available on all sides, the faith healers (including Latino *curanderos*), TV hucksters, the traffic in astrology and omens, the New Age books, even the glitz of Christmas. Latino Catholicism incorporates more popular religion than non-Latino Catholicism, and a debate rages today as to how much it should accept and encourage (see Espin 1994).

Of the four boundaries, which is the one most often crossed? It is a question no one can answer. The third and fourth boundaries (with secular individualism and with popular religion) have no clear demarcation, institutional or otherwise, and they really resemble a broad grey belt rather than a distinct boundary as such. People can cross both of them while remaining Catholics by the official definition, and in the Protestant baby boomer studies the researchers found many who were members of Protestant churches but held secular relativistic beliefs. Had these people crossed a boundary, or did no boundary exist? Given the trends in American culture, we expect more and more young adult Catholics to explore the boundaries and cross some of them.[8]

The Dysfunction of Boundaries

Group boundaries are functional for some purposes, as we have argued, yet they are dysfunctional for others. They are functional for uniting in-groups but dysfunctional for uniting the larger society. Boundaries around exclusive clubs or societies, for example, exclude everyone else. High-status groups such as yacht clubs put up barriers around themselves so that very few outsiders can join; this enhances the status of the in-group, but it causes tension between it and the larger society.

Group boundaries are dysfunctional for unification of the larger society and creation of a wider identity. Sociological studies of building new nations furnish plenty of examples. Newly independent governments, such as in Nigeria or Sri Lanka, wish to end inter-ethnic strife and to build a new identity of nationhood, but ethnic identities and traditional boundaries stand in the way. To build a nation out of separate tribes requires a period of time having improved communications, rising levels of trust, and establishment of new institutions transcending old boundaries.

For the Catholic Church the biggest boundary issue is the question of ecumenism. While strong boundaries to the Catholic Church can strengthen subjective identity, they may at the same time weaken ecumenical attitudes. We have arrived at a central theological issue: if Catholic identity and ecumenism cannot both be increased simultaneously, which should take priority over the other? Embedded here is a prior empirical question, namely, can Catholic identity and ecumenism *both* be increased? Or do they exist in a fixed-sum relationship so that in general as one strengthens the other inevitably weakens? Put differently, do religious groups with strong identities and boundaries discourage ecumenical goodwill and cooperation? We have heard theoretical arguments stating that the answer is *yes*, and other arguments that it is *no*. Some assert that having a strong Catholic identity frees and empowers Catholics to reach out to others. Others disagree, saying that sustained ecumenical contacts inevitably cause Catholics to see Catholic distinctiveness as less important.

The available empirical research on the question is not consistent enough to be conclusive. One repeated finding is that ecumenical attitudes are relatively stronger among Christians with the least traditional beliefs (Stark and Glock 1968, Kelley 1972, Iannaccone 1994); this is not totally pertinent, since our concern is with denominational identity, not traditional beliefs. Another finding is that laity who have switched denominations report relatively weaker denominational identity, and congregations with high numbers of switchers are less concerned about denominational identity (Ammerman 2000). A third finding, noted earlier, is that relativism and church commitment are not strongly associated either way in surveys of lay persons (J. Kelly 1979, Smith 1998). The empirical research thus indicates that among Christians stronger denominational identity is at least weakly associated with less ecumenical commitments. In some studies the relationship is very weak. The research does not support the proposition that stronger Catholic identity will produce *stronger* ecumenism.

We have arrived at a dilemma, and more theological and empirical study is needed. From what we know, it seems to be difficult in present-day cultural reality to achieve both stronger Catholic identity and stronger ecumenism.

The discussion of ecumenism is sensitive in Catholicism as well as in other denominations. Present-day culture puts pressure on all groups to express respect for other denominations and to offer cooperation leading to future union. At the same time, institutional pressures pull in the opposite direction. Institutional leaders responsible for churches, seminaries, schools, and institutions of specific denominations worry about specific denominational identity of the young. Who, they ask, will support our churches and schools? Who will feel loyalty to our specific tradition and give us the financial help we will need? These concerns pull in an anti-ecumenical direction, and the result of the opposing forces is a confusion of empty phrases and mixed signals. Not only theological statements, but specific institutional commitments, influence what the churches do. Church leaders need to see clearly the conflicting forces behind the discussions of Catholic identity and ecumenism.

CHAPTER 10

·⟨⟨◦⟩⟩·

Conclusion

· · · ·

In the first nine chapters of this book we have reported our research findings and our first-level interpretations. We have tried to show how our study contributes to a better understanding of young adult Catholics today. In this final chapter we capsulize these findings and add our own reflections in a broader discussion of the future of Catholicism in America. These reflections are drawn from the rich experiences we have had in undertaking this research. We have learned a lot and thought a lot. We do not claim that the personal reactions in this final chapter are above dispute, but we believe they offer themes that will benefit all levels of the Church concerned with ministry to young adult Catholics.

First we will synthesize the research findings in chapters 2 through 9 by describing five problematic issues facing the Church. Then, in the last portion of this chapter, we will report the main recommendations to church leaders made by the young adults we interviewed and add our own recommendations.

YOUNG ADULT CATHOLICS TODAY

Catholic Vitality

There are positive signs of young adult Catholic vitality today. Most young adults like being Catholic and cannot imagine themselves being anything other than Catholic. The overwhelming majority see the sacraments and devotion to Mary as essential to the Catholic faith. Some want to play a more active role in the life of the Church. Most consider themselves spiritual, pray regularly, and support the Church's social mission. Their sense of Catholicism is not a depoliticized or socially retreatist faith.

Young adult Catholics differ from mainline Protestants in that they (especially Latinos) have a stronger ethnic identity, a stronger identification with their church, and a more basic feeling that Catholicism is the "real thing." They see Catholicism as the oldest and most central expression of Christianity, in continuity with the apostolic tradition and hallowed by the ages. Catholics seem to have a "glue" that Protestants do not have. They see Catholicism as a basic part of their being. In spite of beliefs and practices that are sometimes divergent, they remain "Catholic." (This also makes the Catholic Church more difficult to manage, since many dissidents refuse to leave.) Many young adult Catholics also take pride in the global dimensions of Catholicism and in the media visibility of a pope whose personal integrity and firmness on moral and ethical questions are admired and respected even when not always followed personally.

Alongside these positive signs, however, we also find the following areas of concern in light of our research experiences.

Institutional Affiliation

Our study confirms previous social science findings that many young adult Catholics have a weaker and more tentative affiliation with the institutional church than previous generations (McNamara 1992, Davidson et al. 1997, D'Antonio 1996). We emphasize four things in this regard: First, young adults differ from older, baby-boomer Catholics. They are not as alienated from the Church and its teachings as some observers have asserted (Ludwig 1995) and not as alienated as many older baby boomers. Like baby boomers, young adults have beliefs and practices at odds with certain Church doctrines. Some see elements of Catholic life as arbitrary, irrelevant, and out of touch with reality. Others feel that being Catholic produces a constraint on their desire to explore, investigate, and experiment. And where many seek a church of community, they often encounter one of hierarchy. As we noted earlier, ten percent have left Catholicism. Tension exists regarding the role of women in the Church and around issues related to marriage, divorce, sexuality, and the desire for more democratic structures.

Most young adult Catholics today, however, are not angry at the Church. They are simply distanced from it. Their knowledge, understanding, and familiarity with the tradition are limited and hollow. They are less interested in the institutional church and its rules. Their affiliation is more tentative. A percentage of young adults are searching, looking for new moorings, and desiring to know more about the tradition. These persons want to negotiate their relationship with an institution that has not caught their imagination or about which they have faint or ambiguous feelings.

Second, what is noteworthy—and different from the mainline Protestant experience—is that in spite of this weaker institutional connection, the majority of young adult Catholics "like being Catholic," can't imagine themselves "being anything other than Catholic," and continue to identify themselves as Catholic. This tendency to identify positively with Catholicism stems from social inertia, ethnic factors (especially among Latinos), and from the fact that many persons simply like more aspects of Catholicism (e.g., its universalism, sacramentalism, social justice agenda) than they dislike. Their Catholic loyalty also springs from a conviction that the individual can define Catholicism on his or her own terms independent of church authority.

Third, this loose affiliation with institutional Catholicism can be understood from what individuals construed as core and peripheral to Catholic identity. As in the Davidson study (1997), our data suggests that young adult Catholics hold certain foundational issues (divinity of Christ, Resurrection, Incarnation, Trinity) as core. However, while obviously central to Christianity, these doctrines are not specific to Catholicism.[1]

In our Princeton poll, four of the six factors rated "most essential" to Catholic identity were distinctively Catholic: belief that God is present in the sacraments; belief that Christ is really present in the Eucharist; devotion to Mary the Mother of God; and having religious orders of priests, sisters, brothers, and monks. The problem, however, is that these factors (along with the more general doctrines of the divinity of Christ, etc.) are increasingly taken as *sufficient* indicators of Catholic identity independent of issues of ecclesiology. This is problematic because

while a distinct Catholic identity includes these beliefs, it also includes—
as theologians assert and Vatican II affirmed—that core to Catholicism
is a sense of the unique role of the institutional church in salvation, the
primacy of the papacy, the role of the Church's teaching authority, and
the importance of sacramentalism (including the sacramental nature of
the Church itself). However, our data show that significant numbers of
young adult Catholics today no longer see the Roman Catholic Church
as unique or essential, the pope as necessary, the Church's structures as
important, or tradition as a source of objective truth. Their actual connection with the Church's sacramentalism is also limited.

A fourth point relating to the weakening commitment to the institutional church is that this problem is not unique to Catholics. It is not
exclusively a failure of leadership. It is part of the larger alienation
from *all* authoritative institutions that is taking place in all American religious communities. Martin Marty reports:

> Whereas once inherited loyalties to a particular ecclesiastical tradi-
> tion—for example, Catholic, Quaker, Orthodox, Jewish—prevailed,
> increasingly, people have come to adopt a more arbitrary, pick-and-
> choose approach to communal expression of faith. An individual
> chooses a spiritual trajectory and then, so long as and insofar as an
> institution matches his or her course, the institution is favored—
> often only to be later dropped more casually than it might have been
> in the past. (1993:14)

While Marty's statement is somewhat extreme to fit all American
Catholics today, it illustrates the changes we have found. This pick-and-
choose dynamic is also expressed in the limited commitment of young
adults to reforming the Church. Many live as self-defined Catholics
without depending on the Church for normative authority to do so.

Identity Coherence

Many young adult Catholics have a difficult time articulating a coherent
sense of Catholic identity. While they like being Catholic, they are not
sure what is distinctive about Catholicism. They believe it is relatively
harder to be a Catholic, but often have little sense of the tradition as

something "handed down," or of what Catholic heritage actually means. They are not well-versed in Catholicism's core narratives. As a result, their sense of the boundaries of Catholicism is diffused and ambiguous. This is why we find the concept of "communal Catholic" (Greeley 1976:1–20) (sometimes "cultural Catholic") of limited value in describing today's young adults. We spoke with many persons who were communal Catholics as described by Greeley: people who like being Catholic and are at ease with their Catholicism, but who have limited interest in the institutional church and do not listen very seriously to what it has to say. But Greeley's notion of a "communal Catholic" includes people with some lived familiarity with Catholicism as a culture system. The life experiences of communal Catholics were shaped to some degree by a church they experienced as a distinct community and cultural tradition (Greeley 1976:11). Post–Vatican II young adult Catholics are not communal Catholics in this regard; they are the *product* of communal Catholicism. Their knowledge of the language and symbolism of the tradition is more limited and sparse—as is their experience of Catholicism as a tight-knit culture system. In addition, few have overlapping memberships in Catholic organizations or associations that would reinforce a distinctive Catholic identity. And few are old enough to have constructed a new Catholic identity over and against the old one, as did many pre–Vatican II and baby-boomer Catholics.

Even as late as the 1960s, young American Catholics would know about Catholic holy days, devotions, ritual rules and (in general) Church moral teachings. Today knowledge about all of these is weaker. We find less self-consciousness of Catholics as being Catholic, less acquaintance with the tradition and its history and symbols, and a weaker Catholic identity. The question of whether young adults are communal Catholics is more complicated in the case of Latinos because of the residual strength of the ethnic factor as a carrier of Catholic religiosity and because Latinos are generally a less assimilated population than Euro-American Catholics.[2]

Waning Centrality

A third factor affecting the future of Catholicism among young adults is the centrality of Catholic identity. As explained in chapter 8, centrality refers to the importance an individual attaches to something relative to other parts of his or her personal identity.

Much of the research on post-conciliar Catholicism has focused on gaps between Church teaching and what Catholics actually believe and do (McNamara 1992, Seidler and Meyer 1989, D'Antonio 1996). These findings are problematic enough. In addition, a more serious issue is the decline in the centrality of Catholic institutional identity. That is, it matters less to large numbers of young adult Catholics if they are Catholic in any institutional or communal sense, in spite of affirmations about liking to be Catholic in more subjective terms. In this respect, the largest type in our sample are young adult Catholics who are all but indistinguishable from mainline Protestants. These spiritual and contingent Catholics (chapter 8) give selective assent to Church teachings. They have no interest or desire to change other people's beliefs. They eschew biblical fundamentalism. They do not make the official language of the Church their own, nor are they consistently involved in the Church's institutional or sacramental life. They are disinclined to adhere to institutional clear-cut standards for being a "good Catholic," and they want a more egalitarian, participatory, and democratic Church. They are "good enough" Catholics (Wilkes 1996) who view Roman Catholicism as one denomination among others of equal legitimacy. As various respondents put it, being Catholic is largely a matter of "accident" (birth) and/or incidental to the individual's relationship with Jesus Christ. The Catholic Church is just "another human institution" that was "constructed by people." Accordingly, God "doesn't care" about religious (denominational) identity. Since one institution cannot have the whole truth, the Roman Catholic Church is merely "one guide" among others, or simply a "different way of looking at something." Nor is any religion false "as long as you get out of it what you need." In addition, where there is truth in religion, it is only true for the individual.

A thirty-year-old mother of two summarized these views in remarking that it was "definitely false" that Catholicism was "the one true religion." However for her,

It's *my* one true religion. For me and for my children and my family, it's the one true church. But to God, I don't think it's the one true church. . . . I really believe that the God that I think is out there isn't really going to care that the Episcopalians do things one way and Catholics do it another way. . . . There's no one true race that is right for God, and religionwise, it's the same thing.

Spiritual and contingent Catholics also separate spirituality and religion and see little essential connection between the two. They are a large part of the 64 percent who believe one can be a good Catholic without going to Mass.

The loss of Catholic distinctiveness and the waning centrality of Catholic identity are also evident in the area of social concerns. While young adult Catholics rank social justice high in what they regard as essential to their faith, the relationship between social justice and a *specifically Catholic identity* remains unclear. While they see social justice as core to Catholic identity, most individuals interpret this to mean approaching social problems with acts of charity. As we observed in chapter 7, many young adult Catholics espouse a religion-as-ethics-and-social-justice perspective similar to what Ammerman has identified as operative among mainline "Golden Rule Christians" (Ammerman 1997). This conflation of religion with ethics and disconnectedness from specific Catholic social teachings implicitly demotes a distinct Catholic identity. Being religious simply means being a "good person," doing good deeds. That is what counts. If the relationship between social justice and a *specifically Catholic identity* were more immediate to young adult Catholics, their perspective might be more concerned with structural approaches, aggregate effects, power, and institutional systems—in keeping with contemporary Church teachings regarding social justice.

Also, as we saw in chapter 7, the multiple sources of spirituality today, the weakening of traditional Catholic devotionalism, the diminishing of the saints as models of spiritual virtuosi, and the emergence of evangelical Catholicism that minimizes the mediational role of the Church are further expressions of a weakening centrality of Catholic identity.

Religious Individualism

As we observed in chapter 1, religious individualism is a revered part of the American experience. It has had a deep impact on contemporary Catholicism. In the view of many young adult Catholics, being a

Catholic is less a matter of core identity and more a matter of personal option. These young adults are more individualistic than ever, less inclined to go to church or to confession out of a sense of obligation, less convinced that the Church's rules are God's rules, less convinced that the Church's structures are divinely ordained or necessary, and more inclined to make choices for themselves. Young adults feel at home in the Church insofar as they appropriate it on their own terms.

It is nothing new that people self-construct a religious identity. All personal and cultural identities (gender, sexual, class, ethnic) are self-constructed partly consciously and partly unconsciously, to some degree or another in accordance with changing historical and life experiences (Hall 1992). And as noted in chapter 8, self-identity as choice derives from the openness of social life today, the pluralization of contexts of action, and the non-foundational diversity of authorities in our culture (Giddens 1991). It is also an expression of a more liberal attitude toward conscience and institutional loyalty and to the possibility offered by class and ethnic fluidity.

The impetus toward a self-constructed religious identity on the part of many young adult Catholics stands in contrast to Catholic identity in the past. Although we reject any sense of a Golden Age of dutiful, harmonious, and monolithic pre–Vatican II Catholicism, we believe that Catholicism's outsider status in nineteenth- and early twentieth-century America, the general compliance with hierarchical and institutional norms, and the formative power of Catholic culture in its religious and ethnic dimensions powerfully shaped Catholic identity. This was true more so for Euro-American than for Latino Catholics. Indeed, the consolidation of hierarchical and institutional control over the construction of Catholic identity (via Vatican I, 1869–1870, the condemnation of Americanism by Leo XIII, 1899, and the opposition to modernism by Pius X, 1907) is one of the central *leitmotifs* of American Catholic history in the hundred years prior to Vatican II. Today, by contrast, personal choice and religious individualism are dominant. It is this situation—the transformation of Catholicism from a perceived church of obligation and obedience to a church of choice—that has accelerated dramatically in the wake of the 1960s.

Our study shows that this transformation continues today, driven in large part by an exaggerated individualism. Catholic identity construction in America's culture of choice is much less amenable to ecclesiastical control and institutional influence than in the past. Church authorities cannot force compliance behavior outside the narrow parameters of institutional life; nor is the control of deviance as effective as in the past. Church authority among Catholics, as among many other denominations, is more symbolic of group identity than practical (Demerath and Williams 1992). Many young adults simply construct "being Catholic" on their own terms—which also explains, in part, why many see no compelling reason to leave the Church. For many young adults, Catholicism is not so much a binding community of discipleship as a cultural tool kit of symbolic religion/spiritual wares from which it is possible to construct a personal religious identity.

As our data indicate, this self-constructed Catholic identity does not greatly affect foundational doctrines regarding God, Mary, and the sacraments, but it is problematic for core elements of Catholic ecclesiology emphasizing the role of the Church as a hierarchically structured community essential to God's plan for salvation.

On the positive side, this shift toward individual religious identity construction allows a greater assumption of responsibility within the tradition by many young adult Catholics for their religious and spiritual life—as mandated by Vatican II. In market economy terms, many young adults have moved from a Catholicism of spiritual consumers to one of spiritual producers. This approach implicitly expresses the Church's collective self-understanding (the "people of God") and explains, in part, the waning of clerical and hierarchical hegemony. It suggests that there are various legitimate ways of being Catholic in the post-conciliar Church, and that diverse Catholics are choosing styles that are relevant to them.

Among a small but sophisticated number of young adult Catholics, Catholic identity is derived from a knowledge of the faith wherein the individual claims the authority to interpret doctrine and autonomy to offer doctrinally grounded reasons in favor of change. These individuals empower themselves to critique Church doctrine and practice as an act of Catholic identity itself (see Dillon 1999). We make this point as a way of emphasizing that the shift in Catholic identity construction is not driven exclusively by the culture of individualism and choice but can be legitimated within the tradition itself, as Dillon has argued. This comes from Catholicism's emphasis on the dignity of the human person, respect for the primacy of informed conscience, the compatibility of faith and reason, the necessity of an enculturated Catholic identity, and emphasis on an embodied and living faith relevant to its cultural context.

Commitment Mechanisms

A final issue concerns the lack of commitment among young adult Catholics. The recent work by Christian Smith and his colleagues on American evangelicals (1998) is relevant in this regard. The central issue raised in Smith's study is the question of what factors contribute to a strong and vital religious tradition in our cultural context?

Smith argues that evangelicalism is a strong tradition today because its adherents have a strong commitment to basic evangelical beliefs. Evangelicals see the faith as highly salient to their lives, and they have a robust church participation and a strong commitment to mission. Evangelicalism is a form of "engaged orthodoxy"; it avoids the twin Achilles' heels of complete enculturation and accommodation (the problem of mainline Protestantism) on the one hand, or a defensive separatism (the problem of fundamentalism) on the other.

If we apply Smith's criteria for religious vitality to contemporary Catholicism, the results are not encouraging. On most of the factors that make evangelicals strong, young adult Catholics are weak. On the issue of belief, surveys point to substantial gaps between certain Church teachings and the views of rank and file Catholics. As we suggested earlier, we do not find the Catholics-share-core-beliefs-so-all-is-well argument convincing with regard to a distinct Catholic identity. Unlike their evangelical counterparts, the current generation of young adult Catholics is less theologically orthodox than their elders.

On the matter of faith group participation, Catholics are also weaker. Most young adult Catholics do not have high participation rates in parish life or programs. In our one-on-one interviews, many complained of the absence of meaningful young adult ministries and activities in their parishes—even where they evaluated parishes high on spiritual satisfaction issues. Most make limited investments of time and energy in parish life. As we have shown, the spirituality of most young adult Catholics remains parish-formed or parish-bound only in limited ways. Few participate in small faith communities within their parishes. Nor is the social network of many young adults predominantly Catholic. As a result, many lack a sense of solidarity with other Catholics or faith group participation that would reinforce a strong Catholic identity. Finally, few young adult Catholics indicated that they spend any significant amount of time proselytizing or sharing their faith with others; this is not a Catholic "thing." Thus, aside from activities associated with involvement with church social justice initiatives and intermittent use of the sacraments, it is not clear what, behaviorally speaking, constitutes commitment to the mission of the Church among many young adults. Institutional Catholicism is simply not of central importance in their lives.

Discussion

For many young adults, Catholic identity is weak, focused outside the institutional church, and only moderately central to their lives. We have talked about the reasons for this, both internal to the Church and external. The implications are portentous. If many young adults now believe that Catholicism is simply another denomination, that it "doesn't really matter that much whether you're Catholic or not," that there is nothing unique or distinctive about Catholicism, or that all that really counts is a generic Christian lifestyle, Catholicism's institutional vitality, public witness, and capacity to retain its young are in jeopardy. Weak centrality of Catholic identity will have a snowballing effect on a variety of behaviors adversely impacting the Church, including moral choices, choices about marriage partners, child rearing practices, Catholic schooling, church attendance, and others. Nor can one assume that marriage will continue to serve as a port of entry (or reentry) into the Church. Young adult Catholics are waiting later to marry and therefore experiencing longer periods of disconnectedness from the Church. As we noted in chapter 3, 50 percent of all non-Latino Catholic marriages are now to non-Catholics. Increasing numbers of Catholics marrying non-Catholics are doing so outside the Church (Davidson 1999). These trends will have serious ramifications for the future. As we saw in chapter 8, contemporary Judaism's experience with high interfaith marriage rates is instructive in this regard, and something to which Catholics should pay attention.

We pointed out earlier that one of the primary reasons Catholic identity was stronger in the past was because of prejudice, discrimination, and the perception of Catholics as outsiders in American society. These conditions contributed to Catholicism's internal solidarity following the axiom: external threat, internal cohesion. Today, however, Catholics, like Jews, find themselves in the ironic situation of having their institutional identity and coherence threatened more by tolerance than intolerance. Factors that contributed to a strong Catholic identity in the past (anti-Catholicism, anti-modernism, anti-communism) have not been supplanted by new ones that put the Church in the right amount of tension and oppositional engagement with mainstream society in a way that would contribute to the tradition's vitality. Where the potential for tension exists in relation to official doctrines, elements of these teachings (e.g., sexual issues) often lack credibility among young adults, in part because the doctrines do not evolve out of dialogue with them or because young adults seek principles and not rules in this regard (Morris 1997:430). Many of the old symbols of Catholicism that have been weakened or discarded have yet to be reappropriated or replaced by viable new ones.

What Type of Catholic Identity?

Any consideration of how to enhance Catholic identity presupposes a definition of what is essential to Catholic identity. Who defines that identity and in accordance with what theological and canonical norms? What kind of identity will Catholics find energizing and what kind of identity will facilitate the Church's cultural witness? In sociological terms, these questions raise the perennial issue of whether Catholicism will be a church or a sect. What degree of tension and attendant boundary strictness should characterize Catholic identity today?

Without a distinct sense of identity, a shared faith and some common elements of religious life relating to sacraments, discipleship, community, tradition, and hierarchy, there is no Catholicism.

Tension relating to these characteristics exists internally in disputes over the boundaries with popular religion. Externally, tensions exist in Catholicism's boundary relationship with non-Catholic Christians and with secular American society. However, tension with the boundaries of popular religion and non-Catholic Christian traditions has loosened in the wake of Vatican II: in the case of popular religion, through Catholicism's embrace of pluralism and enculturation; in the non-Catholic churches with ecumenism and recognition of the ecclesial validity of other traditions. These boundaries are now more diffuse and less tension-laden than in the past. In contrast, Catholicism's boundaries with secular society are more distinct and tension-laden, especially in reference to values in American society (materialism, greed, narcissism, consumerism, individualism, sexual morality, instrumental rationality) that are at variance with official Catholic social teachings.

If Catholic leadership moves toward higher boundary maintenance in regard to non-Catholic Christian identity, as suggested by the recent Vatican declaration *Dominus Iesus,* (On the Unicity and Salvific Universality of Jesus Christ and the Church), or in regard to popular religion, a risk is created of implicitly denigrating the ecumenical movement and the new pluralism (enculturation) in the Church. However, the potential clearly exists for higher tension with secular culture that will accentuate Catholic boundaries and work to some degree to strengthen Catholic identity. Such an approach need not contravene Catholicism's mission to transform the culture in positive and inclusive ways.

What Did Young Adult Catholics Recommend?

In our personal interviews and focus groups with young adults we included this question: "What if you had a chance to address the American Catholic bishops, and they wanted to hear from young people? What if you were selected to speak for the young people today? What would you say?"

Four main themes emerged in their recommendations. Not everyone agreed, and we do not present divergent views here, but we heard several main themes.

First, the Church should be more welcoming to young adults, more willing to address issues and concerns relevant to them, and more willing to listen seriously to them instead of issuing authoritative pronouncements or asserting that issues are closed and cannot be discussed. Interviewees often expressed the conviction that their views and concerns were not taken seriously by those in leadership positions in the Church, that fiat rather than dialogue is the norm.

Second, ways must be provided in which young adults can become meaningfully involved in Church life. This is especially important with regard to parishes. Many of our respondents complained of the absence of programs and activities for them, and especially for single adults in parish settings. While the needs of adolescents, of married couples, and other groups were met, ministries and programs geared toward young adults were absent.

Third, they asked for more adult education, especially more study of Scripture and knowledge of the faith and its traditions. The latter issue relates to everything from knowledge of Vatican II, to a better understanding of social justice teachings of the Church, and to how these teachings connect with Catholicism's ecclesial and theological foundations.

Fourth, it is clear that a number of Church teachings, particularly in the realm of human sexuality, erode the Church's credibility among many young adult Catholics. Our interviewees repeatedly mentioned birth control, homosexuality, women's place in the church, married priests, and women priests as the most problematic issues.

OUR RECOMMENDATIONS

In light of the findings of our study of young adult Catholics, we present the following recommendations:

I. A "Preferential Option" for Young Adult Catholics[3]

Church leadership should initiate a "preferential option" for young adult Catholics. This means a dynamic and sustained program of outreach. Resources and energies should be directed toward helping young adult Catholics feel wanted, welcomed, and actively involved in the life of the Church. Liturgy is a primary venue for such outreach, since it is the institutional context in which the vast majority of young adults experience themselves as church.

Efforts must be made to develop programs, ministries, and initiatives in parish settings specifically directed toward young adults. We cannot assume that programs which are efficacious for adolescents or married couples are also appropriate for young adults. Respondents told us that while some young adult groups in parishes were faith sharing, others were little more than de facto singles groups. Parish and diocesan levels should highlight particular issues for young adult subpopulations—single life, marriage, work, elderly parents, children, ethics, social justice, sexuality, and the problems of relationships and intimacy—and develop appropriate programs.

Young adult Catholics who have stopped practicing the faith and who return to the Church on the occasion of a wedding or funeral or baptism should not be greeted with the question, "Are you registered in this parish?" Such queries will drive many away. Parishes must be pastorally sensitive. Young adult Catholics need to be welcomed and encouraged to reconnect with the Church before being confronted with juridical requirements.

II. Promote a Distinct Catholic Identity

Young adult Catholics should be imbued with a positive and distinct sense of Catholic identity. While ecumenical dialogues should continue, Catholic religious educators should re-focus some of their energies on promoting the distinctiveness of Catholic identity. This means responding creatively to the yearning for core values and faith content alluded to by young adults. As one respondent cogently put it: "I want to be a Catholic. I want to know more about my faith. I want some substance."

We concur with Davidson et al. (1997) in bringing attention to the negative consequences of religious education that emphasizes ecumenism and a common Christian heritage but that fails to include a focus on what is distinctive about being Catholic and why that matters. To continue this generic orientation will have detrimental consequences to the future of the Church.

III. Build Catholic Identity in a Positive Way

Emphasizing the distinctiveness of Catholic identity can be done in a positive way. Approaches based on exhortations to obligation, duty, or obedience will likely fall on deaf ears. Such exhortations may produce momentary compliance, but not the positive motivations which are foundational to spiritual growth. We believe that the strengthening of Catholic identity will necessitate more than a simplistic emphasis on learning traditional doctrinal positions. Young adult Catholics must be listened to and consulted regarding their own values and concerns and in terms of their own visions of what they can contribute to the future of the Church. The type of positive approach associated with the Rite of Christian Initiation of Adults (RCIA) with its emphasis on mentoring, deliberation, community, and discipleship is a helpful model in this respect. Church efforts to enforce boundaries, rules, regulations that are not widely accepted by those involved are likely to be counterproductive. Nor will Catholic identity be strengthened by disparaging what is different about non-Catholic traditions.

In chapter 8 we saw that elements in the total identity structure achieve more or less centrality and more or less influence over other elements, depending on how well they serve the total spiritual needs of the person. Elements of an individual's personal identity which enhance self-confidence will grow in importance. The reverse is also true. If church leadership wants to strengthen Catholic identity, what is done must contribute to the confidence and strength of the individual believer. People who experience empowerment through the Church will become stronger Catholics.

We believe that Catholic distinctiveness can be accentuated in positive ways by special emphasis on three dimensions of Church life: (a) sacramentalism (especially the Mass as noted below), (b) the struggle for peace and justice in a fashion that builds on distinct elements of contemporary Catholic theology, and (c) the centrality of community and promotion of the common good. All three are distinctive to Catholic identity. And they are values and orientations that counter many of the prevailing forces of materialism, secularism, and exaggerated individualism in American society. They can be affirmed in ways that are not excessively sectarian or that imply a return to pre-conciliar

Catholic triumphalism. In combination, they can provide a healthy and necessary tension with society conducive to the commitment of young adult Catholics to the Church and its mission.

IV. The Liturgical Context

The Mass has a compelling power in the spiritual life of many young adult Catholics. Although not the only context, it is one in which many Catholics encounter community, the Word, and the sacred. The solidarity expressed in the liturgy is fundamental to Catholic identity and critical to a generation of young adults concerned with problems of intimacy and caring. Parish resources of every type should be poured into enhancing the quality (spiritual, communal, aesthetic) of liturgies. Young adult Catholics must not experience liturgies as outdated, mechanical, irrelevant, or boring. This means that young adults themselves must be *meaningfully integrated into the liturgical act in a variety of ministerial roles*. Appropriate room must also be made in the liturgy for musical, artistic, and cultural forms with which young adults can resonate.

V. Build Better Community

The communal nature of the Church should be emphasized. More attention and energy should be given to building community in parish life. But the liturgy alone should not bear the entire burden of this task. Small faith communities and action-oriented projects will also be important.

This community building initiative should not be construed simply as bringing back young adults who are feeling isolated and in need of social support and intimacy. Young adults must see that community is an ecclesial dimension that is intrinsic to their Catholic identity, that being Catholic is not something simply between the individual and God or even between the individual and the hierarchy representing God; they must feel it is a communally mediated and articulated identity.

VI. Better Young Adult Religious Education

There is a critical need for credible and relevant adult religious education. As one young adult observed, "The Church settles for less than the best." This is especially true in three areas: Bible study, Vatican II theology, and the Church's social teachings.

Disputation over Vatican II's meaning and implementation is an undercurrent in the contemporary Church. It is still a source of polarization and division among Catholics. Yet many young adult Catholics know little about the Council, its deliberations, documents, and theology, and what is known is piecemeal and superficial. A respondent's comment that "My understanding of the Vatican Council was it made the Latin Mass become non-Latin and . . . changed some of the words in prayers," is emblematic of the situation. This is a serious lacuna in Catholic life today—as is the general lack of knowledge regarding Catholic social teachings since Vatican II.

The three areas—Bible, Vatican II, and social teachings—need to be addressed with programs that are intellectually edifying and challenging, action-oriented, community building, and helpful for integrating young adults into parish life. Many young adult Catholics are eager for instruction in their faith and will prove receptive to initiatives.

The problem of Catholic young adult religious education transcends the issues of content and the development of curriculum; it is also one of pedagogy. Greater attention needs to be given to the training of teachers and those involved in young adult education. Resources should be directed to these ends, along with the development of youth groups, community service projects, and retreat programs which implement these teachings.

VII. Better Marriage Preparation

One of the most challenging areas in our interviews was the relationship of the respondents to people of other faith traditions. The topic is broad and includes everything from knowledge of Catholicism and of non-Catholic traditions to feelings of vulnerability and insecurity in defending Catholicism.

Attention should be paid to the specific needs of the large number of Catholics who are marrying people of other faiths or no faith—and, where possible, to the increasing number who are marrying outside of the Church. The rate of interfaith marriage is high. Parishes need to develop programming that will address interfaith questions ranging from basic information about different faiths to issues of child rearing, religious education, and holiday celebrations.

VIII. More Recruitment to the Priesthood, Religious Life, and Lay Ministry

The low percentage (15 percent) of young adults who indicated that they had been encouraged to think about a vocation to the religious life or priesthood is a cause of concern. We believe that efforts to empower the laity to take their rightful place in the Church do not preclude the invitation of some young adults to consider religious life and priesthood and the education of all young adults about the various ways of life in the Church. Young adult Catholics should be brought to greater awareness of ministry in service in the Church and the world. This involves both encouragement for new forms of non-ordained lay ministry and encouragement for priests, brothers, and sisters. One young woman told us that she had never been taught about the option of religious life. She said her religious education focused on "Christian lifestyles" but only presented the options of marriage and single life.

For those who were encouraged to think of a vocation to the priesthood and religious life, the encouragement came primarily from their family. Our findings suggest the Church should explore why more intensive recruitment does not come from within the priesthood and religious life itself.

Attention should also be paid to the vocation of lay ministry. While the Church often talks about the laity assuming more ministerial roles in the future, we found that very few young adults were employed in full-time work within the Church. Will lay ministers in the Church continue to be found in older generations alone?

IX. Spirituality, Prayer, and Meditation

The Church needs to continue to teach young adults about its many rich and diverse sources of spiritual renewal. Efforts should be made to assist young adult Catholics in reappropriating specifically Catholic symbols and spiritual traditions. This is especially important in view of the fact that most of their spiritual seeking occurs within the tradition (chapter 7). This reappropriation will facilitate their sense of connectedness and continuity with Catholicism, even while these symbols and traditions are transformed in a new cultural and historical context. The Church's emphasis on prayer and meditation in conjunction with social action is also important.

We learned from our interviews that retreat experiences in particular are effective in the above respects. There should be more and a greater variety of retreat opportunities that are affordable, relevant, and offered at convenient times and locations.

X. Young Adult Catholic Initiatives

The effort to incorporate young adults into a more meaningful experience of the life of the Church is not a one-way street. While persons in leadership positions in the Church have responsibilities in this regard, so do young adults themselves. Young adult Catholics should try to take the spiritual offerings and mission of the Church more seriously. This involves learning more about the Church and its rich intellectual tradition and investing more time in its institutional, sacramental, and liturgical life. Making the effort to get to know Catholics who are parish-connected will help reinforce the sense of community and solidarity essential to Catholic life. Peer relationship will also make a difference in encouraging Mass attendance and participation in small groups or parish service projects.

Conclusion

The Catholic Church in the United States is reconstituting itself. This is a dynamic process that is hardly new, but the tensions surrounding this process have been exacerbated by the speed, scope, and nature of change in the Church and society over the last half century. The Church in the United States has transformed from living in a hostile culture to living in an accommodating culture; from a church apart to a church included; from uniformity to diversity; and from a Church dominated by clergy to one in which laity share more leadership and authority.

Historically, Catholicism achieved a measure of success in keeping people and their descendants within a single Church largely through the pressures of minority status, the cultural affinities between ethic and religious identity, and the authority and discipline of its ecclesial structures. With few exceptions it did so without falling prey to formal schism, or to a divisive pluralism of subcultures and communities that negated its communal unity and doctrinal moorings. This situation has changed substantially by the end of the twentieth century.

As Catholics enter the new millennium, the Church's capacity to transform culture and to bear witness to the redeeming love of Christ will depend in large part on its institutional vitality. Some semblance of a distinct and coherent Catholic identity must be maintained. The young need to be successfully socialized into the tradition, and there should be some successful evangelization. The Church should also avoid the temptations of hyper-sectarianism on the one hand and anemic culture religion on the other. Tendencies that would reduce Catholicism to moralism and a social service agency at the expense of its sacramental, symbolic, and communal character must be resisted.

Realistically, many of the transformations of society that have created the new cultural situation cannot easily be changed by church leadership. As we have briefly stated, however, there are programmatic initiatives that can strengthen Catholic identity and loyalty among young adults.

In America's culture of exaggerated individualism, and in the context of pluralism, ecumenism, and Catholicism's loss of outsider status, the Church cannot function as a lazy monopoly (ignoring competition from others), simply assuming that the next generation of Catholics will remain Catholic in the old way or automatically return to the Church in keeping with life cycle patterns, or that it can be reached in the same way previous generations were reached. In the culture of choice, where compliance behavior cannot be forced, where lifestyles are adopted rather than handed down, where identity and boundaries are diffuse and polymorphous, and where the religious domain is similar to a pluralistic free market, Catholicism will need to present itself as distinct, vital, relevant, and worthwhile—as a living tradition of discipleship, community, and sacramental consciousness. The challenge for

Catholic leadership is to convince young adults that in such a climate, there is no reason to apologize or hesitate to take measures to promote the distinctiveness and value of Catholic identity. In light of the dictum that the demise of a religious tradition is not about the death of the old, but the failure to retain the young, we believe this is the agenda for the twenty-first century.

Appendix A

Methods Used in the Telephone Survey
And Personal Interviews

Pilot Study

In September 1994 we received a planning grant from the Lilly Endowment to undertake a pilot study. Our advisory committee recommended that we gather a sample of Latino Catholics and a sample of non-Latinos (that is, all other Catholics) who are twenty to thirty-nine years old and who were confirmed as adolescents.

In early 1995 we embarked on a pretest to see if a study of confirmands would be possible. We worked in eight parishes, four predominantly non-Latino and four predominantly Latino. The former were in the Washington D.C. area, and the latter were in Los Angeles, California; Tucson, Arizona; San Antonio, Texas; and Miami, Florida. We hired and trained bilingual research assistants to work in each Latino parish. We wish to thank Marcos Sanchez, Rosie Garcia, Otto Santa Ana, and Rev. Jorge Presmanes for their work.

We found that all parishes have good confirmation records, and we encountered no problem drawing random samples of names. The difficult problem was to locate the target persons and interview them by phone. We relied on paid helpers in each parish to find as many as possible. The parishes varied greatly in the percent of the target persons we could locate. In rural parishes we could locate more than in urban parishes, and in upper-income parishes we could locate many more than in working-class parishes. The worst situations were urban parishes with shifting population and few homeowners.

The difficulty in finding Latinos was similar to the difficulty in find-ing non-Latinos, and the level of cooperation by respondents was also similar. This encouraged us, since other researchers had told us that the Latino sample would be nearly impossible to gather.

How valid were the interview responses? Our Latino interviewers detected that some respondents tended to give responses which they thought were appropriate but not necessarily honest. In chatting with respondents after the interviews the interviewers found that some per-sons admitted giving too-favorable responses to our questions about the church. To estimate this bias we considered the idea of purchasing a Gallup poll alongside our own survey (but abandoned the idea due to cost). Also we convened a committee of Latino theologians and re-searchers to get advice.

To raise the percentage of confirmands found, we decided to hire a professional tracker to help locate the target persons.

Sampling Frame

We decided on a sample of 200 non-Latinos twenty to twenty-nine years old, 200 non-Latinos thirty to thirty-nine, 200 Latinos twenty to twenty-nine, and 200 Latinos thirty to thirty-nine, for a total of 800. We designed the non-Latino sample to include all ethnic groups, not just European whites, so we estimated how many Asians and African-Americans would be needed to have them represented proportionally in the sample.

Not all Catholic children are confirmed. Our sample could there-fore not be representative of *all* persons this age who grew up Catholic, but only those who were confirmed. What percentage were con-firmed during adolescence? We searched for reliable data on this question and found none. Thus we needed to rely on expert esti-mates, and we consulted fifteen experts on all nationalities of Catholics (veteran pastors, diocesan staff, and catechesis officials). The consensus estimate was that the percentage of Catholic children confirmed during adolescence in the 1980s (the median years of our sample) in the non-Latino portion of the Catholic community was between 60 and 70 percent, and in the Latino community between 30 and 40 percent.

Based on data from the United States Catholic Conference, we calculated that as of 1980 (near the midpoint of the confirmation years) three percent of Catholics were African-American and two percent were Asians or Pacific Islanders. Of non-Latino Catholics they would represent approximately 3.5 and 2.5 percent respectively.

We also needed to get a proper mix of nationalities in the Latino sample. U.S. census data for 1980 indicate the following origins of the Hispanic population: 59 percent Mexican, 14 percent Puerto Rican, 6 percent Cuban, and 21 percent other. We adopted these percentages as targets. From the *Official Catholic Directory* and U.S. census data we identified regional distributions of non-Latino and Latino Catholics in the nine U.S. census regions. The non-Latino sample was taken disproportionately from the Mid-Atlantic and East North Central regions (52 percent of the total), and the Latino sample was taken disproportionately from the West South Central, Mountain, and Pacific regions (67 percent of the total).

In each of the eight regions we chose about half of the sample dioceses for convenience (near our homes) and the other half by random chance. We wrote to the bishops of the desired dioceses, asking for permission to do the study. Three refused, requiring us to substitute neighboring dioceses. In New England our final sample diocese was in Massachusetts; in the Mid-Atlantic region we had two, in Pennsylvania and New York; in the Southeast we had two, in Virginia and Florida; in East North Central it was in Ohio; in West North Central it was in Kansas; in West South Central it was in Texas; in Mountain it was in New Mexico; and in Pacific we had two in California. Thus we worked in eleven dioceses in all.

Finding and Interviewing the Confirmands

After the bishops gave permission, we worked with chancery officials to select representative parishes for the study. We picked the correct percentage of urban, suburban, and rural parishes in each diocese, and we insisted that no parishes be specialized or unusual (for example, no campuses or vacation communities). All parishes were as typical as possible and representative of the diocese in income level. The parishes could not be selected entirely randomly because of the disinclination of some pastors to cooperate with research studies. In all, we worked in forty-four parishes.

After each pastor agreed to participate, we traveled to the parish, explained the study to the staff, and took random samples of names from the confirmation books. Based on the age of confirmation in that parish's past (usually at twelve to fourteen years), we selected names from the appropriate confirmation years (usually 1971 to 1991). We typically took between thirty and sixty names from each parish, but in five Latino parishes we took more.

The most difficult task was locating the confirmands today. Our search method was first to hire a person in each parish to find as many as possible, then to give the remaining names to a tracker using a nationwide phone list on CD-Rom and phoning people with the same surnames.

The difficulty in tracking the confirmands varied greatly from parish to parish. It was more difficult for Latinos than non-Latinos, and it was the most difficult in urban working-class neighborhoods. Once we found the address and telephone number of a target person, we sent the person a letter telling of the study and including a short letter from the pastor. Then we tried calling them as many as fifteen times before giving up.

Early in the process we noted that the Latino sample was more difficult, since the target persons were harder to find and to interview by phone. Therefore in five Latino parishes our interviewers went door to door, and this worked. Some respondents were more willing to talk to an interviewer in person than on the telephone. Also, halfway through the process we began offering $10 to Latinos for interviews. In a few places we experimented with offering $20.

For the Latino sample we hired bilingual interviewers locally so that the respondents could choose the language, and the interviewer's accent and local knowledge would put the respondents at ease. Most of the Latinos preferred English. Only 4 percent were interviewed entirely in Spanish, and another 5 or 10 percent were interviewed in English with additional explanations in Spanish by the interviewers.

We kept records on the percent of confirmands we were able to find and the percent we interviewed. We considered a person "found" if we got the correct phone number for the person. A person whose phone number turned out to be wrong was designated as not "found." A few persons had died, one or two were in jail, and several were out of the country. About fifty turned out to be too young or too old for the study, so we excused them. All ineligible names were removed before we calculated the percentage found.

In the non-Latino sample we succeeded in finding 74 percent of the target list, and of them we succeeded in interviewing 74 percent. Seven percent refused to be interviewed, and 19 percent were unreachable or impossible to schedule. In the Latino sample, we found 51 percent of the target list, and of them we interviewed 73 percent. Nine percent refused and 18 percent were unreachable or impossible to schedule. Our inability to interview persons once we found them was mainly because we could not reach them by phone or schedule an interview. Some were evasive. Outright refusals were infrequent.

Regional variations in success in the non-Latino sample were small; we had similar rates in all parts of the nation. But in the Latino sample the rates varied greatly from region to region. We had the highest rates of finding and interviewing people in the Midwest and West South Central. Our rates in California were somewhat lower, and in the greater New York City area they were much lower. The New York area was especially difficult because of the transiency of the Latino population, the large size of the urban parishes, and the difficulty in catching people at home. Many of the Latinos work long hours.

Biases in the Telephone Survey

What biases resulted, either due to our inability to interview some of the confirmands or our inability to get honest information? We are certain that the biases are greater in our Latino sample than in our non-Latino sample, since our success rate was lower with the Latinos.

We believe the bias in the non-Latino sample is small. Without doubt our final sample is a bit more educated and a bit more church-involved today than average, but the bias is not great. In the Latino sample the total bias is larger. We know of four specific biases.

(1) We have too many educated, too few uneducated persons. We noticed during the data collection process that educated persons were easier to locate and to interview. By contrast, people with only high

school education or less were harder to find and more hesitant to be interviewed. Certainly we did not get as high a percentage of them.

(2) We found many of the confirmands through local contacts and family connections. Thus we were disproportionately able to find people who had not moved out of town. Transient persons and transient families were very difficult to find. Thus we have a mild bias of too many local sedentary persons.

(3) Some Latinos were inclined to give us socially desirable responses rather than true opinions. Thus without doubt some social desirability bias exists in the Latino sample. All past researchers studying Hispanics and Latinos have reported the same problems in interviewing.[1] That is, some Latinos agree to be interviewed but mask their true feelings by saying they support social authorities (including the Church) more than is really true. They tend to show deference to authority. As a result, our sample is biased toward reporting higher levels of church involvement and more positive feelings than are really true.

(4) As noted earlier, a lower percentage of Latino children were confirmed than non-Latino children. This does not constitute a bias as such, but the reader should keep in mind that the list of Latino confirmands with which we started is more limited to children of active Catholic parents than is the case with the non-Latino list.

We were able to check yea-saying tendencies of non-Latinos and Latinos by comparing items stated in opposite directions, and we found more yea-saying by Latinos on both conservative and liberal theological and ecclesiological statements. An average of the differences on both kinds of statements revealed a yea-saying bias among Latinos about five percentage points higher than among the others.

Comparisons with Other Surveys

One way to estimate bias in our samples is to compare our responses with those in other surveys. Most helpful is a comparison with the nationwide phone survey of young Catholics which we commissioned in autumn 1997. It included self-identified Catholics twenty to thirty-nine years old, and it identified persons who had been confirmed earlier. It was nationwide, with weighted data, gathered by Princeton Survey Research Associates.

A second comparison is with the 1995 nationwide phone survey of Catholics commissioned by James Davidson and his colleagues, reported in the book *The Search for Common Ground* (1997). That survey interviewed self-identified Catholics of all ages in the U.S., and it weighted the data. We look at the responses of all persons who said they were raised as Catholics. See Table A.1.

We see that our sample reports similar levels of Mass attendance, Bible study participation, and prayer group participation. But it professes more loyalty to the Catholic Church than did the 1995 Davidson sample. For example, 13 percent more in our sample agreed that "There is something very special about being Catholic which you can't find in other religions"; 19 percent more agreed that "I cannot imagine myself being anything other than Catholic", and 9 percent more agreed that "The Catholic Church is the one true church." These differences are no doubt due to our sample, which included confirmands only.

Taped Interviews and Focus Groups

We decided to get seventy-five personal interviews from Catholic confirmands now twenty to thirty-nine years old. We selected persons who were convenient, not any random sample. The four research partners did most of the interviews, but we hired two Latino interviewers to do ten interviews to reduce biases. Most of the interviews were ninety minutes in length, recorded on tape.

We carried out seven focus groups with an average of seven persons in each. One involved only African Americans, and one involved only Latinos. They were audio-recorded.

TABLE A.1

Comparison of Three Surveys

	Our 1997 Confirmands*	1997 Confirmed	1995 Raised Catholic
In the last year, how often have you attended Mass on the average? Would you say once a week or more, about once a month, less often, or what? (in percents)			
Once a week or more	31	33	30
Two or three times a month	25	8	—
Once a month	12	26	—
Less than once a month, or never	32	32	—
In the last year or so, how often have you taken part in a Scripture study or a Scripture discussion class? Weekly.	6		4
How often have you attended a prayer group or faith sharing group? Weekly.	5		4
Strongly agree or agree:			
One can be a good Catholic without going to Mass.	64		74
The Church should stick to religion and not be involved in economic or political issues.	54		59
There is something very special about being Catholic which you can't find in other religions.	69		56
The Catholic Church is the one true church.	52		43
I could be just as happy in some other church; it wouldn't have to be Catholic.	22		51
Lay people are just as important a part of the Church as priests are.	89		86
I cannot imagine myself being anything other than Catholic.	76		56
Catholics have a duty to try to close the gap between the rich and the poor.	77		60

*Combined from our two samples: 80 percent Anglo and 20 percent Latino.

Appendix B

Detailed Results of the Phone Survey

TABLE B.1
Ethnicity of Samples (*in percents*)

	Non-Latinos	Latinos
Ireland	12	
Germany	20	
Poland	5	
Italy	6	
France, French Canada	2	
England, Scotland, Wales	3	
Czechoslovakia, Greece	4	
Spain		6
Mexico		58
Puerto Rico		13
Cuba		4
Dominican Republic		4
Other Central or South America	1	2
Philippines	1	
Other Asia	1	
African American	4	
Mixed European	36	
Latino mixture	11	
Other mixture	4	1
Don't know	3	2

TABLE B.2

Level of Formal Education Completed (*in percents*)

	Non-Latinos	Latinos
Less than a high school diploma	1	6
High school diploma	18	28
Attending vocational school or technical school, or finished vocational school	6	5
Some college but no B.A. or B.S. degree	21	37
In college now	4	5
B.A. or B.S. degree	41	17
In graduate or professional school now	2	1
Graduate or professional degree	8	2

TABLE B.3

Occupations (*in percents*)

	Non-Latinos	Latinos
Homemaker, housewife	9	7
Professor, college administrator	1	0
Teacher, counselor, school administrator	6	6
Physician, dentist	1	1
Helping profession: social worker, nurse	8	5
Engineer, computer expert, systems analyst	10	3
Manager, business owner, supervisor	13	10
Accountant, CPA, lawyer	5	3
Writer, musician, artist	1	1
Secretary, bank teller, clerical worker	9	16
Sales, real estate agent	7	8
Manual or skilled worker	19	28
Farmer	1	0
Full-time student (in 20–29 groups: 16% and 13%)	8	7
Unemployed	2	2
Other	2	6

TABLE B.4

Formally Joining Other Denominations (*in percents*)

	Non-Latinos	Latinos
Did you ever leave the Catholic Church and formally join another church or religious body? Yes	6	8
(For those saying yes:)		
What group did you join?		
Episcopalian	4	0
Lutheran	8	0
Methodist	8	6
Presbyterian	4	0
Baptist	12	16
Other Protestant (incl. Pentecostal, Mormon)	28	34
Non-denominational church	32	31
"Protestant" or "Christian," unspecified	0	13
Buddhist; eastern religion	4	0
How old were you at the time?		
21 or younger	29	22
22–27	38	51
28 or older	33	28
Mean age:	25.3	24.4
What was the main reason?		
Moved and switched to nearby church I liked	4	0
Influence of spouse, dating partner, or relative	36	22
New church had better preaching	0	3
New church had better programs for children	0	3
New church had better priest or minister	0	3
More emphasis on the Bible; better Bible teaching	16	34
New church had better worship or liturgy	12	6
Old church had too strict demands (divorce, marriage, annulment)	8	3
Conversion; I was born again	8	9
Other	16	16

TABLE B.5

Persons Who Became Inactive (*in percents*)

	Non-Latinos			Latinos		
	All	*20–29*	*30–39*	*All*	*20–29*	*30–39*
Percent who became inactive in church life, that is, for a time did not attend as often as 12 times a year.	59	52	65	62	61	64
(Of those ever inactive:) Age the inactivity began:						
15 or younger	9	10	8	16	17	15
16–19	47	55	43	34	46	23
20–23	26	28	25	29	28	30
24 or older	17	7	25	21	9	33
Mean age:	20.0	18.9	20.8	20.0	18.6	21.3
Reason for becoming inactive:						
Left home, moved, away from family	19	22	18	8	11	4
Conflict or disagreement with parents	3	2	4	2	2	1
Too busy, lack of interest, lazy	35	44	27	41	42	41
Bored	3	4	3	2	2	2
Disagreed w. church, felt alienated	12	15	11	7	7	6
Too busy with family or babies	1	1	1	4	5	4
Life-style in conflict with church	1	0	2	3	2	5
Doubted, questioned, lost faith	5	4	6	4	4	5
Conflict or disagreement with spouse	2	0	3	2	1	4
Didn't like the parish or priest; felt unwelcome	3	1	5	5	4	7
No more parental pressure	5	3	6	6	6	7
Influence of spouse or dating partner	2	2	2	2	2	3
Disliked liturgy or homilies	2	2	1	0	0	0
Other or don't know	7	3	11	14	14	13

TABLE B.6

Persons Who Became Active Again (*in percents*)

	Non-Latinos			Latinos		
	All	*20–29*	*30–39*	*All*	*20–29*	*30–39*
(Of all persons who went inactive:)						
Are you active now, that is, attending any church 12 times a year or more?						
Yes, active	48	42	54	45	38	53
(Of those active again:)						
At what age did you become active again?						
19 or younger	4	7	3	7	12	3
20–23	34	43	28	34	58	19
24–27	36	48	19	28	28	27
28–31	15	2	22	19	2	31
32 or older	11	0	17	12	0	21
Mean age	25.1	23.0	26.4	25.5	22.4	27.7
In what kind of church?						
Catholic	86	(Too few)*		86	(Too few)	
Episcopalian	4			0		
Lutheran	1			0		
Methodist	3			1		
Presbyterian	1			1		
Baptist	2			0		
Other Protestant, Mormon	2			5		
Non-denominational church	2			7		
Other or mixed	1			1		
Main reason you became active:						
Had children, thought of family, rel.ed.	24	(Too few)		21	(Too few)	
Settled down locally, psychosocially	15			7		
Spouse influenced me	5			5		
Other family or friends influenced me	5			8		
More time available now	4			7		
I found a good church, pastor, fellowship	6			3		
Returned to old church or community	5			4		
Spiritual need: felt empty or guilty	26			28		
Conversion experience: saved, born again	2			5		
Had marital problems, wanted to improve	1			1		
Other	5			7		
No particular reason; don't know	2			4		

*The subsample has too few cases to be reliable.

TABLE B.7

Scores on Five Attitude Scales

	Non-Latinos		Latinos	
	Mean	% High	Mean	% High
Traditional Doctrine Scale	4.38	70	4.60	79
Catholicism Only Scale	3.85	50	4.11	52
Relativism Scale	3.53	38	3.58	37
Catholic Duty Scale	4.07	62	4.29	69
Empowerment of Women and Laity Scale	4.07	61	4.14	62

TABLE B.8

Intercorrelations of the Attitude Scales

	Tradit. Doctrine	Cath. Only	Relativism	Catholic Duty
Total Sample:				
Traditional Doctrine				
Catholicism Only	.31			
Relativism	−.10	−.10		
Catholic Duty	.12	.12	.02	
Empowerment	.00	−.04	.08	.27
Non-Latinos:				
Traditional Doctrine				
Catholicism Only	.35			
Relativism	−.13	−.22		
Catholic Duty	.08	.09	.01	
Empowerment	−.01	−.09	.05	.32
Latinos:				
Traditional Doctrine				
Catholicism Only	.22			
Relativism	−.07	.01		
Catholic Duty	.14	.13	.02	
Empowerment	−.02	.01	.10	.22

Note: Correlations stronger than .11 are significant at .05.

CONSTRUCTION OF THE FIVE ATTITUDE SCALES

All scales were built using the combined non-Latino and Latino samples.

(1) Traditional Doctrine

This scale was constructed from three items. The first two were scored strongly agree = 5, moderately agree = 4, don't know = 3, moderately disagree = 2, and strongly disagree = 1:

Q45J. In Mass the bread and wine actually become the body and blood of Christ.
Q64C. I believe in a divine judgment after death where some shall be rewarded and others punished.

The third was scored differently:

Q65. What do you believe about Jesus Christ? He was God or the Son of God = 5; another religious leader, never actually lived, or other = 1; don't know = 3.

The scale score was the mean of the items if at least two were answered. Cronbach's alpha = .50, Mean = 4.49, s.d. = .74, N = 848. The mean was very high, since the respondents agreed on most items.

(2) Catholicism Only Scale

On this three-item scale, two were scored strongly agree = 5, moderately agree = 4, don't know = 3, moderately disagree = 2, and strongly disagree = 1. One item (Q45C) was scored in reverse.

Q45C. I could be just as happy in some other church; it wouldn't have to be Catholic. (Score reversed)
Q45D. There is something very special about being Catholic which you can't find in other religions.

Q45H. I cannot imagine myself being anything other than
Catholic.

These items were asked only of Catholic respondents. A high score indicates an attitude that the Catholic Church is special. The scale score
is the mean; no cases were lost due to missing data. Cronbach's alpha
= .72, Mean = 3.98, s.d. = .98, N = 762.

(3) Relativism Scale

This three-item scale expresses the belief that religious truth claims
are relative. The items were scored strongly agree = 5, moderately
agree = 4, don't know = 3, moderately disagree = 2, and strongly disagree = 1:

Q64B. All the major world religions are equally good ways of
helping a person find ultimate truth.
Q64F. All the great religions of the world are equally true and
good.
Q64H. In the realm of morality, the final authority about good
and bad is the individual's informed conscience.

The last of the three (Q64H) intercorrelated weakly with the first two;
its correlations were .28 with Q64B and .27 with Q64F. Q64B and
Q64F correlated at .58. These questions were asked of all respondents, not just Catholics. Cronbach's alpha = .65, Mean = 3.56, s.d. =
.99, N = 848.

(4) Catholic Duty Scale

This three-item scale was composed of items asked only of
Catholic respondents. The items were scored from 5 to 1 as in the last
scale. The items were:

Q45M. Catholics have a duty to try to end racism.
Q45N. Catholics have a duty to try to close the gap between the
rich and the poor.

Q45O. Catholics have a duty to try to live more simply in order to preserve the environment.

The scale score is the mean of the three. Cronbach's alpha = .74, Mean = 4.18, s.d.=.89, N = 762.

(5) Empowerment of Women and Laity Scale

This three-item scale expresses the attitude that women and laity should be given more power and participation in church life. The items were scored from 5 to 1 as in the earlier scale:

Q45I. It is important that the Catholic Church put more women in positions of leadership and authority.

Q45K. The Catholic Church should facilitate discussion and debate by the laity on doctrinal issues such as divorce, remarriage, and human sexuality.

Q45L. The Catholic Church should allow women greater participation in all ministries.

These items were asked only of Catholic respondents. The scale score is the mean of the three. Cronbach's alpha = .63, Mean = 4.11, s.d. = .79, N = 762.

Alternative Scoring of the Scales

For some purposes we needed to categorize scale scores as high or low, and we designated as "high" on each scale the respondents who agreed with all the items. For example, on the Catholicism Only Scale, we scored respondents "High" if they strongly or moderately agreed on all three items. (In the case of reversed Q45C, it would be those who strongly or moderately disagreed.)

Notes

INTRODUCTION

1. United States Catholic Conference, *Sons and Daughters of the Light: A Pastoral Plan for Ministry with Young Adults* (Washington, D.C.: U.S.C.C., 1997).

2. Tom W. Smith, "American Catholics," Report on General Social Survey Results, 1998 (University of Chicago: National Opinion Research Center, 1999).

3. Researchers differ in their estimates of the percentage of American Catholics who are Latinos. Our guess is about 30 percent. The Bureau of the Census says that the U.S. had about 28.5 million Latinos in 1998, and if we assume that 65 percent are Catholic, that would be 18.5 million, or 30 percent of all Catholics. See chapter 5 below.

CHAPTER 1: CATHOLICISM IN AMERICAN CULTURE

1. The continued polarization gave rise to the Common Ground Project, an initiative launched by the late Cardinal Joseph Bernardin of Chicago to ameliorate the left/right conflict among American Catholics.

CHAPTER 2. PAST RESEARCH ON YOUNG CATHOLICS

1. See Karl Mannheim, "The Problem of Generations," Ch. 7 in his *Essays on the Sociology of Knowledge* (New York: Oxford University Press, 1952), pp.276–320.

Also see Daniel Yankelovich, *New Rules: Searching for Fulfillment in a World Turned Upside Down* (New York: Random House, 1981); Philip Blumstein and Pepper Schwartz, *American Couples: Money, Work, Sex* (New York: Pocket Books, 1983); Landon Y. Jones, *Great Expectations: Americans and the Baby Boom Generation* (New York: Ballantine Books, 1980).

2. For earlier research see John N. Kotre, *The View from the Border: A Social-Psychological Study of Current Catholicism* (Chicago: Aldine Atherton, 1971); Joan L. Fee, Andrew M. Greeley, William C. McCready, and Teresa A. Sullivan, *Young Catholics: A Report to the Knights of Columbus* (Los Angeles: Sadlier, 1981); and E. Nancy McAuley and Moira Mathieson, *Faith without Form: Beliefs of Catholic Youth* (Kansas City: Sheed & Ward, 1986). An impressive study of parish life was done at Notre Dame; see Jim Castelli and Joseph Gremillion, *The Emerging Parish: The Notre Dame Study of Catholic Life since Vatican II* (San Francisco: Harper & Row, 1987).

3. In a recent article we compared our survey findings with Beaudoin's depiction of GenXers, and we stressed that typical Catholic young adults are more conventional in their religious lives and more concerned about relationships and family than Beaudoin tells us. See Mary Johnson, Dean Hoge, William Dinges, and Juan L. Gonzales, "Young Adult Catholics: Conservative? Alienated? Suspicious?" *America*, March 27, 1999, pp. 9–13.

4. For a more detailed report on this analysis see Dean R. Hoge, "Catholic Generational Differences," *America*, October 2, 1999, pp. 14–20.

5. The 1992 survey was done by the Gallup poll for the Catholics Speak Out organization (802 cases); the 1996 survey was done by the University of Maryland Survey Research Center for a Small Faith Community Study (644 cases); and the 1997 survey was done by the Roper agency for Ignatius Press (1000 cases). Used by permission.

CHAPTER 3. YOUNG ADULT CATHOLICS: SURVEY RESULTS

1. The experience of the Gallup organization in doing a 1985 phone survey of Hispanic Catholics is instructive here. They tried to get a random sample in the forty largest Hispanic communities in the nation; they made no attempt to interview farm workers. Bilingual interviewers did the phoning, and they offered to use either Spanish or English. Forty-five percent of the interviews were done in Spanish and 55 percent in English. But the interesting part was that the preference for English rose with each generation after immigration. Among the first-generation interviewees, over 70 percent chose Spanish. Among the second generation, 19 percent, and among the third and higher generations, almost none chose Spanish. See Gonzalez and LaVelle (1985:4).

Stephen Steinberg reports, concerning earlier European immigrants: "Studies conducted by Joshua Fishman indicate an almost complete breakdown in the transmission of non-English languages between the second and third generations. For example, when Fishman collected his data in 1960, there were 2,300,000 second-generation Italians who spoke Italian, but among the third generation, the figure plummeted to 147,000. Similarly, between the second and third generations, the number speaking Yiddish dropped from 422,000 to 39,000. For Poles, the comparable figures are 1,516,000 and 87,000; for Swedes, 187,000 and 17,000." See Steinberg (1989:45).

2. The Latinos in our sample did not marry earlier than the non-Latinos, in contrast to the pattern in the total U.S. population. Census data show that Latinos in the U.S. marry at younger ages. The median age of first marriage in the total U.S. in 1990 was 26.1 for men and 23.9 for women, but for Latinos it was approximately 20 for men and 19 for women. Here is more evidence that our Latino sample is more assimilated than average. See Gonzales (1993a).

3. The interfaith marriage rate for American Jews was 57 percent in a large 1990 survey (see Kosmin et al. 1991:14). This is only slightly higher than the non-Latino rate in our sample. The high rate of interfaith marriage is a problem distressing to many American Jewish leaders, since it has long-term effects of weakening Jewish identity in the families of intermarried persons. The same consequence can reasonably be expected for intermarried Catholic persons.

4. New research by Nancy Ammerman clarifies the denominational comparisons. She found in a large survey that within Protestantism, denominational switching varied widely. Lutherans and African American Baptists did much less switching than members of other Protestant groups. More broadly, Greek Orthodox and Catholics did little switching. Ammerman concluded that denominations with (a) strong ethnic consciousness and (b) a distinct worship tradition have less out-switching than others. It would follow that evangelicals (who have neither strong ethnic consciousness nor distinct worship) should have the most switching and the least denominational loyalty. This hypothesis was confirmed. This research goes far to explain the denominational differences. See Ammerman (1999).

5. C. Kirk Hadaway, Penny Long Marler, and Mark Chaves, "What the Polls Don't Show: A Closer Look at U.S. Church Attendance," *American Sociological Review* 58 (December 1993): 741–52; Mark Chaves and James C. Cavendish, "More Evidence on U.S. Catholic Church Attendance," *Journal for the Scientific Study of Religion* 33:4 (December 1994): 376–81.

6. In 1995, Davidson and his collaborators asked their nationwide random sample of Catholics about agreement or disagreement with the statement "Women should be allowed to be priests." Of persons twenty to thirty-nine years

old, 67 percent agreed. We did not ask the same question, though our other results are similar to Davidson's.

7. In 1991, researchers at the National Catholic Educational Association estimated that 38 percent of Catholic children five to thirteen years old were enrolled in parish religious education programs, and 21 percent of Catholic children 14 to 17 were enrolled in such programs. See Schaub and Baker (1993).

8. We are not the only researchers to find evidence that religious commitments can be strong even if the person tends to be relativistic about truth claims of religious traditions. In a study of American evangelicals, Christian Smith found evidence parallel to ours. See Smith (1998:219–20).

9. The word *Latinas* is the feminine plural in Spanish. The word *Latinos* has two meanings, denoting either men only or both men and women together, depending on the context. We use *Latinos* to refer to both genders, *Latinas* to refer to women, and *Latino men* to refer to men.

CHAPTER 4. FIVE TYPES OF CATHOLIC INVOLVEMENT

1. We are not the first to distinguish types of Catholics in this way. A well-known categorization was done by Joseph Fichter in the 1950s. He studied three urban parishes in New Orleans and found four types of Catholics: "nuclear Catholics," three percent; "modal," 46 percent; "marginal," 12 percent; and "dormant," 39 percent. The "dormant" Catholics never or rarely went to church, so Fichter considered them out of parish life entirely. In his book (1954) he described each type in detail. We have also identified four types among the confirmands, plus a fifth—persons not Catholic any more.

2. Seven factors were removed from Table 4.2 because they had only negligible effect: (1) whether the person had attended Catholic elementary school; (2) whether the person had attended Catholic high school; (3) whether the person had attended religious education at the parish, such as C.C.D.; (4) whether a man had ever been an altar boy; (5) level of formal education; (6) whether the person had ever been married; and (7) whether the person was born in the U.S. (for the Latinos only). We tested whether the cumulative effect of Catholic elementary and high school might have a detectable effect, but we found no evidence. We could not test for the combined effect of Catholic high school and Catholic college because there too few cases.

3. Figure 4.1 is drawn from the means on three of the scale scores at the top of Table 4.3. This method produces smoother relationships. The vertical dimension is truncated from the total range of one to five since most persons had high scores on the scales. All five groups are represented on the Traditional Doctrine

Scale, but non-Catholics were not asked the questions in the Catholicism Only Scale and the Catholic Duty Scale.

4. We can be specific about which churches the non-Catholics now attend. In the non-Latino sample (forty-nine persons), ten now go to nondenominational churches, three are Baptists, three are Methodists, three are Lutherans, two are Presbyterians, two are Mormons, two are Pentecostals, one is Episcopalian, one is Brethren, and one is Jewish. In the Latino sample (thirty-nine persons), nine now go to nondenominational churches, six go to Pentecostal or evangelical churches, four are Mormons, three are Baptists, two are Methodists, and two belong to other denominations.

Chapter 5. Latino Young Adults

1. Estimates of undocumented immigrants have been made by several government offices. Our figure of four to five million is from the Immigration and Naturalization Service, as reported in the *Washington Post*, August 28, 1995, and October 5, 1995.

2. We wondered if the Latinos born outside the United States were different from those born here. We checked and found no differences.

Chapter 6. Experiences with Religious Education

1. These changes in religious education began with the Second Vatican Council's "Decree on the Pastoral Office of Bishops in the Church." The decree mandated that a directory for the "catechetical instruction of the Christian people" be developed (Abbott 1966:428). The appearance of the new *Catechism of the Catholic Church* in 1994 necessitated revision of the 1971 *Directory*, thus the *General Directory for Catechesis* was promulgated by the Congregation for the Clergy in 1997.

An important distinction is made in the *Directory* when it says that the *Catechism* and the *Directory* are two "distinct but complementary instruments." The *Catechism of the Catholic Church* is "a statement of the Church's faith and of Catholic doctrine," while the *General Directory for Catechesis* provides "the basic principles of pastoral theology taken from the Magisterium of the Church, and in a special way from the Second Vatican Council" (1997: 114). Article 167 of the *Directory* states the importance of sound catechesis: "All the baptized, because they are called by God to maturity of faith, need and have therefore a right to adequate catechesis." The *Directory* sets forth detailed directions, and it emphasizes teaching the social vision of the Church:

By means of catechesis, in which due emphasis is given to her social teachings, the Church desires to stir Christian hearts to "the cause of justice" and to a "preferential option of love for the poor" so that her presence may be light that shines and salt that cures. (1997:17)

Chapter 7. Young Adult Spirituality

1. In this chapter the term "spirituality" refers to the personal, subjective, internal dimensions of religion in contrast to the institutional and external dimensions. For a thorough discussion of the problematic aspects of the various definitions of "spirituality" see Farina (1989). For analysis of the structuring of spirituality *qua* theology see Neuman (1982).

2. Representative works on Catholic spirituality in America include Chinnici (1979; 1996); Dolan (1977); Portier (1996); and Lescher (1997).

3. This critique was also evident in Pius XII's 1947 encyclical on the liturgy, *Mediator Dei*.

4. "Catholics in the United States," Report by the Survey Research Center, University of Maryland, done for William D'Antonio, Small Christian Communities Research Project, Catholic University of America, 1996.

5. As noted, clerical and religious life have been closely aligned with the category of saints as an institutional norm of Catholic spirituality. Interviewee comments about the importance of individual priests and nuns as role models in their spiritual formation were diverse and, therefore, difficult to generalize. Fewer young adult Catholics have attended Catholic schools. Coupled with the overall decline in the number of priests and religious, opportunities for interaction have diminished. What is most significant is that while *individual* clerics and religious can have positive (or negative) influences as models of Catholic spirituality, the category of clerical or religious life as the norm of spiritual virtuosity has less credibility among many of today's young adult Catholics.

6. Cavendish, Welch, and Leege (1998) note that Mass attendance is a type of "obligatory devotionalism." It is conceivable, therefore, that one could score high on this measure without being especially religious or spiritual in other ways.

7. The survey of Kellsted et al. (1995) of 4001 Americans in 1992 identified 3.6 percent of the Catholic population as "evangelical" in relation to affirmation of four key evangelical traits: salvation comes only through faith in Jesus; "born again" experience; necessity of spreading the Gospel ("witnessing"), and belief that Scripture is true.

8. Fourteen percent of our sample do not consider themselves as "spiritual persons."

9. This occurs, paradoxically, in spite of widespread ecumenical interest in traditional forms of Catholic spirituality (e.g., monastic retreat experience); in Catholic devotional literature (Teresa of Avila, John of the Cross, Julian of Norwich, Thomas Merton, Henri Nouwen); and in Catholic traditions and practices popularized by non-Catholic writers such as Kathleen Norris (Leonard 1999).

CHAPTER 8. CATHOLIC IDENTITY OF YOUNG ADULTS

1. Analysis of the Catholic identity of institutions lies beyond our present interest. See Butler (1994) and Provost and Walf (1994). Also the various meanings of "identity" as used by psychologists are beyond our concerns here. We can merely say that the most pertinent tradition of identity analysis is in social psychology, and the leading theorists are William James, Sheldon Stryker, and Morris Rosenberg. We are not looking at identity development during youth, as studied by Erik Erikson and James Marcia; that topic is less important to our concerns here.

2. On the influence of motivation to enhance self-esteem see Hogg and Abrams (1988), Allen, Wilder, and Atkinson (1983), and Yost, Strube, and Bailey (1992).

3. We do not have the space to explore the concept "salience," which is part of identity theory. Salience describes elements of the self-concept which become important in a particular time and place. Its relevance here is mainly that Catholicism is more salient in social contexts with few Catholics than in contexts where Catholics are a majority and Catholicism is culturally dominant. Catholic dioceses in the U.S. where Catholics are a distinct minority, such as in states of the Old South, have higher rates of producing seminarians, subscriptions to Catholic literature, and financial contributions, due to this factor. See Hoge and Augustyn (1997) and Stark (1998).

4. On the Jewish debates over interfaith marriage and identity, see Shapiro (1992), Neusner (1994), Lipset and Raab (1995), Goldberg (1996), Dershowitz (1997), Gordis (1997), and Tobin (1999).

CHAPTER 9. CATHOLIC IDENTITY AND TRADITION

1. The concept "institutional church" has various meanings. In this book it includes all of the institutional structure and its rules, from the Vatican to the local parish. We utilize this inclusive definition because it is widely used by young adult Catholics, who often say something like this: "Well, I'm a believer and a spiritual person, but I'm not into the institutional church."

2. For more reflections on the 1997 Princeton Survey Research Associates study see our article in *Commonweal*, "A Faith Loosely Held: The Institutional Allegiance of Young Catholics," March 21, 1998, pp. 13–18. Hoge's recent article on Catholic generational differences makes use of the 1997 survey in showing that the generational differences are more on peripheral than on core issues. See Dean R. Hoge, "Catholic Generational Differences," *America*, October 1, 1999, pp. 14, 16–20.

3. Sociological theorizing about religion has come to a consensus that the religious market is diverse and is best served by a diversity of groups, programs, and regimens. Stark and Bainbridge state this clearly: "No single religious organization can offer the full range of religious services for which there is substantial market demand. No one church can minister to the needs of everyone" (1985: 108). Analysts of church growth and decline agree, stressing that individual churches and parishes need a diversity of groups and programs (see Hunter, 1996). An opposing argument states that church members, given a choice of parishes, will self-select into homogeneous parishes whose presence inadvertently damages Christian unity.

4. The literature on group boundaries is mostly social psychological and theological. For a review of the former see Hogg (1992) and Smith (1998). For the latter see McBrien (1980), Dulles (1985), and Phan (1998).

5. For an extensive discussion of boundaries around Protestant evangelicalism see Smith (1998); on the theories of boundaries see Barth (1969) and Hogg and Abrams (1988).

6. Polls provide ample evidence that anti-Catholicism almost disappeared after the 1960s. For example, a 1952 Gallup poll asked Americans, "Do you think the Catholics are trying to get too much power in the U.S. or not?" and 41 percent of the Protestants said yes. In 1974 only 11 percent said yes. See D'Antonio, et al. (1996:12).

7. Another example of the same distinction is that between "claimed authority" and "accepted authority," as explained by D'Antonio, et al. (1996:25–27). A leader may make a pronouncement claiming authority, but whether the people will accept and obey it is another matter, and it is best measured through empirical research. A further example of this distinction is used early in the present chapter, between core elements of Catholicism as defined theologically and core as felt by laity.

8. Christian Smith (1998) provides a useful discussion of the boundaries of the present-day evangelical movement which helps us understand Catholic boundaries. Evangelicals, unlike Catholics, are uninterested in specific denominations and denominational loyalties. The boundary they talk most about is that which distinguishes them from non-evangelical Christians; its main symbolic markers

are that evangelicals have a personal relationship with Jesus Christ and are obedient to the authority of the Bible (1998:124). Anyone lacking one or both of these qualities is not an evangelical. A second important boundary is between evangelicals and "the world," by which is meant the American consumer culture, values of permissiveness in sexual matters, and relativistic attitudes that all religions are basically the same. Anyone holding these values or beliefs is not an evangelical. The most interesting difference is that, for evangelicals, specific denominations and external church institutions do not define boundaries. There is no concept of loyalty to specific institutions. To evangelicals, whether a person is a Baptist, Lutheran, or non-denominational Christian is not crucial. Though Smith does not tell us, probably a strong belief in a particular church or denomination is seen as a negative, not a positive, indicator of evangelical identity.

Chapter 10. Conclusion

1. The Davidson et al. study (1997) also included as "pan-Vatican II beliefs" two specifically Catholic items: Mary as the Mother of God and belief in the Real Presence.

2. On a related issue, Ana Maria Díaz-Stevens (1993) has suggested that because Latinos often experienced a Catholicism with minimal clerical presence, they may be the model of the future Catholic Church in the United States as institutional Catholicism faces declining numbers of priests. Anthony M. Stevens-Arroyo also notes that the concept of a "cultural Catholic" introduced by Andrew Greeley in the 1970s for Euro-American Catholics, appears a great deal like an experience that is four hundred years old among Latino Catholics (1995:37).

3. The phrase, "preferential option for young adult Catholics" was coined by Father John Cusick of the Archdiocese of Chicago, a nationally recognized expert on Young Adult Ministry.

Appendix

1. The problems of getting reliable information when polling Latinos are well known. For a thorough discussion see Rodolfo O. de la Garza, *Ignored Voices: Public Opinion Polls and the Latino Community* (Austin, Tex.: Center for Mexican American Studies, 1987). Also see Gerardo Marin and Barbara V. Marin, *Research with Hispanic Populations*, Applied Social Research Methods vol. 23 (Newbury Park, Calif.: Sage Publications, 1991), and Alan Riding, *Distant Neighbors: A Portrait of the Mexicans* (New York: Vintage Books, 1986).

References

Abbott, Walter M., ed. *The Documents of Vatican II.* New York: Guild Press, 1966.

Albom, Mitch. *Tuesdays with Morrie.* Garden City, N.Y.: Doubleday, 1997.

Allen, Vernon L., David A. Wilder, and Michael L. Atkinson. "Multiple Group Membership and Social Identity." Ch. 5 in Theodore Sarbin and Karl Scheibe, eds., *Studies in Social Identity*, pp. 92–115. New York: Praeger, 1983.

Ammerman, Nancy T. *Bible Believers: Fundamentalists in the Modern World.* New Brunswick, N.J.: Rutgers University Press, 1987.

————. "Golden Rule Christianity: Lived Religion in the American Mainstream." In David D. Hall, ed., *Lived Religion in America*, pp. 196–217. Princeton: Princeton University Press, 1994.

————. "New Life for Denominationalism." *Christian Century*, March 15, 2000, 302–7.

————. "Postmodern Trends in Religious Organization." Paper presented to the annual meeting of the American Sociological Association, August 7, 1999.

Barth, Fredrik, ed. *Ethnic Groups and Boundaries.* London: George Allen & Unwin, 1969.

Baumeister, Roy F. "How the Self Became a Problem: A Psychological Review of Historical Research," *Journal of Personality and Social Psychology* 46 (1987), 163-76.

Beaudoin, Tom. *Virtual Faith: The Irreverent Spiritual Quest of Generation X.* San Francisco: Jossey-Bass, 1998.

Bellah, Robert. *The Broken Covenant: American Civil Religion in Time of Trial.* New York: Seabury Press, 1975.

Bellah, Robert, et al. *Habits of the Heart: Individualism and Commitment in American Life.* Berkeley: University of California Press, 1985.

Berger, Peter L. *A Far Glory: The Quest for Faith in an Age of Credulity.* Garden City, N.Y.: Doubleday, 1992.

————. *The Sacred Canopy*. New York: Anchor Books, 1967.

Beyer, Peter. *Religion and Globalization*. London: Sage, 1994.

Braungart, Richard G., and Margaret M. Braungart. "Life-Course and Generational Politics," *Annual Review of Sociology* 12 (1986), 205–31.

Butler, Francis J., ed. *American Catholic Identity: Essays in an Age of Change*. Kansas City: Sheed & Ward, 1994.

Cadena, Gilbert R. "Religious Ethnic Identity: A Socio-Religious Portrait of Latinas and Latinos in the Catholic Church." Ch. 2 in Anthony Stevens-Arroyo and Gilbert Cadena, eds., *Old Masks, New Faces: Religion and Latino Identities*, pp. 33–59. New York: PARAL, City University of New York, 1995.

Callahan, Daniel. *The Mind of the Catholic Layman*. New York: Charles Scribner's Sons, 1963.

Campbell, Dennis M. "Study of United Methodism and American Culture," cited in *Christian Century*, October 11, 1995, 920.

Casarella, Peter, and Raul Gomez, S.D.S., eds. *El Cuerpo de Cristo: The Hispanic Presence in the U.S. Catholic Church*. New York: Crossroad, 1998.

Cavendish, James C., Michael R. Welch, and David C. Leege. "Social Network Theory and Predictors of Religiosity for Black and White Catholics: Evidence of a 'Black Sacred Cosmos'?" *Journal for the Scientific Study of Religion* 37 (1998), 397–411.

Cavis, Cary, Carl Haub, and JoAnne L. Willette. "U.S. Hispanics: Changing the Face of America." Ch. 1 in Edna Acosta-Belen and Barbara Sjostrom, eds., *The Hispanic Experience in the United States*, pp 3–55. New York: Praeger, 1988.

Chaves, Mark, and James C. Cavendish. "More Evidence on U.S. Catholic Church Attendance," *Journal for the Scientific Study of Religion* 33:4 (December 1994), 376–81.

Cherlin, Andrew J. *Public and Private Families: An Introduction*. New York: McGraw-Hill, 1996.

Chinnici, Joseph P. *Living Stones: The History and Structure of Catholic Spiritual Life in the United States*. Maryknoll, N.Y.: Orbis, 1996.

————. "Organization of the Spiritual Life: American Catholic Devotional Works, 1791–1866," *Theological Studies* 40 (June 1979), 229–55.

Coalter, Milton, John M. Mulder, and Louis B. Weeks. *Vital Signs: The Promise of Mainstream Protestantism*. Grand Rapids, Mich.: Eerdmans, 1996.

Cohen, Steven M. *American Modernity and Jewish Identity*. New York: Tavistock, 1983.

Coleman, John A. *An American Strategic Theology*. Mahwah, N.J.: Paulist, 1982.

————. "Young Adults: A Look at the Demographics." *Commonweal*, September 14, 1990: 483–490.

Congregation for the Clergy. *General Directory for Catechesis*. Washington, D.C.: United States Catholic Conference, 1997.

D'Antonio, William V., James D. Davidson, Dean R. Hoge, and Ruth A. Wallace. *Laity American and Catholic: Transforming the Church.* Kansas City: Sheed & Ward, 1996.

Davidson, James D. "Outside the Church: Whom Catholics Marry and Where," *Commonweal,* September 10, 1999: 14–16.

Davidson, James D., et al. *The Search for Common Ground: What Unites and Divides Catholic Americans.* Huntington, Ind.: Our Sunday Visitor, 1997.

Deck, Allan Figueroa, S.J. "Hispanic Ministry: Reasons for Our Hope." *America,* April 23, 1994, 12–15.

———. "Models." Ch. 1 in Allan Figueroa Deck, Yolanda Tarango, and Timothy Matovina, eds., *Perspectivas: Hispanic Ministry,* pp. 1–6. Kansas City: Sheed & Ward, 1995.

———. *The Second Wave: Hispanic Ministry and the Evangelization of Cultures.* New York: Paulist Press, 1989.

de la Garza, Rodolfo, Louis De Sipio, F. Chris Garcia, John Garcia, and Angelo Falcon. *Latino Voices: Mexican, Puerto Rican, and Cuban Perspectives on American Politics.* Boulder, Colo.: Westview Press, 1992.

Demerath, N. J., and Rhys H. Williams. *A Bridging of Faiths: Religion and Politics in a New England City.* Princeton: Princeton University Press, 1992.

Dershowitz, Alan M. *The Vanishing American Jew.* New York: Simon & Schuster, 1997.

Díaz-Stevens, Ana Maria. "Latinas and the Church." Ch. 7 in Jay P. Dolan and Allan F. Deck, eds., *Hispanic Catholic Culture in the U.S.: Issues and Concerns,* pp. 240–277. Notre Dame, Ind.: University of Notre Dame Press, 1994.

———. *Oxcart Catholicism on Fifth Avenue.* Notre Dame, Ind.: University of Notre Dame Press, 1993.

Díaz-Stevens, Ana Maria, and Anthony M. Stevens-Arroyo. *Recognizing the Latino Resurgence in U.S. Religion: The Emmaus Paradigm.* Boulder, Colo.: Westview Press, 1998.

Dillon, Michele. *Catholic Identity: Balancing Reason, Faith, and Power.* New York: Cambridge University Press, 1999.

Dinges, William D. "Roman Catholic Traditionalism." In Martin E. Marty and R. Scott Appleby, eds., *Fundamentalisms Observed,* vol. I, pp. 43–79. Chicago: University of Chicago Press, 1991.

Documents of Vatican II. Ed. Walter M. Abbott. Trans. by Joseph Gallagher. New York: Guild Press, 1966.

Dolan, Jay P. *The American Catholic Experience: A History from Colonial Times to the Present.* Garden City, N.Y.: Doubleday, 1985.

———. *Catholic Revivalism in the United States, 1830–1990.* Notre Dame, Ind.: University of Notre Dame Press, 1977.

Dolan, Jay P., and Allan Figueroa Deck, S.J. *Hispanic Catholic Culture in the U.S.* Notre Dame, Ind.: University of Notre Dame Press, 1994.

Downey, Michael. "Christian Spirituality: Changing Currents, Perspectives, Challenges." *America*, April 2, 1994, 8–12.

Dulles, Avery. *The Catholicity of the Church.* Oxford: Clarendon Press, 1985.

Eisenstadt, S. N. *From Generation to Generation: Age Groups and Social Structure.* New York: Free Press, 1956.

Elizondo, Virgilio. *The Future Is Mestizo: Life Where Cultures Meet.* New York: Crossroad, 1988.

————. *Guadalupe: Mother of the New Creation.* Maryknoll, N.Y.: Orbis Books, 1998.

Erikson, Erik H. *Identity: Youth and Crisis.* New York: Norton, 1968.

Espin, Orlando O. "Popular Catholicism among Latinos." Ch. 9 in Jay P. Dolan and Allan Deck, eds., *Hispanic Catholic Culture in the U.S.: Issues and Concerns*, pp. 308–59. Notre Dame, Ind.: University of Notre Dame Press, 1994.

Farina, John. "The Study of Spirituality: Some Problems and Opportunities." *U.S. Catholic Historian*, Spring, 1989, 15–31.

Fichter, Joseph H. *The Catholic Cult of the Paraclete.* New York: Sheed & Ward, 1975.

————. *Social Relations in the Urban Parish.* Chicago: University of Chicago Press, 1954.

Firebaugh, Glenn, and Kenneth E. Davis. "Trends in Anti-Black Prejudice, 1972–1984: Region and Cohort Effects." *American Journal of Sociology* 94 (September 1988), 251–72.

Gallup Organization. *The Gallup Poll: Public Opinion 1997.* Annual Report. Wilmington, Del.: Scholarly Resources, Inc.

Glenn, Norval D. "Values, Attitudes, and Beliefs," In Orville G. Brim, Jr., and Jerome Kagan, eds., *Constancy and Change in Human Development*, pp. 596–640. Cambridge, Mass.: Harvard University Press, 1980.

Giddens, Anthony. *Modernity and Self-Identity.* Palo Alto, Calif.: Stanford University Press, 1991.

Gillis, John R. *Youth and History.* New York: Academic Press, 1981.

Goldberg, J. J. *Jewish Power.* Reading, Mass.: Addison-Wesley, 1996.

Goldstein, Sidney. *Profile of American Jewry: Insights from the 1990 National Jewish Population Survey.* New York: Council of Jewish Federations, 1993.

Gonzales, Juan L. "A Comparison of Fertility Rates and Family Size among Latino Families: Mexican American, Puerto Rican, and Cuban." Paper presented to the Southwestern Social Science Association, New Orleans: March 18, 1993(a).

————. *Racial and Ethnic Groups in America.* 2d edition. Dubuque: Kendall/Hunt, 1993(b).

Gonzalez, Robert, and Michael La Velle. *The Hispanic Catholic in the U.S.* New York: Northeastern Pastoral Center, 1985.

Gordis, Daniel. *Does the World Need the Jews? Rethinking Chosenness and American Jewish Identity.* New York: Charles Scribner's Sons, 1997.

Gordon, Chad. "Self-Conceptions: Configurations of Content," In Chad Gordon and Kenneth J. Gergen, eds., *The Self in Social Interaction,* pp. 115–36. New York: Wiley, 1968.

Greeley, Andrew M. *American Catholics: A Social Portrait.* New York: Basic Books, 1977.

———. *The Catholic Myth.* New York: Charles Scribner's Sons, 1990.

———. *The Communal Catholic: A Personal Manifesto.* New York: Seabury Press, 1976.

———. "Defection among Hispanics (Updated)." *America,* September 17, 1997, 12–13.

Greenberg, Irving. "Jewish Survival and the College Campus." *Judaism* 17, Summer 1968, 260–81.

Hadaway, C. Kirk, Penny Long Marler, and Mark Chaves. "What the Polls Don't Show: A Closer Look at U.S. Church Attendance." *American Sociological Review* 58 (December 1993), 741–52.

Hall, Stuart. "Cultural Identity and Diaspora." In Jonathan Rutherford, ed., *Identity: Community, Culture, Difference,* pp. 222–37. London: Lawrence & Wishart, 1992.

Hammond, Phillip E. *Religion and Personal Autonomy.* Columbia: University of South Carolina Press, 1993.

Herberg, Will. *Protestant, Catholic, Jew: An Essay in American Religious Sociology.* New York: Anchor, 1960.

Hitchcock, James. *Catholicism and Modernity: Confrontation or Capitulation?* New York: Seabury Press, 1979.

Hoge, Dean R. *Converts, Dropouts, Returnees: A Study of Religious Change among Catholics.* Washington, D.C.: United States Catholic Conference, 1981.

———. "Summary of General Social Survey Trends, 1972–1996." Unpublished paper, 1998.

———. "What Is Most Central to Being a Catholic?" *National Catholic Reporter,* October 29, 1999, pp. 12–13, 15.

Hoge, Dean R., and Boguslaw Augustyn. "Financial Contributions to Catholic Parishes: A Nationwide Study of Determinants." *Review of Religious Research* 39:1 (September 1997), 46–60.

Hoge, Dean R., Benton Johnson, and Donald A. Luidens. *Vanishing Boundaries: The Religion of Mainline Protestant Baby Boomers.* Louisville, Ky.: Westminster/John Knox Press, 1994.

Hogg, Michael A. *The Social Psychology of Group Cohesiveness.* New York: New York University Press, 1992.

Hogg, Michael A., and Dominic Abrams. *Social Identifications*. London: Routledge, 1988.

Holy See, the. *Catechism of the Catholic Church*. Washington, D.C.: United States Catholic Conference, 1994.

Hunter, George G., III. *Church for the Unchurched*. Nashville: Abingdon Press, 1996.

Iannaccone, Lawrence R. "Why Strict Churches Are Growing." *American Journal of Sociology* 99:5 (March 1994), 1180–1211.

Imbelli, Robert. "Vatican II: Twenty Years Later." *Commonweal*, October 8, 1982, 522–26.

Kelley, Dean M. *Why Conservative Churches Are Growing*. New York: Harper & Row, 1972.

Kellstedt, Lyman. "Simple Questions, Complex Answers: What Do We Mean by 'Evangelicalism'? What Difference Does It Make?" *Evangelical Studies Bulletin* 12:2 (Fall 1995), 1–4.

Kelly, George A. *The Battle for the American Church*. Garden City, N.Y.: Doubleday, 1979.

Kelly, James R. "The Spirit of Ecumenism: How Wide, How Deep, How Mindful of Truth?" *Review of Religious Research* 20:2 (Spring 1979), 180–94.

Kiecolt, K. Jill. "Recent Developments in Attitudes and Social Structures." *Annual Review of Sociology* 14 (1988), 381–403.

Komonchak, Joseph A. "Modernity and the Construction of Contemporary Roman Catholicism." *Cristianesimo Nella Storia* 18 (1997), 353–85.

Kosmin, Barry A., Sidney Goldstein, Joseph Waksberg, Nava Lerer, Ariella Keysar, and Jeffrey Scheckner. *Highlights of the CJF 1990 National Jewish Population Survey*. New York: Council of Jewish Federations, 1991.

Kosmin, Barry A., and Seymour P. Lachman. *One Nation under God: Religion in Contemporary America*. New York: Harmony Books, 1993.

Kselman, Thomas A., and Steven Avella. "Marian Piety and the Cold War in the United States." *The Catholic Historical Review* 72 (1986), 403–24.

Lakeland, Paul. *Postmodernity: Christian Identity in a Fragmented Age*. Minneapolis: Fortress Press, 1997.

Lazerwitz, Bernard, J. Alan Winter, Arnold Dashefsky, and Ephraim Tabory. *Jewish Choices: American Jewish Denominationalism*. Albany, N.Y.: State University of New York Press, 1998.

Lee, Che-Fu, and Raymond H. Potvin. "A Demographic Profile of U.S. Hispanics." In Eugene Hemrick, ed., *Strangers and Aliens No Longer: The Hispanic Presence in the Church of the United States*, pp. 35–62. Washington, DC: National Conference of Catholic Bishops, 1992.

Leonard, Bill J. "Forum: American Spirituality." *Religion and American Culture: A Journal of Interpretation* 9:2 (Summer 1999), 131–58.

Lescher, Bruce. "American Catholic Spirituality." In Michael Glazier and Thomas J. Shelley, eds. *The Encyclopedia of American Catholic History*, pp. 45–52. Collegeville, Minn.: Liturgical Press, 1997.

Lippy, Charles H. *Being Religious, American Style: A History of Popular Religiosity in the United States*. Westport, Conn.: Greenwood Press, 1994.

Lipset, Seymour Martin, and Earl Raab. *Jews and the New American Scene*. Cambridge, Mass.: Harvard University Press, 1995.

Lipset, Seymour Martin, and Philip G. Altbach, eds. *Students in Revolt*. Boston: Houghton Mifflin, 1969.

Ludwig, Robert A. *Reconstructing Catholicism for a New Generation*. New York: Crossroad, 1995.

Marcia, James E. "Development and Validation of Ego Identity Status." *Journal of Personality and Social Psychology* 3 (1966), 551–58.

Marin, Gerardo, and Barbara V. Marin. *Research with Hispanic Populations*. Applied Social Research Methods, vol. 23. Newbury Park, Calif.: Sage Publications, 1991.

Marty, Martin E. "Where the Energies Go." *Annals of the American Academy of Political and Social Science* 527 (May 1993), 11–26.

McBrien, Richard. *Catholicism*. Minneapolis: Winston, 1980.

McCutcheon, Alan L. "Denominations and Religious Intermarriage: Trends among White Americans in the Twentieth Century." *Review of Religious Research* 29:3 (March 1988), 213–27.

McGreevey, John T. *Parish Boundaries: The Catholic Encounter With Race in the Twentieth-Century Urban North*. Chicago: University of Chicago Press, 1996.

———. "Thinking on One's Own: Catholicism in the American Intellectual Imagination, 1928–1960." *Journal of American History*, June 1997, 97–131.

McLemore, S. Dale, and Ricardo Romo, eds. *The Mexican American Experience*. Austin: University of Texas Press, 1985.

McNamara, Patrick H. *Conscience First: Tradition Second*. Albany: State University of New York Press, 1992.

Morris, Charles R. *American Catholics: The Saints and Sinners Who Built America's Most Powerful Church*. New York: Times Books, 1997.

Moore, Joan. "The Social Fabric of the Hispanic Community since 1965." Ch. 1 in Jay Dolan and Allan Figueroa Deck, eds., *Hispanic Catholic Culture in the U.S.: Issues and Concerns*, pp. 6–49. Notre Dame, Ind.: University of Notre Dame Press, 1994.

Neuman, Matthias. "The Religious Structure of a Spirituality." *American Benedictine Review* 33 (1982): 115–48.

Neusner, Jacob. *Fortress Introduction to American Judaism*. Minneapolis: Fortress Press, 1994.

Niemi, Richard G., John Mueller, and Tom W. Smith. *Trends in Public Opinion: A Compendium of Survey Data*. New York: Greenwood Press, 1989.

O'Connell, Timothy E. *Making Disciples: A Handbook of Christian Moral Formation*. New York: Crossroad, 1998.

O'Dea, Thomas. *American Catholic Dilemma*. New York: Sheed & Ward, 1958.

Orsi, Robert A. *The Madonna of 115th Street: Faith Community in Italian Harlem, 1880–1950*. New Haven, Conn.: Yale University Press, 1985.

Phan, Peter C. "To Be Catholic or Not to Be: Is It Still the Question? Catholic Identity and Religious Education Today." *Horizons* 25:2 (1998), 158–80.

Philibert, Paul J. "Pastoral Approaches to Generation X." Notre Dame University: Unpublished paper, 1999.

Portes, Alejandro, ed. *The New Second Generation*. New York: Russell Sage Foundation, 1996.

Portes, Alejandro, and Ruben G. Rumbaut. *Immigrant America: A Portrait*. Second edition. Berkeley: University of California Press, 1993.

Portier, William L. "Spirituality in America: Selected Sources." *Horizons* 232:1 (Spring 1996), 140–61.

Provost, James H., and Knut Walf, eds. *Catholic Identity*. *Concilium* No. 5. London: SCM Press, 1994.

Rodriguez, Jeanette. *Our Lady of Guadalupe: Faith and Empowerment among Mexican American Women*. Austin, TX: University of Texas Press, 1994.

Rohr, Richard, and Joseph Martos. *Why Be Catholics? Understanding Our Experience and Tradition*. Cincinnati: St. Anthony Messenger Press, 1989.

Roof, Wade Clark. *A Generation of Seekers*. San Francisco: Harper, 1993.

———. *Spiritual Marketplace: Baby Boomers and the Remaking of American Religion*. Princeton, N.J.: Princeton University Press, 1999.

Roof, Wade Clark, and William McKinney. *American Mainline Religion: Its Changing Shape and Future*. New Brunswick, N.J.: Rutgers University Press, 1987.

Rosenberg, Morris. *Conceiving the Self*. New York: Basic Books, 1979.

Sanchez, George J. *Becoming Mexican American: Ethnicity, Culture and Identity in Chicano Los Angeles, 1900–1945*. New York: Oxford University Press, 1993.

Schaub, Maryellen, and David Baker. "Serving American Catholic Children and Youth." Report by the Life Cycle Institute, Catholic University, Washington D.C., 1993.

Schreiter, Robert J. *Constructing Local Theologies*. Maryknoll, N.Y.: Orbis Books, 1985.

Searle, Mark. "The Notre Dame Study of Catholic Parish Life." *Worship* 60:4 (1986), 332.

Seidler, John, and Katherine Meyer. *Conflict and Change in the Catholic Church*. New Brunswick, N.J.: Rutgers University Press, 1989.

Shapiro, Edward S. *A Time for Healing: American Jewry since World War II*. Baltimore: Johns Hopkins University Press, 1992.

Sharry, Frank. "A Nation of Immigrants." *Washington Post*, September 13, 1999, A26.

Smith, Christian. *American Evangelicalism: Embattled and Thriving*. Chicago: University of Chicago Press, 1998.

Smith, Dennis A. "Coming of Age: A Reflection on Pentecostals, Politics, and Popular Religion in Guatemala." Study paper. Guatemala City: CELEP, 1991.

Stark, Rodney. "Catholic Contexts: Competition, Commitment and Innovation." *Review of Religious Research* 39:3 (March 1998), 197–208.

Stark, Rodney, and Williams Sims Bainbridge. *The Future of Religion*. Berkeley: University of California Press, 1985.

Stark, Rodney, and Charles Y. Glock. *American Piety*. Berkeley: University of California Press, 1968.

Steinberg, Stephen. *The Ethnic Myth: Race, Ethnicity, and Class in America*. Boston: Beacon Press, 1989.

Steinfels, Peter. "Signs and Numbers." *Commonweal* 122:2 (January 27, 1995), 11.

Stevens–Arroyo, Anthony M., ed. *Discovering Latino Religion: A Comprehensive Social Science Bibliography*. New York: Bildner Center for Western Hemispheric Studies, 1995.

Stevens–Arroyo, Anthony M., and Gilbert R. Cadena, eds. *Old Masks, New Faces: Religion and Latino Identities*. New York: PARAL, City University of New York, 1995.

Stoll, David. *Is Latin America Turning Protestant?* Berkeley: University of California Press, 1990.

Stryker, Sheldon. "Identity Theory." In Edgar F. Borgatta and Marie L. Borgatta, eds., *Encyclopedia of Sociology*, vol. 2, pp. 871–76. New York: Macmillan, 1991.

Stryker, Sheldon, and Richard T. Serpe. "Identity Salience and Psychological Centrality: Equivalent, Overlapping, or Complementary Concepts?" *Social Psychology Quarterly* 57:1 (1994), 16–35.

Taves, Ann. *The Household of Faith: Roman Catholic Devotions in Mid-Nineteenth Century America*. Notre Dame, Ind.: University of Notre Dame Press, 1986.

Tentler, Leslie Woodcock. "On the Margins: The State of American Catholic History." *American Quarterly* 45:1 (March 1993), 104–27.

Tobin, Gary A. *Opening the Gates: How Pro-Active Conversion Will Revitalize the Jewish Community*. San Francisco: Jossey-Bass, 1999.

United States Bureau of the Census. *Statistical Abstracts of the United States 1998*. Washington, D.C.: U.S. Department of Commerce.

United States Catholic Conference. *Sons and Daughters of the Light: A Pastoral Plan for Ministry with Young Adults*. Washington, D.C.: United States Catholic Conference, 1997.

Vidal, Jamie R. "Hispanic Catholics in America." In Michael Glazier and Thomas J. Shelley, eds., *The Encyclopedia of American Catholic History*, pp. 635–42. Collegeville, Minn.: Liturgical Press, 1997.

Walch, Timothy. *Catholicism in America: A Social History*. Malabar, Fla.: Robert E. Krieger, 1989.

Waters, Mary C. *Ethnic Options: Choosing Identities in America*. Berkeley: University of California Press, 1990.

Weaver, Mary Jo, and R. Scott Appleby. *Being Right: Conservative Catholics in America*. Bloomington, Ind.: Indiana University Press, 1995.

Wilder, Esther I. "Socioeconomic Attainment and Expressions of Jewish Identification, 1970 and 1990." *Journal for the Scientific Study of Religion* 35:2 (June 1996), 109–27.

Williams, Andrea, and James D. Davidson. "Catholic Conceptions of Faith: A Generational Analysis." *Sociology of Religion* 57:3 (Fall 1996), 273–90.

Wilkes, Paul. *The Good Enough Catholic: A Guide for the Perplexed*. New York: Ballantine Books, 1996.

Wittberg, Patricia S.C. "Deep Structures in Community Cultures: The Revival of Religious Orders in Roman Catholicism." *Sociology of Religion* 58:3 (Fall 1997), 239–59.

Wuthnow, Robert. *After Heaven: Spirituality in America since the 1950s*. Berkeley: University of California Press, 1998.

———. *The Restructuring of American Religion*. Princeton, N.J.: Princeton University Press, 1988.

Yost, John H., Michael J. Strube, and James R. Bailey. "The Construction of the Self: An Evolutionary View." *Current Psychology: Research and Reviews* 11:2 (Summer 1992), 110–21.

Index

teachings, 64
values, 140
Christmas, 188, 190
Christmas and Easter Catholics, 181
church
    authority, 27, 226
    involvement, 44–45
    leaders, 34, 231, 239
    shopping, 46, 98. *See also* switching
church-as-choice Catholics, 170–71
civil rights movement, 11
Coleman, John, 18
college. *See* Catholic education
college students (general), 21, 23, 28
communal Catholics, 23–25, 28, 51, 222
communion of Saints, 169
community service, 140–41, 165
confirmation. *See* religious rituals
consumer Catholicism, 16
contingent Catholics, 181, 194, 223, 224
conversion. *See* switching
core Catholics, 17, 158, 172
core versus periphery (discussion),
    195–205
Coronado, Cecilia (interviewee), 85–90,
    181
cultural Catholicism, 17. *See also* ethnic
    Catholics
cultural pluralism, 212
culture of death, 147, 166
curanderos / as. *See* folk healers
Cusick, John (Father), 267n3
Cursillos, 160, 169

D'Antonio, William V., 266n7
data (or data analysis). *See* methodology
Davidson, James, 18, 33–35, 43, 55, 56,
    57, 155, 232, 267n1
Davidson study. *See* polls
Day, Dorothy, 152

Deck, Allan Figueroa, 113, 120
Dershowitz, Alan, 193
Deutsch, Karl, 19
Diaz-Stevens, Ana Maria, 267n2
Dignitatis Humanae, 151
Dillon, Michele, 197, 213, 226
divine judgment, 153
divorce. *See* special issues
doctrines (Catholic), 36, 55, 61–62, 66
dropping out. *See* inactive Catholics
Durkheim, Emile, 202
Dylan, Bob, 10

Easter, 188
Eastern spiritual movements, 155
ecclesiastical Catholics, 24
ecclesiology, 124–25, 220, 231
ecumenical, 125, 265n9
    goodwill, 206
    settings, 143–44
ecumenism, 173, 216–17, 238
education, 124. *See also* Catholic
    education
espiritismo, 123
ethnic Catholics, 26, 194
the ethnic factor, 220
the Eucharist, 53, 104, 159, 161, 202. *See
    also* real presence
Euro-American Catholics (Euros), 9,
    70, 225. *See also* non-Latino
    Catholics
evangelical Catholics, 264n7
evangelical church. *See* non-
    denominational churches
evangelicals, 227, 266n8–267
ex-Catholics, 97
exogamy. *See* interfaith marriage

faith journeys, 173
faith sharing groups. *See* groups